Falling Backwards

AN EXPLORATION OF TRUST

AND SELF-EXPERIENCE

Doris Brothers

Ph.D.

W. W. Norton & Company • New York • London

By the Same Author

The Shattered Self: A Psychoanalytic Study of Trauma
(with Richard B. Ulman)

Printed in the United States of America

First Edition

Composition by Bytheway Typesetting Services, Inc.
Manufacturing by Haddon Craftsmen, Inc.

Library of Congress Cataloging-in-Publication Data

Brothers, Doris.
    Falling backwards : an exploration of trust and self-experience /
Doris Brothers.
        p.   cm.
    Includes bibliographical references (p.   ) and index.
    ISBN 0-393-70177-8
    1. Trust (Psychology) 2. Betrayal—Psychological aspects.
3. Psychic trauma—Case studies. 4. Psychoanalysis. I. Title.
BF575.T7B76   1995
158'.2—dc20   94-40263 CIP

W. W. Norton & Company, Inc., 500 Fifth Avenue, New York, NY 10110
W. W. Norton & Company, Ltd., 10 Coptic Street, London WC1A 1PU

1 2 3 4 5 6 7 8 9 0

To my mother

CONTENTS

ACKNOWLEDGMENTS

This book was written at a time of mingled sorrow and joy. My father's death in March 1993 deprived me of a powerful source of love and inspiration. His exuberance and strength helped me through the book's rough beginnings. I wish he were here to help me celebrate its completion.

I am deeply grateful for the sustaining presence of many others in my personal and professional life. It is my good fortune to count as friends and supporters my colleagues at the Training and Research Institute for Self Psychology (TRISP). A number of faculty members and candidates served as sounding boards for various ideas contained in the book and contributed valuable suggestions. Special thanks go to Charles Strozier for encouraging my earliest efforts and for offering helpful advice. Richard Ulman's input proved invaluable, as ever. I am indebted to both men as well as to Joanne Gates, Mark Miller, Harry Paul, and Peter Zimmermann, among others, who attended my first informal presentation of *Falling Backwards*, for helping me find a name for a central construct in this book: self-trust.

My efforts were also greatly benefited by the talented clinicians I have had the good fortune to supervise. Ellen Lewinberg's sensitive work with her patients led to many refinements of my clinical thinking. In lively case discussions with Mary Ellen Bowles I felt challenged to explain a number of concepts with greater clarity. I also gained many insights in supervising Lisa Abram, Kathy Gordon, Paulette Landesman, Marcia Lavipour, Maria Miliora, and Pat Walter. However, it was my patients who taught me the most. I cannot begin to thank them enough for their faith in me.

My work on this book was guided by Susan Barrows Munro, my editor and the director of Professional Books at Norton. I thank her for her unfailing helpfulness, wisdom, and support. Superb copyediting was provided by Regina Dahlgren Ardini, associate editor. Assistance with German and French translation was graciously given by Ruth Manoff. I am indebted to my husband, Jack Sherin, for designing the beautiful jacket with the assistance of Don Ledwin.

Writing a book can be a lonely enterprise. My loneliness was always eased by thoughts of my children, Laurence and Karen, my mother, and my husband. Jack helped me in innumerable ways, from changing the ribbon in my printer to serving as first reader. But mainly I am thankful to him for being there, always, with outstretched arms.

PREFACE

Well before I knew the word for it, the idea of trust intrigued me. In my family, children, particularly female children, were regarded as delicate treasures too fragile to withstand the onslaughts of grim reality. Secrets abounded. Why, I wondered, was I not trusted with the truth? Did the grownups trust one another? Did they trust themselves? How much could I trust the rosy version of life they presented to me? Always needing to search for hidden meanings, I might have grown up to be a suspicious, mistrustful person. How is it that, instead, I am someone who trusts far too easily?

The graduate program in clinical psychology at Yeshiva University provided my first opportunity to subject this puzzling realm to scientific investigation. I designed a scale to measure trust for my "pre-doc" and my dissertation (Brothers, 1982) examined trust disturbances in rape and incest victims. My work on *The Shattered Self: A Psychoanalytic Study of Trauma*, coauthored with Richard B. Ulman (1988) convinced me that trust disturbance is inextricably bound up with trauma. But trust, like love, yields its secrets reluctantly. Although this book records my attempts to solve some of the mysteries of trust, countless more remain.

This book owes its evocative title, *Falling Backwards*, to the splendid imagination of my daughter, Karen Elena Brothers. She was inspired by the trust-building nonverbal activity often used in sensitivity or T-groups. In a typical version described by Watson (1972), "One member stands in the center of a tight circle of his peers, closes his eyes, and lets himself fall backward. The others catch him; they may roll him around the group" (p. 157).

Upon learning the name of this book, a number of people shared their experiences of falling backwards with me. I was particularly delighted by this note dated April 27, 1992 from my colleague, Dr. Laura Josephs, about her son, Aaron, then nine months old:

> Re: your book "Falling Backwards"—I was reminded of it by my son—if I am sitting behind him, he will let himself fall backwards onto me, even hurl himself backwards onto me (at times he seems to be paying no attention to the fact that I'm even there, but he obviously is). I've never seen him do this onto anything else, the rug, his crib, etc.

This book is divided into two parts. Part I, Toward a Psychology of Trust, consists of five chapters. Chapter 1 introduces the notion that trust is universally prized because the experience of self is impossible in its absence. It explores possible reasons that psychoanalysis has not produced a comprehensive psychology of trust. One hypothesis concerns traumatic betrayals of trust in Freud's early life. It is suggested that his self-restitutive efforts in the aftermath of these betrayals led him to develop a theory of human nature in which trust has little relevance. Ferenczi's valiant attempts to address this oversight were poorly received in his day. In addition to his contributions, those of Balint, Suttie, Erikson, Benedek, Mahler, Rogers, and Winnicott are examined. The remainder of the chapter is devoted to a discussion of the advantages of using psychoanalytic self psychology as a theoretical framework for a psychology of trust.

Chapter 2 describes self-trust, "the glue of self-experience." Straddling the world of selfobject fantasies and the world of subjective reality, self-trust is the realm of trust vital to cohesive selfhood. Four separate yet complexly interrelated dimensions of self-trust are described. A review of research on caretaker-infant relationships supports the notion that the four self-trust dimensions are to be found, in nascent form, at the earliest beginnings of life. The chapter concludes with an examination of the developmental transformation of self-trust. Highly individual criteria for self-trust are shown to become more realistic, abstract, complex, and differentiated over the course of development.

That betrayed self-trust lies at the heart of trauma is the subject of Chapter 3. This conceptualization refines the "shattered fantasy" theory of trauma (Ulman & Brothers, 1988). When the meaning of an event is construed as a self-trust betrayal, the glue of selfobject relatedness loosens and unconscious selfobject fantasies shatter. The restoration of selfobject fantasies, the unconscious organizers of self-experience, depends on the reestablishment of trust in self and/or others as providers of selfobject experiences. As a means of regaining trust in oneself or in others after it has been betrayed, the experience of subjective reality is often altered. This chapter describes the various elements involved in the alteration of subjective reality and helps to explain the dissociative nature of trauma. Among the topics explored are the bidirectional nature of self-trust disturbance, the creation of "black holes" in self-experience, and various psychological strategies commonly employed to fill in these black holes. Two illustrative clinical examples are presented.

Chapter 4 is devoted to the "rescripting" of trauma scenarios. Faced with the threat of retraumatizing betrayals, trauma survivors often attempt to change the meaning of their original traumas through enactments in their present lives. These enactments, usually sadomasochistic in character, represent efforts to revise old traumas in order to make them conform with the survivors' new ways of experiencing reality. Masochism in this context refers to fantasies of being betrayed or of being vulnerable to betrayal by those needed as providers of selfobject experience and the behavioral enactment of these fantasies. Sadism refers to fantasies of betraying others who are dependent upon one for the provision of selfobject experiences, or related behaviors. Sadistic activities often entail revenge, a shift from betrayed to betrayer. This formulation offers an alternative to Freud's theory of a repetition compulsion insofar as retraumatization is seen as an inadvertent consequence of efforts to rescript trauma. Chapter 4 also examines sadomasochistic enactments in Freud's relationships with Fliess, Jung, and Adler that appear to represent his efforts to rescript trauma scenarios of his early life.

Paranoid experience, the subject of Chapter 5, is viewed primarily as a trust disorder, the result of early and repeated self-trust betrayals and the formation of disorganized/disoriented attachments with caretakers (Liotti, 1992). Paranoid phenomena, including delusions of persecution and grandeur, are understood both as attempts to establish the actuality of traumatic betrayals and as extreme measures to alter subjective reality in their aftermath. Paranoid projection is understood as a search for alter ego selfobject experiences. Because huge portions of self-experience antithetical to the paranoid person's altered subjective reality are sucked into experiential black holes, alter ego selfobjects who embody these repudiated aspects of self are required to assure a sense of self-cohesion. Aspects of Freud's famous case study of Daniel Paul Schreber are reinterpreted from a self-trust perspective.

Part II, Toward a Psychotherapy of Trust, opens with Chapter 6 in which a self-trust perspective on disorders of self-experience and their treatment is presented. Since betrayals of self-trust are viewed as aspects of all psychological disorders, their dissociative manifestations must be addressed in every therapeutic relationship. The familiar principles of self-psychological technique refined by intersubjectivity theory are employed in an effort to resolve the self-trust dilemma confronting every psychotherapy patient and his or her therapist. The hope of restoring trust in self and others as selfobjects places both partners in the therapeutic relationship at risk for retraumatizing betrayals. Treatment is understood as involving three recurring and interconnected elements: testing, reconstructing, and working-through. Testing tends to be most prominent in the initial phase of treatment; reconstructing, in the middle phase; and working-through, in the final phase. When events in the therapeutic relationship threaten patients or therapists with retraumatization, attempts may be made to rescript trauma scenarios through sadomasochistic enactments.

In Chapter 7, two in-depth treatment cases are presented to illustrate the clinical advantages of a self-trust perspective. Events in the early lives of both patients led to severe self-trust betrayals: Ruth, a middle-aged educator, was stricken with crippling polio at the age of three; Mark, a young medical student, was incestuously abused by an uncle following the death of his father when he was six. Both cases demonstrate how testing, reconstructing, and working-through are colored by the unique configurations created by the therapist's self-trust organization in relation to that of the patient. And both cases illustrate the rescripting of trauma scenarios by means of sadomasochistic enactments within the therapeutic relationship.

A person's self-esteem, security, and well-being, not to mention his or her very humanness, depend on meriting and receiving the trust of others. Self-as-trustworthy, the dimension of self-trust that pertains to the need to be trusted, is the focus of Chapter 8. Patients with disturbances in this realm may experience themselves as either indifferent to the psychological needs of others or overly invested in providing for them. The therapeutic relationship provides an ideal medium for addressing disturbances in this self-trust dimension. Two illustrative treatment cases are presented.

Chapter 9 summarizes the other chapters in a question-and-answer format. Some implications of a self-trust perspective are reviewed and areas for future study are suggested. The reader may wish to turn to this chapter for a more detailed overview of the contents of the book.

Part I

TOWARD A PSYCHOLOGY
OF TRUST

IN SEARCH OF A THEORY

When we discover that someone we trusted can be trusted no longer, it forces us to reexamine the universe, to question the whole instinct and concept of trust. For awhile, we are thrust back onto some bleak, jutting ledge, in a dark pierced by sheets of fire, swept by sheets of rain, in a world before kinship, or naming, or tenderness exist, we are brought close to formlessness.

Adrienne Rich (1979)

Silent and invisible, trust rarely occupies the foreground of conscious awareness. We are no more likely to ask ourselves how trusting we are at any given moment than to inquire if gravity is still keeping the planets in orbit. However, when trust is disturbed it claims our attention as urgently as would any irregularity in the gravitational field. Throughout the ages, theologians, philosophers, poets, and writers have directed their creative energies to the problem of lost or damaged trust. Indeed, it is difficult to think of a single great work of literature in which injured trust does not figure importantly. Oedipus, Hamlet, Anna Karenina, Emma Bovary, and Gregor Samsa are only a handful of the innumerable characters who assume tragic celebrity as betrayed or betrayers.

It is trust that makes the world feel safe, comfortable, and familiar. You have only to consider waking one morning without the "confident expectation" (Benedek, 1938) that the sun will rise, that your body will respond to your wish to get out of bed, that the ground will remain firm beneath your feet, that water for your coffee has not been contaminated during the night and that loved ones will greet you with recognition to begin to appreciate how indispensable trust is for the maintenance of life as we know it.

Trust and gravity also warrant comparison in that, for all their ubiquity, both elude the complete grasp of science. Moreover, revolutions in the fields of physics and psychoanalysis have produced fresh insights into their mysteries. With the advent of Einstein's theory of relativity physicists gained a set of elegant, yet simple rules that accorded with their intuition in an aesthetically satisfying way, immeasurably enhancing their understanding of gravity. And, as Mitchell (1988) argues, a "paradigm shift" (Kuhn, 1962) comparable in impact to Einstein's theory has also occurred in psychoanalysis. The model of human experience derived from Freudian drive theory in which a relatively asocial individual is viewed as torn by conflict over sexual and aggressive drives pressing for discharge has been largely replaced by what Mitchell terms a "relational model" in which relations with others are viewed as the basic elements of psychological life. (See also Atwood & Stolorow, 1984; Balint, 1969; Erikson, 1982; Stolorow & Atwood, 1992; Stolorow, Brandschaft, & Atwood, 1987.)

Concomitant with the shift in emphasis from events occurring within a person to events occurring between people is a dramatic change in the psychoanalytic understanding of self-experience. As Mitchell (1988) observes, "there is no 'self' in a psychologically meaningful sense, in isolation, outside a matrix of relations with others" (p. 33). It is this new perspective on self-experience that paves the way for a deeper and more complete understanding of trust. Once it is accepted that, from birth to death, we are utterly dependent on one another for the provision of psychological experiences essential to selfhood, the need to trust others and to be trusted by them assumes a supraordinate position in mental life. Paraphrasing Mitchell, there is no self without trust.

Ironically, although few psychoanalysts would deny that trust is a basic variable in personality and indispensable to the practice of psychoanalytic psychotherapy, psychoanalysis has not produced a comprehensive psychology of trust. As a brief review of some of its fundamental tenets should make clear, a view of trust as central to psychological existence is intrinsically incompatible with much of classical Freudian theory. First, as already mentioned, the fact that Freud conceived psychoanalysis as a "one-person" theory (Balint, 1969) ineluctably relegated trust to the periphery of scientific investigation. Trust has little meaning outside the context of relationships.

Second, the dual-drive theory of motivation (Freud, 1920) is antithetical to an appreciation of the centrality of trust. Wispe (1978) observed that hedonism is the "natural enemy" of altruism and trust. Under the sway of libido, the sexual drive, humans are essentially hedonistic. According to Freud's pleasure principle, drive reduction is associated with pleasure gain. To the extent that the need to maximize pleasure and avoid pain takes precedence over the need for human attachment, trust loses significance as an organizer of self-experience. Indeed, from this perspective, the very existence of trust between people seems doubtful.

The notion of an innate aggressive drive is equally inimical to a belief in a universal need for trust. In Freudian theory, as Kohut (1977) observed, biologically determined destructiveness is the psychological "bedrock" of human personality; "the behavioral baseline with regard to aggressiveness is the raging destructive baby" (p. 118). It is difficult to imagine such a baby trusting its caretakers and itself, let alone eliciting the trust of others who must care for it.

The third and, perhaps, most important reason for the neglect of trust by traditional psychoanalytic thinkers is Freud's positioning of the Oedipus complex at the center of human experience. The need to trust and be trusted pales in comparison to this dramatic saga of sexual longing and murderous rivalry. Because the Oedipus complex occurs early in development and its vicissitudes are thought to shape personality so decisively, traditionally psychoanalysis accepted a view of psychological development as essentially completed with its resolution. The notion that trust plays a significant role in maintaining self-experience throughout life would have had little meaning for most of the early analysts.

OEDIPUS BETRAYED

A number of writers (e.g., Bloch, 1989; Bunselmeyer, 1989; Kohut, 1981; Miller, 1986; Stolorow & Atwood, 1979; Suttie, 1988) suggest that Freud's highly idiosyncratic use of Sophocles' *Oedipus Rex*, the drama around which so much of psychoanalytic thought revolves, was prompted by unexamined aspects of his own personality. Freud claimed to have discovered the Oedipus complex during the course of his self-analysis. Soon after recovering memories of his infatuation with his mother and jealousy of his father, he became convinced of the universality of these experiences. Moreover, as Peter Gay (1988) observed, Freud strongly identified with Oedipus, "the bold discoverer of mankind's secrets, the eponymous hero of the 'nuclear complex,' the killer of his father, and the lover of his mother" (p. 442).

A rereading of the myth suggests that the tragic events in Oedipus's life cannot be attributed to his lust or his aggressiveness. Far from desiring his mother or feeling murderous rivalry toward his father, Oedipus committed patricide and incest inadvertently, following desperate attempts to avoid these horrors by self-exile. The most deliberate crimes in the myth were perpetrated against Oedipus, not by him (Bunselmeyer, 1989; Miller, 1986; Suttie, 1988). As an infant he was left alone to die by his self-concerned father and, in old-age, he was spurned by his sons. Rather than enjoying his ill deeds, Oedipus was tormented by remorse. It is noteworthy that abandonment and ostracism were Oedipus's fate. If humans cannot maintain a sense of self in isolation, surely the most heinous crime is the deprivation of human companionship.

Heinz Kohut (1981), struck by the degree to which the "intergenerational relationship" between Laius and Oedipus has been misconstrued by analysts, asks, "Is it not the most significant dynamic-genetic feature of the Oedipus story that Oedipus was a rejected child?" (p. 97). In borrowing the myth of Oedipus to illustrate what he deemed the central conflict of human development, Freud ignored the poignant irony of Oedipus's life: He is as much the victim as he is the victimizer. He is as much the betrayed as he is the betrayer.

That Freud experienced himself as injured by the deceitfulness of others repeatedly throughout his own life is corroborated by many of his biographers. For example, Jones (1961) observed, "How often in later years did Freud complain of the times he had been 'betrayed,' to use his expression, by his friends; in turn Breuer, Fliess, Adler, and Jung had promised to aid or even inspire him in his great search and then deserted him" (p. 381).

Devastating as these desertions were for the adult Freud, they appear to have been far less traumatic than the betrayals he experienced in childhood. Many who have researched Freud's early life (e.g., Gay, 1988; Jones, 1961; Schur, 1972; Stolorow & Atwood, 1979; Suttie, 1988) suggest that Freud sustained his first psychological injuries with the births of his siblings. Freud was only eleven months old when his brother Julius was born. As the adored first-born of a vivacious, beautiful young woman, Freud apparently experienced Julius's arrival as a terrible threat to his position as his mother's "indisputable favorite." He acknowledged having felt "malevolent wishes and genuine childish jealousy" toward Julius (Gay, 1988, p. 11) and, when his infant brother's death eight months later fulfilled his wishes, that "self-reproaches" were aroused in him that remained throughout his life (Jones, 1961, p. 7).

The distress he again experienced at age 2½, with the birth of his sister Anna, was apparently compounded by the fact that her appearance on the scene coincided with the dismissal of a nursemaid who had been a key figure in his early life. Accused of petty theft by Freud's half-brother, Philipp, she was subsequently arrested and imprisoned. Speculating in a letter to Fliess (October 3, 1897) on the cause of his (Freud's) "mild hysteria," Freud wrote:

> in my case the "prime originator" [*Urheberin*] was an ugly, elderly but clever woman [the nursemaid] who told me a great deal about God Almighty and hell and instilled in me a high opinion of my own capacities . . . She was my teacher in sexual matters and complained because I was clumsy and unable to do anything . . . Moreover, she washed me in reddish water in which she had previously washed herself. (Masson, 1984, p. 215)

Thus, Freud appears to have had a very intense and ambivalent relationship with this woman which may have included sexual abuse.

Freud, as might any child, appears to have experienced the births of his siblings as betrayals by his mother. Far from acknowledging his rage and disappointment in her, however, Freud's references to his mother invariably ring with praise, sexual longing, and love. It is to the "bad treatment" he received from his old nursemaid that he attributes his neurotic suffering. The unswerving nature of Freud's conscious loving feelings toward his mother reflects a defensive idealization (Stolorow & Atwood, 1979) intended to protect her from his unconscious rage at her infidelity. Moreover, Freud's theories of psychosexual development, insofar as they neglect the actual behavior of parents toward their children in favor of an innate biologically determined sequence, served to further protect his mother from blame (Stolorow & Atwood, 1979; Suttie, 1988). Suttie (1988) interpreted Freud's belief in an innate destructive drive and his emphasis on sex over love as "the work of a thwarted infant revenging itself on mother" (p. 249). He saw Freud as "the older, anxious child" who never came to terms with his mother's infidelity (p. 254). Gay (1988) suggested that it was not merely that his mother gave birth to his siblings in quick succession that tormented young Freud, but also that his half brother, to his mind a far better match for her than his father, seemed likely to displace him as his mother's favorite.

In contrast to his strenuous efforts to maintain an untarnished view of his mother's perfection, Freud appears to have been keenly aware of his disappointments in his father. He recounted the following anecdote told by his father involving an act of anti-Semitism. A Christian man knocked his father's new fur cap into the muck and shouted, "Jew, off the sidewalk." When Freud asked his father what he did in response, Jacob Freud replied, "I stepped into the road and picked up my cap." Freud reported that his father's submissive response "did not seem heroic to me," and that it raised doubts in him that his father was a "big strong man" (Gay, 1988, p. 12). Other writers (e.g., Bloch, 1989; Levinson, 1983; Mitchell, 1988) suggest that Freud had great difficulty in coming to terms with his father's "secrets and hypocrises" (Mitchell, 1988, p. 42). In letters to Fliess written in 1896 and 1897, Freud baldly asserted that his father had sexually abused several of his siblings and was responsible for their neuroses (Masson, 1985, p. 231). Bloch speculated that after his father died, Freud's need to exonerate him led to his retraction of the seduction theory according to which he believed "in all cases, the *father*, not excluding my own, had to be accused of being perverse" (Masson, 1985, p. 264).

The biographical record seems to leave little doubt that Freud experienced betrayals by all of his most trusted caretakers. By allowing her adoring gaze to fall on so many rivals, his mother appears to have prematurely and suddenly deprived him of a needed experience of being special to her. By revealing himself as weak and corrupt, and possibly incestuously abusive, his father disappointed his natural wish for a strong, masculine figure worthy of respect and emulation, a source of protection and security. By becoming intimately involved with him (perhaps sexually) and then abruptly disappearing, his nursemaid undoubtedly shook Freud's faith in her goodness and loyalty. Yet, Freud never mentioned having been betrayed in childhood.

As will be explained at greater length in Chapter 4, the means by which Freud attempted to restore his self-experience foreclosed the possibility of his recognizing how profoundly his childhood trust had been betrayed. It seems likely that his neglect of trust was not an oversight on the part of a genius. Rather, Freud could not give issues of trust and betrayal prominence in his work without opening a Pandora's box of dangers to his self-experience.

FREUD, FERENCZI, AND THE "CONFUSION OF TONGUES"

On April 26, 1886, in a speech before members of the Society for Psychiatry and Neurology in Vienna, Freud proposed that traumatic sexual experiences in childhood caused hysteria. Only a year and five months later (September 21, 1887), Freud wrote a letter to Fliess confessing, "I no longer believe in my neurotica [theory of neurosis]" (Masson, 1984, p. 108). Freud explained that if his original theory were true, the fathers of most of his hysterical patients would be guilty of incest, a possibility, given the high incidence of hysteria, he apparently found hard to accept. Instead, he suggested that since truth and fiction cannot be distinguished on an unconscious level, children predisposed to hysteria by hereditary factors, elaborate sexual fantasies which "invariably seize upon the theme of the parents" (Masson, 1984, p. 108; see also Ulman & Brothers, 1988).

As Strozier (1983) suggested, Freud remained ambivalent about the primacy of fantasy over reality throughout his life. Yet, Freud's down-playing of what has come to be known as "the seduction theory" of neurosis in favor of his oedipal theory has had monumental consequences. His followers have tended to discount the effects of actual experiences in their patients' early lives, and concentrate instead on their intrapsychic conflicts over the expression of pathogenic sexual and aggressive fantasies.

Sandor Ferenczi was the only member of Freud's "inner circle" to question his repudiation of the seduction theory of neurosis. As one of Freud's most devoted and loyal disciples, Ferenczi was extremely conflicted over his wish to win Freud's approval on the one hand, and his need to be true to his clinical convictions on the other (de Forest, 1954; Masson, 1984, Thompson, 1955). However, in a 1932 speech commemorating Freud's 75th birthday, Ferenczi's professional integrity apparently won out. This speech, originally entitled, "The Passions of Adults and their Influence on the Sexual and Character Development of Children," caused an irreparable rift in his relationship with Freud. It was posthumously published in English as "Confusion of Tongues Between Adults and the Child: The Language of Tenderness and of Passion" (Ferenczi, 1933).

It is hardly surprising that Freud objected to his birthday tribute. Not only did Ferenczi (1933) assert that "sexual trauma, as the pathogenic factor cannot be valued highly enough" and that it occurred "more often than one had dared to suppose," he also introduced the notion that "people thought to be trustworthy such as relatives (uncles, aunts, grandparents), governesses or servants . . . misuse the ignorance and innocence of the child" (p. 161). With these assertions, Ferenczi raised the specter of trust betrayal that Freud had so determinedly ignored. Resurrecting the discarded seduction theory, Ferenczi argued that sexual fantasies, innate disposition, and constitution were not primary causal factors; neuroses were caused by the mistreatment of children by trusted adults!

Ferenczi's phase "confusion of tongues" refers to the gross misunderstanding of children by adults who confuse a child's wish for "tenderness" with an adult's wish for actual sexual relations. Mistaking the child's playful emulation of its parents for the seductive behavior of a sexually mature person, the adult initiates sex with the child "without consideration of the consequences." The extremely harmful consequences, according to Ferenczi, include profound disturbances in the child's trust.

Urgently needing to maintain a trusting relationship with the adult, the child institutes various psychological stratagems, including "identification with the aggressor." Since the aggressor is now introjected, the abusive event becomes intrapsychic instead of extrapsychic and, therefore, ceases to exist as external reality. In a dream-like trance (Ferenczi's apparent reference to the dissociative nature of trauma), the child succeeds in maintaining an illusion that his or her trust had not been betrayed. Moreover, the child "introjects" the guilt he or she imagines the adult should feel and loses trust in self: "When the child recovers from such an attack, he feels enormously confused, in fact split—innocent and culpable at the same time—and his confidence in the testimony of his own senses is broken" (p. 162).

The forcing of adult sexuality on children is not, in Ferenczi's view, the sole cause of psychopathology; pathological consequences are also likely to follow from rejection or the withdrawal of love. It is Ferenczi's great achievement to have discovered that the successful psychoanalytic treatment of adults who have experienced traumatizing childhood betrayals of either kind depends on working through trust disturbances in the therapeutic relationship and the subsequent development of "confidence" or trust in the therapist.

Ferenczi's discoveries about the betrayal of trust in childhood trauma and the crucial importance of trust in the therapeutic relationship derived from his earnest, if unsuccessful, attempts to treat trauma patients in accordance with Freud's theoretical understanding and technical recommendations. While his patients confirmed Freud's insight that traumatized individuals are bound to reexperience their original traumas in the context of the therapeutic relationship (Freud had postulated a repetition compulsion), Ferenczi discovered that the abreaction of their repressed affects was not curative. To his dismay, the condition of patients treated in the recommended manner seemed to deteriorate. They would complain of severe nightmares and anxiety attacks suffered after and even during analytic sessions. Although usually compliant and willing to accept Ferenczi's interpretations, they occasionally accused him of being cold, hard, cruel, selfish, heartless, etc. He came to believe that their seeming compliance hid hatred and rage for him.

Ferenczi explained his patients' efforts to hide their rage at him as stemming from the "paralyzing fear" they suffered following their childhood traumas. Rendered silent by "the overwhelming power and authority" of the adult, they had not dared to criticize him. He described his startling discovery that, in treatment, the unexpressed rage of such patients is often directed toward the "professional hypocrisy" of the therapist. Although, according to Ferenczi, therapists hold out to patients the promise of providing undivided interest and genuine concern, inevitably, because of all sorts of countertransferential interferences, they fail to keep their word. To make matters worse, they refuse to admit breaches of their promises to their patients.

Since the patients' childhood traumas were also denied by the adults who abused them, the therapist's hypocrisy is now unbearable. "Small wonder," Ferenczi (1933) noted, "that our effort produced no better results than the original trauma" (p. 160). Ferenczi's solution to this seemingly insoluble dilemma was deceptively simple:

> The setting free of his critical feelings, the willingness on our part to admit our mistakes and the honest endeavor to avoid them in future, all these go to create in the patient a confidence in the analyst. *It is this confidence that establishes the contrast between the present and the unbearable traumatogenic past.* (p. 160)

The recommendation that therapists must honestly and undefensively acknowledge failures in empathy and other inevitable mistakes, a radical idea in Ferenczi's day, is now the cornerstone of contemporary self-psychological treatment. It was to Ferenczi's enormous credit that he understood that by acknowledging these empathic failures the therapist promotes and restores trust (see Chapter 6).

Trust *per se* was not of special interest to Ferenczi and he did not attempt its systematic investigation. Yet, with his impassioned plea that issues of trust and betrayal be recognized as crucial in pathogenesis and psychoanalytic treatment, Ferenczi addressed the void in Freudian theory. His understanding of the relationship between trauma and trust disturbance and the uses of trust in psychoanalytic treatment anticipated in many respects the views developed in later chapters.

TRUST AFTER FREUD

Ferenczi's discoveries about trust and betrayal were vehemently rejected by most of the leading analysts of his time. Many who heard his "Confusion of Tongues" paper at the 12th International Psycho-Analytic Congress in Weisbaden believed that the dissemination of his ideas would pose a "danger to society" (Masson, 1984). Consequently, efforts were made to suppress the publication of its English translation—efforts that Freud himself appears to have supported. Seventeen years later, Michael Balint, one of Ferenczi's analysands, finally succeeded in having the paper published in *The International Journal of Psycho-Analysis*.

Despite the chilling lesson of Ferenczi's fall from grace (i.e., that efforts to revive the connection between trust betrayal and neurosis are dangerous), the decades following Freud's death have produced a number of major contributions toward a psychology of trust. Many theorists have acknowledged the importance of trust in human development and the clinical situation, among whom Michael Balint, Ian Suttie, Erik Erikson, Therese Benedek, Margaret Mahler, Carl Rogers, and Donald Winnicott gave trust special prominence in their writings.[1] As we shall see, however, for various reasons, none of these writers developed an integrated and systematic theory of trust.

Michael Balint: Trauma and Trust Disturbance

A prolific writer and creative thinker, Michael Balint has gained recognition for proposing important revisions of psychoanalytic theory and technique (e.g., Balint, 1935, 1952, 1957, 1968, 1969) and for introducing such concepts as "primary love," "the basic fault," and "the new beginning" that are highly congruent with many of the latest developments in object relations theory and self psychology.[2] Like Ferenczi, Balint did not set himself the task of elucidating the nature of trust. However, he fully recognized the importance of Ferenczi's insights into trauma and trust disturbance and his contributions broadened the scope of their application.

Building on Ferenczi's understanding of sexual abuse in childhood, Balint (1969) proposed that trauma has a "three-phasic structure." Describing the first phase of trauma in which the immature child is dependent upon adult caretakers, he observed: "[A]lthough frustrations in their relationship may lead to irritation and even to rages at times, the relationship between the child and the adult is mainly trusting" (p. 432).

In the second phase, the adult does something highly exciting, frightening, or painful to the child. Balint agreed with Ferenczi that the abusive behavior is not necessarily "genital-sexual"—it may even be that the adult ignores, rejects, or acts with cold severity toward the child. Although the aftermath of trauma is commonly attributed to this phase alone, Balint suggested that it is the next phase that constitutes the "real completion of the trauma."

---

[1]The importance of trust is implicit in the theoretical formulations of many other writers. However, I have chosen to review only the work of those who specifically devote themselves to the topic.
[2]See Bacal & Newman (1990) for a summary of Balint's contributions.

The third phase of trauma, according to Balint, involves a radical change in the behavior of the abusive adult. Acting as if the previous excitement or rejection had not occurred, the adult coldly rebuffs the abused child's attempts to repeat the "exciting passionate game" and may refuse to offer comfort or consolation when the child shows pain or distress. Adopting an attitude of moral indignation, such an adult is likely to accuse the child of depravity. Balint understood the third-phase behavior of the adult as a consequence of severe guilt feelings and the belief that the best way to remedy the misdeed is to pretend ignorance. However, he also suggested that some abusive adults change simply because they find more satisfactory adult partners.

As Balint (1969) pointed out, his three-phasic structure represents a change from the "purely quantitative considerations" of Freudian trauma theory. Moreover, it shifts the basis of trauma from "the field of one-person psychology, to the study of events in an object relationship, i.e., the field of two-person psychology" (p. 433). An important consequence of viewing trauma as inseparable from the relationship in which it occurs is that disturbances in trust emerge as a central issue. Suggesting that his understanding of trauma may even shed light on the dynamics of such trauma in adult life as accidents, explosions, etc., Balint (1969) noted: "It is very likely that in these situations the starting relationship between the individual and his environment was confident and trusting, the accident struck him unprepared, *destroying his trust*" (p. 432, italics added).

The treatment of adults traumatized as children, according to Balint (1952), must take into account their damaged trust: "Our therapeutic aim is quite clear. These mistrustful people must learn in the course of treatment to be able again to give themselves up to love, to pleasure, to enjoyment, as fearlessly nd innocently as they were able to do in their earliest childhood" (p. 154). Fearing retraumatization in the transference, these patients exhibit intense anxiety against "a full surrender to love" and against its counterpart, "a full surrender to hate." If therapists "control" their countertranference, Balint contended, they can show these patients how they protect themselves against this anxiety in the therapeutic relationship. In the course of these efforts, the situations in which the child's trust was betrayed are discovered.

Balint (1952) proposed that it is not the recovery of the memory of the trauma that results in cure, nor even the awareness of the ways that patients protect themselves against retraumatization. Rather, they have to learn anew "to love innocently, unconditionally, as only children can love" (p. 157). At this point patients arrive at "the new beginning," which is based on "the capacity for an unsuspicious, trusting, self-abandoned and relaxed object relation."

These insights into trauma and trust disturbance inform all of Balint's major contributions. For example, Balint (1968) used the term "the basic fault" to account for the severe narcissistic disorder that results from the traumatic disruption of the "the primary object relationship," the trusting bond between infant and its mother. In treatment, according to Balint (1968), patients who regress to the level of the basic fault experience a deep gulf separating the "child in the patient" from the "grownup analyst" (p. 182). It is the empathic understanding of the analyst that bridges the gap. However, this understanding can not always be conveyed by interpretation but rather by creating the atmosphere that the patient needs. Balint likened this atmosphere to "holding the patient tight," an idea very similar to Winnicott's (1960) "holding environment."

In 1969, one year before his death, Balint proposed that by applying his ideas on trauma and trust disturbance to the "complicated issue" of the etiology of character disorders and neuroses, the traumatic and structural theories of pathogenesis might be united into one integrated theory. Observing that "ego distortions" also have a three-phasic structure, he suggested that in essence they are traumas. With this assertion Balint placed himself in the forefront of contemporary psychoanalysts who urge the return to a "trauma paradigm" (see Chapter 6). Had he lived longer, Balint might well have developed a theory of pathogenesis centered around trauma and trust disturbance. However, Balint's theories are limited by his adherence to a "maturity or reality-morality" (Kohut & Wolf, 1978, p. 423; also see Bacal & Newman, 1990; Mitchell, 1988). That is, he believed that the patient-therapist relationship at the level of the basic fault is "primitive" and must be given up. After some time in treatment, the patient achieves a mature concern for the needs of others. Balint apparently failed to understand that the need to trust others and to be trusted by them to provide essential psychological experiences persists throughout the life span.

Ian Suttie: The Love-Relationship of Trust

The theoretical innovations advanced by Ian Suttie in his extraordinarily prescient 1935 book, *The Origins of Love and Hate*, have been, until very recently, largely ignored by the psychoanalytic community (see Bacal & Newman, 1990; Brome, 1982). Nevertheless, Suttie deserves acclaim not only for anticipating many of the central concepts of object relations theory and self psychology, but also for his deep understanding of the importance of trust in psychological life and its role in the therapeutic relationship. Suttie acknowledged his debt to Ferenczi, but made no reference to Balint despite the similarity of a number of their formulations.

Arguing that "mind is social and society is mental" (1988, p. 13) and that the need for companionship is innate and all-important, Suttie totally rejected Freudian drive theory. Where Freud saw sublimated sexuality, Suttie saw love and tender affection. In contrast to Freud's understanding of anger and hate as expressions of a primary destructive drive, Suttie understood these emotions neither as "death-seeking" nor "death-dealing," but as functioning to preserve the self. For Suttie, the mother's responsiveness to the infant's love is essential for the preservation of its self-experience. When that responsiveness is lacking, the child's anger can be understood as a protest, not an attempt to destroy the mother, which, he noted, "would have fatal repercussions upon the self" (p. 23). Anticipating Kohut by some 50 years, Suttie argued that the child's self-preservative dependency on the responsiveness of others is never outgrown, but undergoes a process of developmental transformation whereby it persists throughout adult life as a need for companionship.

Although Suttie did not often refer to trust or its betrayal explicitly in his discussions of normal and pathological development, his appreciation of the role it plays in preserving self-experience is implicit. For example, describing the emotion of fear as "an appeal to the mother," Suttie noted: "[W]here the child is afraid, it is reassured by her [the mother's] confidence and serenity, but not by her indifference and neglect, which is perhaps the worst of all for the child. Neglect of the fear-appeal is extremely traumatic" (p. 24). Translating Suttie's words into the language of trust we might say that the fearful child needs to experience the mother as self-trusting. Her failure to respond to its fear empathically constitutes a traumatic betrayal insofar as her indifference and neglect threaten its experience of self-cohesion (see Chapter 3).

Suttie also understood children's need to experience themselves as trustworthy providers of psychological experiences for others. As he observed: "The mother-child relationship . . . (to the child's mind) is a true, 'balanced' Symbiosis; and the *need to give is as vital, therefore, as the need to get*" (p. 53). Distrust, Suttie believed, is likely to result when the child's needs are met reluctantly. "One of the most grievous of possible experiences is that of having to accept grudging service, since the unwilling servant shows no satisfaction in our pleasure—rejects our love responses and manifestly refuses to love us. A natural outcome of such an experience is a distrust of love-relationships" (p. 65).

Strongly emphasizing the importance of trust in the therapeutic relationship, Suttie often referred to trust explicitly in this context. Since psychopathology, in his view, is a "disturbance in the love life," he endorsed Ferenczi's assertion that love heals the patient. The therapeutic employment of love (which he defined as a "feeling-interest responsiveness—not a goal-inhibited sexuality" [p. 211]) promotes trust. Only when the patient enters into what he called "the love-relationship of trust" does a transference neurosis develop in which ambivalent feelings for the mother are "played off" on the therapist. The main goal of treatment is "the overcoming of resistances" such that the patient relaxes defenses against the expression of all affects, including hatred.

> The overcoming of resistances might almost be paraphrased as the development of a trust in the analyst-parent *which will be capable of surviving* the reproaches arising from repressed anxiety and rage and which therefore makes repression (and its secondary bitterness, instability and other bad consequences) *unnecessary.* (p. 217)

He was quite specific in outlining therapeutic techniques for promoting trust. First, although therapists need not respond to their patients' emotions with identical or harmonious emotions, they show by their understanding and insight that a "fellowship of suffering" has been established. Second, a "true and full companionship" should be offered the patient that resembles a loving maternal relationship. Warning against a "passive" technique,[3] Suttie argued that "a one-sided, unresponsive, love-relationship must evoke anxiety and cannot be curative." Here, he was in complete agreement with many contemporary object relations theorists and self psychologists who argue that the so-called neutrality of classical analysts often recapitulates for patients the traumas inflicted by unresponsive caretakers. Third, the therapist's own security must not depend on what Suttie termed "neurotic flight" from feeling. Therapists who fear their own affective experience or are afraid to violate our culture's "taboo on tenderness," are likely to resort to such techniques as persuasion, suggestion, and hypnosis. These authoritarian measures serve to coerce the patient into "normal" ways of thinking and acting. With this assertion, Suttie demonstrated his sensitivity to the "intersubjective" nature of the therapeutic relationship.

Although Suttie's formulations certainly go a long way toward preparing the groundwork for a psychology of trust, they fall short of completing one. For example, he failed to elucidate his suggestion that psychoanalytic treat-

---

[3]Suttie appears to allude to Ferenczi's (1919) recommendation that analysts adopt an "active" technique.

ment heals damaged trust with a clear explanation of how trust is damaged in the first place, much less the ways in which damaged trust leads to psychopathology. Since it is love in the child's early relationships rather than trust that he celebrated, and love that he hailed as the significant curative agent in psychotherapy, Suttie had no need to develop his understanding of trust more fully. For example, he neither distinguished the many aspects of trust one from another, nor examined the possibility that trust changes with development. He ignored the positive functions of mistrust as well as the maladaptive aspects of intensified trust.

Nevertheless, Suttie was among the first psychoanalysts to recognize the centrality of trust in the therapeutic relationship and in human life. Describing a successful therapeutic outcome, he observed that "the patient [who finds] confidence in himself and trust in others . . . finds thereby the interests whereby mental intercourse – intellectual or aesthetic – the companionship of speech, is developed; and the patient is now 'well'" (p. 247).

Erik Erikson: Basic Trust

With his conceptualization of basic trust as the "first component of a healthy personality" (1964, p. 50), "the most fundamental prerequisite of mental vitality" (1968, p. 96), Erikson was more influential than any other theorist in putting trust on the psychoanalytic map. His discoveries about trust appear to derive from his conviction that to understand human development and psychopathology we must reach beyond the psychosexual to the psychosocial and the historical, beyond a "single person's inner 'economics' of drive and defense" to "an ecology of mutual activation within a communal unit such as the family" (1982, p. 21).

Erikson envisioned psychosocial development in terms of an epigenesis consisting of eight stages, each of which is characterized by polarities of basic (i.e., unconscious) attitudes. An interaction between the emerging potentialities of the person and societal pressures and sanctions determines the nature of these attitudes. At each of the eight stages, which range from infancy to old age, a crisis evolves reflecting the need to master a particular developmental task. The first of these crises is basic trust versus basic mistrust.

According to Erikson (1968), a sense of basic trust derives from experiences in the infant's first year of life. It depends less on the amount of nurturance provided than on the quality of the maternal relationship. We are not born with trust. Rather, trust is *created* in children by mothers who respond to their needs sensitively and who, most importantly, transmit "a firm sense of personal trustworthiness within the trusted framework of their community's life style" (p. 103).

The crisis of basic trust versus basic mistrust coincides with what Erikson viewed as the incorporative mode of infancy, a general approach to the world that subsumes the psychosexual phase of orality in Freudian theory. There are two incorporative phases, the earlier being passive, and the later, an active biting phase characterized by rages that crucially test the trusting maternal relationship. Inevitably, the child develops some mistrust from disappointments in life such as those accompanying weaning. In Erikson's (1959) view, the child acquires a ratio of basic trust and mistrust which, if balanced toward trust, will promote the successful resolution of later crises.

Erikson (1968) recognized that basic trust contributes importantly to a "sense of identity." He summarized his multifaceted use of the term identity as referring to "a conscious sense of individual uniqueness . . . an unconscious striving for a continuity of experience, and . . . a solidarity with a group's ideals" (p. 208). The earliest sense of identity, according to Erikson (1950), arises out of the trustworthiness and "mutual recognition" of the mother-infant relationship. Disturbances in these mutually trusting experiences interfere with the need to consolidate a sense of identity in adolescence. Erikson (1959) related the alternatives of "time perspective vs. time diffusion" (i.e., a loss of the ego's function of maintaining perspective and expectancy) in adolescence to the crisis of basic trust versus basic mistrust in infancy. If they have not emerged from infancy with the conviction that predictable satisfaction awaits them, adolescents find themselves "at odds with time itself" (1968, p. 181).

The absence of basic trust, according to Erikson (1968), is responsible for the most severe forms of psychopathology, including infantile schizophrenia and shizoid and depressive states in adults. He suggested that the reestablishment of trust is a "basic requirement" for therapy of such patients. However, he did not specify the therapeutic methods helpful in reestablishing trust. Ultimately, basic trust is "the ontologic source" of hope and faith. Religion, Erikson (1950) argued, is the most lasting institution to serve the ritual restoration of a sense of trust in the form of faith.

Reviewing the rich variety of Erikson's theoretical formulations about trust, some open doors to deeper and more systematic investigation, while others appear to close them. The following critique aims at identifying both aspects of his work. Erikson's appreciation of the complex, multidimensional nature of trust provides a generous and sturdy foundation for theory building. Consider the richly nuanced conceptualization of trust offered by Erikson (1968):

> The general state of trust . . . implies not only that one has learned to rely on the sameness and continuity of the outer providers but also that one may trust oneself and the capacity of one's own organs to cope with the urges; that one is able to consider oneself trustworthy enough so that the providers will not need to be on guard or to leave. (p. 102)

However, he was quite vague about the developmental transformations of basic trust. Although he asserted that "the psycho-social quality" of basic trust becomes more differentiated with ego development, he did not describe the process whereby it becomes more differentiated, nor spell out how changes in the experience of trust result from this process of differentiation. His explanation about the relationship between trust and identity is similarly imprecise. He asserted that all eight phases of the life cycle constitute an "epigenesis of identity" without describing the ways in which trust promotes a sense of identity in each of the phases. The "mutuality of trust" of the mother-infant relationship, an important first step in the development of a sense of identity is connected to the adolescent's need for "men and ideas to have *faith* in" (Erikson, 1968, p. 128) as well as "the emergence of the strength of fidelity" (Erikson, 1982, p. 60). However, it is not clear if and how trust affects identity in the years between infancy and adolescence and the years that follow it.

The imprecision in Erikson's formulations about trust development may be attributed, at least in part, to his reliance on a theory of epigenesis in which development proceeds from one phase devoted to a specific clinical issue to another. In recent years, the epigenetic perspective seems to have lost favor with developmental theorists. As Stern (1985) noted, "The quantum shifts in the social 'presence' and 'feel' of the infant can . . . no longer be attributed to the departure from one specific developmental task-phase and the entrance into the next. Instead, the major developmental changes in social experience are attributed to the infant's acquisition of new senses of the self" (p. 10). It is difficult to imagine how trust might develop beyond the crisis of the first phase of the life cycle during subsequent phases devoted to different clinical issues. If, for example, during the second year of life, the child is caught up in the crisis of autonomy versus shame and doubt, what role, if any, does trust play in the resolution of the crisis?

The difficulty of tracing the vicissitudes of trust from infancy to adolescence is further compounded by Erikson's implicit belief that the goal of childhood development is separation and individuation. Although the initial crisis of trust versus mistrust places development within the context of mutual relatedness, the successful resolution of the next four crises involves move-ment toward ever greater autonomy and independence, qualities that do not depend on trust (see Gilligan, 1982). Another difficulty inherent in Erikson's epigensis is that basic trust is contrasted with its polar opposite, basic mistrust, in a way that unavoidably lends negative meaning to mistrust. Mature trust, as I argue in later chapters, involves a generous helping of skepticism and doubt. Moreover, disturbed trust often takes the form of intensified trust, as, for example, when a person places trust in someone whose behavior warrants suspicion.

Roazen (1976) referred to "tensions with Erikson's work between the Freudian loyalist and the erring rebel" (p. 9). The lack of clarity in Erikson's theorizing about the relationship between trust and identity appears to reflect this tension, especially in his attempt to relate the term "identity" to both ego, the Freudian construct, and self, or self-representation, as Hartmann (1950) used the term. According to Erikson (1968): "One can then speak of ego identity when one discusses the ego's synthesizing power in light of its central psychosocial function, and of self-identity when the integration of the individ-ual's self- and role-images are under discussion" (p. 211). To the extent that Erikson retains the Freudian concept of ego (he mentions Freud's references to the ego's attitudes toward the self) he is still wedded to a "single person" theory. While one's sense of self, a purely psychological construct, cannot exist independent of one's relationships with others, ego comes into existence as an autonomous biological entity. Thus, although Erikson recognized that a firm sense of identity depends on trust in self and in others, to the extent that identity involves ego, the relationship between trust and identity is attenuated.

In a number of respects, Erikson's (1968) ideas about trust seem free from Freud's pessimism about human nature. In discussing the Freudian notion of an oral character, Erikson (1968) observed that

> there is an optimistic oral character, too, one who has learned to make giving and receiving the most important thing in life. And there is "orality" as a normal substratum in all individuals, a lasting residuum of this first period of dependency on powerful providers. It normally expresses itself in our depend-encies and nostalgias, and in our all too hopeful and all too hopeless states. The integration of the oral stage with all the following ones results, in adulthood, in a combination of faith and realism. (p. 102)

On the other hand, Erikson (1968) proposed that trust originates in a crisis of the "second oral stage" stemming from, among other things, the infant's "more violent drive to incorporate," (p. 101) and the mother's gradual turning away from the baby toward other pursuits. Erikson (1968) protests that the term "crisis" does not connote "impending catastrophe" but, rather, "a necessary turning point, a crucial moment, when development must move one way or another, marshaling resources of growth, recovery, and further differentiation" (p. 16). Nevertheless, according to his developmental scenario, the extent to which a person is trusting or mistrustful is determined by a turn taken at a crossroads encountered very early in life. What is more, this turn is decided, at least in part, by a person's innate aggressiveness.

Erikson (1959) warned that even if the outcome of the crisis of the first year leads to a ratio of greater basic trust than basic mistrust, this should not be regarded as a lasting achievement. He noted that even under optimal conditions in which the mother weans the child gradually, experiences of this period are bound to leave a person with "some sense of basic loss," and "a dim but universal nostalgia for a lost paradise" (p. 61). He added, "It is against the combination of these impressions of having been deprived, of having been divided, and of having been abandoned, all of which leave a residue of basic mistrust, that basic trust must be established and maintained" (p. 61).

Thus, Erikson appeared to view the sense of trust as an extremely fragile and precarious state of affairs, established and maintained only after arduous struggle. In chapters to come, I describe a very different understanding of trust as an inborn potential that, under normal circumstances, matures and strengthens over the course of a lifetime and is disturbed only as a consequence of traumatic betrayals.

Therese Benedek: The Concept of Confidence

Born in Hungary, Therese Benedek was one of the early European analysts who gained recognition as an educator and theorist in the United States. She published many papers between 1931 and 1968 on the relationship between psychological and somatic processes in women, the early mother-infant relationship, and personality development in adulthood. Although she embraced much of Freud's libido theory, arguing, for example, that each phase of motherhood is accompanied by a regression to the oral phase of development, her discoveries about confidence are highly compatible with recent developments in psychoanalysis.

Benedek (1952) described her use of the term as follows:

Confidence is used as a term to designate an emotional state of the infant which has developed through multiple repetitions of the gratifying experience of symbiosis. This concept implies an ego organization in which the effects of the libidinal relationship with the mother through introjection have become a part of the mental organization of the child. (p. 362)

According to Benedek (1938) her concept of confidence found an "identical twin" years later in Erikson's concept of trust. As she observed, both confidence and trust are attributable to the same primary processes between mother and infant and both function to facilitate object relationships. However, if Benedek's confidence is, in certain respects, a close relative of Erikson's basic trust, it is hardly an identical twin. Benedek herself pointed to differences reflected in their respective word choices:

> I chose the word confidence because this word for me implies reciprocity, mutuality, con-fideo. Erikson feels that he chose the word trust because it implies "complete reliance" vested in the trusted person . . . trust would be a man's word—reliance on the self, trusting because he is trusted; confidence is the woman's word—it relates always to another person who shares the trust. (p. 127)

Although Erikson (1968) explained that he preferred the word "trust" to "confidence" because "there is more naivete and more mutuality in it" (pp. 247–248), Benedek's descriptions of the infant-mother relationship emphasize much more strongly than do Erikson's the infant's contribution. From Benedek's perspective, confidence is not dependent solely upon the mother's ability and willingness to give, but also upon the infant's congenital or acquired ability to receive.

Benedek was also critical of Balint's (1952) concept of primary object love, a concept she viewed as similar to confidence, for its failure to posit an expectation of reciprocity. Balint's infant would express primary object love with the words, "I should be loved and satisfied, but without the least return of love on my part." Benedek (1938) argued, "Observations show undoubtedly that an infant, as soon as the relationships with the environment develops, instinctively returns as much love as lies within its physiologic maturity" (p. 119).

Another difference between Erikson's trust and Benedek's confidence lies in the fact that, for Benedek (1956), the mother's self-confidence stands to gain as much as the infant's from their early interactions: "Parallel with the developmental process which leads to confidence in the infant, the mother, through introjecting the gratifying experiences of successful mothering, establishes her self-confidence, her trust in her own motherliness" (p. 363).

Benedek (1959) conceptualized parenthood as a developmental phase; the mother's new-found confidence in herself enables her to achieve a greater integration of her personality. Since the mother's "self-concept" is enhanced through her association of "good, thriving infant and good mother—good self," she is helped to resolve infantile conflicts with her own mother. If, however, the mother does not develop trust in her motherliness but instead experiences herself as inadequate, a regressive spiral may be established in which the infant's negative reactions increase the mother's inability to furnish the right response. The mother's repeated failures, in turn, make it difficult for the infant to experience confidence which, itself, serves to intensify the mother's sense of inadequacy.

Benedek's understanding of confidence, more than Erikson's understanding of trust, foreshadows the ideas I develop in this book. In contrast to Erikson, who argued that trust is "created" in the infant by the mother, Benedek viewed confidence as integral to the relationship between infant and caretaker. Benedek's appreciation of the infant as an active participant in early relationships not only anticipates the perspective of such contemporary developmental theorists as Beebe and Lachmann (1988a, 1988b), Lichtenberg (1983), and Stern (1985), but is also highly congruent with the intersubjective understanding of trust to which I subscribe.

Margaret Mahler: Trust as the "Midwife" of Psychological Birth

Mahler was another of the transplanted Europeans whose work greatly influenced American psychoanalysis. Although she did not offer an original conceptualization of trust, her account of the "psychological birth" of the individual (Mahler, Pine, & Bergman, 1975) makes use of Benedek's concept of confidence as well as Erikson's concept of basic trust and, therefore, warrants our consideration. Working within the mainstream of psychoanalytic ego psychology, Mahler (1967, 1979; Mahler et al., 1975) attempted to develop a theory of early object relations based on direct observations of children and caretakers.

Mahler (1967) outlined a detailed sequence of development during which the child forms a differentiated sense of self and others. On emerging from what she termed a "normal autistic phase" that marks the first weeks of life, the infant enters the symbiotic phase, "a twilight stage of still primary narcissism" (p. 219) characterized by a "need-satisfying object relationship." According to Mahler, Pine, and Bergman (1975), "The essential feature of symbiosis is hallucinatory or delusional somatopsychic *omnipotent* fusion with the representation of the mother and, in particular, the delusion of a common boundary between two physically separate individuals" (p. 45).

Successful symbiosis, she argued, depends on the mother's actual trustworthiness, i.e., she must be available and predictable. Gross failures by the mother in providing trustworthy symbiotic gratification may lead to severe psychopathology, e.g., autism or symbiotic psychosis. But even less serious failures in symbiosis may have important repercussions on the development of the child's confidence and trust, which, in turn, greatly affects subsequent development.

The peak of the symbiotic phase in the third quarter of the first year, coincides with the onset of the separation-individuation phase, which is further subdivided into the phases of differentiation, practicing, rapprochement, and "on the way to libidinal object constancy." During differentiation, which occurs at about four months of age, the infant begins to "hatch," that is, to take the first steps toward breaking away from psychological unity with the mother. For Mahler (1972), the stranger reactions that occur during this period strongly reflect the quality of the infant's confidence and trust that develop during symbiosis.

> In children for whom the symbiotic phase has been optimal and "confident expectation" has prevailed (Benedek, 1938), curiosity and wonderment are the predominant elements of their inspection of strangers. By contrast, among children whose basic trust has been less than optimal, an abrupt change to acute stranger anxiety may make its appearance; or there may be a prolonged period of mild stranger reaction, which transiently interferes with pleasurable inspective behavior. (p. 225)

The following subphase, practicing, which typically occurs from 10 to 18 months of age, is characterized by the maturation of the infant's motoric capacities, which enable the infant to move physically away from the mother. The mother again must be reliably available as a "home base" for "emotional refueling." Like Benedek, Mahler (1972) emphasized the importance of the mother's self-confidence during this period.

> If the mother's "primary preoccupation" with her infant—her mirroring function during earlier infancy—is unpredictable, unstable, anxiety ridden or hostile; if her confidence in herself as a mother is shaky, then the individuating child has to do without a reliable frame of reference for checking back, perceptually and emotionally, to the symbiotic partner. The result will then be a disturbance in the primitive "self feeling" which would derive or originate from

a pleasurable and safe state of symbiosis, from which he did not have to hatch prematurely and abruptly. (p. 209)

Following the "love affair with the world" (Greenacre, 1957) that characterizes the practicing subphase, the 16-to-18-month-old toddler, who has by now mastered upright locomotion, enters the rapprochement subphase. Increasing awareness of physical separateness leads to intensified separation anxiety. The earlier refueling contact with mother, according to Mahler, "is replaced by a quest for constant interaction at a progressively high level of symbolization." During this subphase, she argued, the child "must gradually and painfully give up his delusion of his own grandeur, often with dramatic fights with mother—less so . . . with father" (Mahler, 1972, p. 231).

Mahler described the task of the fourth subphase, object constancy, as twofold: the achievement of individuality and the attainment of a certain degree of object constancy. It is during this period that the child must resolve a primitive psychic conflict between an all-good, loved maternal imago and an all-bad, hated maternal imago. The mother's continuous libidinal availability, that is, her trustworthiness, makes it possible for the child to fuse these split introjects into a whole object. Both the resolution of "the rapprochement crisis" and the attainment of object constancy depend upon the child's prior attainment of trust and confidence in the mother's ability to satisfy needs and relieve tension.

M. Tolpin (1980) criticized Mahler's developmental scenario on the grounds that it confuses the child's normal psychology with what she calls "the adult's mental disintegration products":

> Mahler's theory that the baby is closed off in an autistic orbit of its own for several weeks, symbiotically merged or fused with a hallucinated object, preobject, of part-object for the next months, dangerously split by drives and defenses which make objects good and bad, prematurely separated, and traumatically deflated and disillusioned, because of normal physical and mental growth, is based on assumptions borrowed from the theory of neurosis and adapted to fit infantile psychology. (p. 53)

Mahler's view of trust as essential to the child's psychological development and her emphasis on what the mother actually does in interaction with the child as importantly affecting the child's trust in self and in others resonate well with the perspective that structures this book. Yet, for the reasons cited by Tolpin, it is difficult to imagine how the psychological birth process described by Mahler and her collaborators could produce a trusting, trustworthy baby.

Carl Rogers: The Person-Centered Approach

If the assumptions that inform Margaret Mahler's theory seem to place it near the low end of a continuum on which humans are viewed as trusting and trustworthy, then Carl Rogers's theory would have to be placed at the other end. As he noted, "Practice, theory, and research make it clear that the person-centered approach rests on a basic trust in human beings, and in all organisms" (1980, p. 117). Although his very eclectic training in theology, education, and counseling familiarized him with psychoanalytic theory, Rogers's work was more influenced by the teachings of Otto Rank than of Freud. Rogers was impressed by Rank's emphasis on therapy as enabling clients to express their personal will, to take command of their lives, and to create their own reality. Generally considered a humanistic psychologist, Rogers was also greatly influenced by the existential philosophy of Buber and Kierkegaard (Rogers & Sanford, 1984).

Rogers (1980) claimed to have developed a "*philosophy* of living and relationships" as well as a method of psychotherapy. Both alone and in collaboration with others, Rogers produced a vast quantity of publications from 1930 to his death in 1987 that dealt mainly with the many applications of his person-centered approach. First known as nondirective therapy, and then as client-centered therapy, this approach was developed as a method for one-to-one treatment and facilitative encounter groups. It has been applied to education, management, leadership, and as a means of resolving interracial and intercultural tensions (Rogers & Sanford, 1984). Its central hypothesis is summarized as follows:

> Individuals have within themselves vast resources for self-understanding and for altering their self-concepts, basic attitudes, and self-directed behavior; these resources can be tapped if a definable climate of facilitative psychological attitudes can be provided. (Rogers, 1980, p. 115)

According to Rogers, three elements constitute this facilitative climate: (1) genuineness, realness, or congruence, that is, the client[4] experiences the thera-

---

[4]Rogers used the word "client" as opposed to "patient" to emphasize his conviction that the medical model is inadequate for dealing with "psychologically distressed or deviant persons" (Rogers & Sanford, 1984).

pist as truly himself or herself, (2) caring, or prizing, "unconditional positive regard," and, (3) empathic understanding. (See Kahn, 1985, 1989 for a comparison of Rogers and Kohut.)

The provision of these conditions depends on the therapist's trust in his or her client and it is this aspect of trust that Rogers emphasizes most strongly. However, he also mentions the importance of the client's trust in self and in others and especially his or her trust in the therapist (1984) and the group (1970). The therapist's trust in the client is intimately related to what he refers to as the "actualizing tendency." Acknowledging his debt to Goldstein (1947), Maslow (1954), Angyal (1941, 1965), and Szent-Gyoergyi (1974), who held similar views, Rogers (1980) claimed,

> There is one central source of energy in the human organism. This source is a trustworthy function of the whole system rather than some portion of it; it is simply conceptualized as a tendency toward fulfillment, toward actualization, involving not only the maintenance but also the enhancement of the organism. (p. 123)

Believing that an actualizing tendency is present in everyone, the Rogerian therapist trusts that the patient will change and grow if he or she provides genuineness, caring, and empathic understanding. Considering the enormous importance of trust in Rogers' person-centered approach, it is somewhat surprising to discover that he did not examine its nature very thoroughly or systematically. Although he referred to trust in several of its various aspects, Rogers seemed to regard trust as a monolithic construct. While he described the conditions that foster trust, he does not specify the ways in which it can be disturbed or lost or the consequences of such disturbance or loss. Nor is it clear from Rogers's writings if he viewed trust as evolving over the course of development or as static and unchanging throughout life.

Donald W. Winnicott:
The Psychological Locale of Trust

The clinical relevance of Winnicott's work by far transcends its lack of theoretical consistency (Bacal & Newman, 1990). Although Winnicott did not attempt to elucidate the essence of trust or describe its complexity, his contribution is invaluable. He discovered the area of psychological life in which trust has its origin, the realm he called transitional space or potential space. In both joining and separating baby and mother, potential space exists between the inner world of the psychological experience and the environment. It is the source of cultural experience, creative living, and play. Winnicott (1967) observed, "From the beginning the baby has maximally intense experiences *in the potential space between the subjective object and the object objectively perceived, between me-extensions and the not-me*" (p. 100).

As a pediatrician and a psychoanalyst, Winnicott was deeply impressed by the importance of the trustworthiness of the mother-figure, that is, the dependability and reliability of her ministrations. In fact, for Winnicott (1967), the mother's love is "displayed or made manifest as human reliability." In his words: "The potential space happens *only in relation to a feeling of confidence* on the part of the baby" (p. 100), and the baby's confidence inturn derives from the trustworthiness of the mother-figure and the environment.

An important element of the mother's trustworthiness for Winnicott (1967) is her ability to adapt to changes in the developing baby's needs. This makes it possible for the baby to distinguish "the not-me from the me" (p. 109), a prerequisite for the establishment of an "autonomous self." Although the notion of an autonomous self is antithetical to the conceptualization of self embraced in this book, we shall see that trust and its disturbance powerfully affects one's experience of subjective reality (Chapter 3).

Winnicott (1967) was also extremely sensitive to the necessity for trust within the therapeutic relationship and the setting in which therapy is undertaken. He extended his notion of the "holding environment" (Winnicott, 1960), by which he meant all of the provisions by the "good-enough" mother, to include the analytic setting as well. It is within a trustworthy holding environment that "relaxation" occurs: "Account has to be taken of the reliability or unreliability of the setting in which the individual is operating. . . . I am trying to refer to the essentials that make relaxation possible" (p. 55). He regarded the relaxation that "belongs to trust" and the "professional reliability" of the therapeutic setting as essential to free association in the treatmentof adults or to spontaneous play in the treatment of children. He recommended the avoidance of premature interpretations as a precaution against interfering with the "natural evolution of the transference arising out of the-patient's growing trust in the psychoanalytic technique and setting" (p. 86).

Winnicott's insights into the psychological locale of trust have enormous relevance to the realm of trust examined in the chapters that follow.

Heinz Kohut's Trusting "Tragic Man"

Nothing even remotely like an elephant could be pieced together from the various accounts offered by the blind men in the fable, each of whom had experienced only one of its parts. And no meaningful psychology of trust could be developed by juxtaposing the disparate contributions by the theorists sampled above. What is needed for both elephant and theory is a unifying perspective. Of the various competing schools of thought, self psychology has much to recommend it as a theory that provides such a perspective. We have seen that many fundamental tenets of classical Freudian theory are incompatible with a view of trust as vital to psychological life. Self-psychological theory, on the other hand, is extremely congenial to such a view. Let us consider the advantages of using self psychology as the unifying perspective for a psychology of trust.

Self psychology is a fundamentally relational theory. Despite the justifiable contention of Stolorow and Atwood (1992) that remnants of "the myth of an isolated mind" persist in self-psychological writings, the major theoretical principles of self psychology place it at the forefront of the relational revolution. Kohut (1971, 1977, 1984) clearly demonstrated that self-experience abhors a vacuum. That is to say, one's self-experience does not exist independent of relations with others who provide psychological experiences necessary for its development, maintenance, and restoration. (I would add that one's self-experience is equally dependent on providing these experiences for others). Kohut coined the term "selfobject" to describe "our experience of another person that relates to this person's functions in shoring up our self" (1984, p. 49). As Wolf (1988) notes, "Precisely defined, a selfobject is neither self nor object, but the *subjective* aspect of a self-sustaining function performed by a relationship of self to objects who by their presence or activity evoke and maintain the self and the experience of selfhood" (pp. 184–185). Lichtenberg, Lachmann, and Fosshage (1992) emphasize the relational aspect of the selfobject concept further by suggesting that it refers to vitalizing experiences rather than internalized functions.

Self psychology is not a drive theory. Kohut (1977, 1981) used the term "Guilty Man" to describe the classical conceptualization of human nature. Reluctant to give up his pleasure and aggressive-destructive aims, Guilty Man lives in hopeless conflict over his need to express them. Although, as Kohut observes, Guilty Man is a psychological and moral view of human nature, it is based on the "quasi-biological" concept of drives. "Tragic Man," on the other hand, the self-psychological conceptualization, is a purely psychological construct. If Guilty Man is bent on satisfying his pleasure seeking drives, Tragic Man strives toward self-fulfillment. Kohut (1981) described Tragic Man as "attempting, and never quite succeeding, to realize the program laid down in his depth during the span of his life" (p. 93).

While this formulation is problematic in certain respects—Stolorow and

Atwood (1992) criticize the notion of an "innate nuclear program" or "inherent design" as inimical to a truly relational theory in which development is continually shaped by one's psychological experiences with others—Kohut leaves little doubt that Tragic Man is utterly dependent on relations with others. It is only when his strivings toward self-fulfillment are frustrated that he experiences driven sexuality and aggression. These experiences are not his biological destiny; they are "disintegration products" (Kohut, 1977, pp. 120–121), the result of failures in selfobject relations.

By replacing the gloomy notion that our pleasure-seeking and aggressive imperatives perpetually embroil us in lonely conflict with the much more hopeful idea that our continual strivings toward fulfillment are facilitated by our relationships with others, self psychology makes room for trust as a key concept.

Self psychology eschews a maturation morality. According to Kohut, we never stop needing selfobject experiences. Unlike many object relations theories in which maturity is equated with separation, individuation, and independence from others, self psychology sees the developmental line of selfobject relations as extending from birth to death. Because selfobject experiences are thought to undergo a process of maturation from archaic to more mature forms, there is no covert pressure to renounce or transcend one's dependence on trusting ties to others.

Self psychology is not an oedipal theory. Although an oedipal stage in which the child experiences sexual and aggressive feelings for its parents is considered universal, the empathic responsiveness of the child's parents to its oedipal strivings is thought to lead to a joyful and healthy outcome. By de-emphasizing the drama of the oedipus complex, self psychology sets the stage for a consideration of trusting relations between child and caretakers throughout development.

Issues related to trust are implicit in the writings of many self-psychological theorists. Kohut (1977) and Tolpin and Kohut (1980) have briefly described the trusting nature of the infant. However, trust has not been thoroughly examined by self psychologists. In the next chapter I describe a realm of trust, the theoretical underpinnings of which derive largely from self-psychological principles.

SELF-TRUST: THE "GLUE" OF

SELF-EXPERIENCE

The potential space between baby and mother, between child and family, between individual and society or the world, depends on experience which leads to trust. It can be looked upon as sacred to the individual in that it is here that the individual experiences creative living.

Donald W. Winnicott (1967)

Trust is a "complex, multi-dimensional construct" (Corrazini, 1977; see also Chun & Campbell, 1974). By means of sophisticated statistical analyses performed on scales designed to measure trust, psychologists have determined not only that various kinds of trust exist, but that each kind is relatively separate from the others. For example, a person may feel great trust in the political system of his or her country but little trust in a particular politician.

Most of the psychological literature on trust (e.g., Isaacs, Alexander, & Haggard, 1963; Deutsch, 1973; Prelinger & Zimet, 1964; Rotter, 1967, 1980) deals with trust in the "outer" world, *the realm of interpersonal relations*. This realm is concerned with reality-oriented (Noy, 1980) interactions between people who experience one another as separate, independent centers of initiative. Because reality cannot be perceived objectively, I shall refer to this realm as *the world of subjective reality*. Self psychology deals primarily with the "inner" or subjective world, *the realm of selfobject relations*. In this region of psychological life others are experienced from a "self-centered" perspective (Noy). They may not be experienced as completely separate from and outside of oneself. Rather, to varying degrees, they may be either experienced as part of oneself, or "in the service of the self and its maintenance and restoration" (Tolpin & Kohut, 1980).

Richard B. Ulman and I (1988) conceptualized the realm of selfobject relations on which self-experience depends in terms of unconscious selfobject fantasies. Although Kohut's later writings pay little heed to unconscious fantasy as central to self-experience, his work before 1977, including his famous monograph *The Analysis of the Self* (1971), contains numerous references to selfobject relations as fantasy formations. His descriptions of his patients' grandiose illusions and their experiences of others as perfectly empathic mirroring selfobjects, omnipotent idealized selfobjects, or identical twin selfobjects vividly convey the phantasmagoric underpinnings of self-experience. Moreover, the notion that fantasizing is a basic form of mental activity is well-established in psychoanalysis. Arlow (1969), Grossman (1982, 1984), and Kris (1956) have all advanced theories of the self as created by unconscious fantasizing. And, many other theorists have written about the centrality of narcissistic fantasy in unconscious mental life (see Ulman & Brothers, 1988 for a review of this literature).

Until 1990, Ulman and I referred to the unconscious fantasies that organize self-experience as "central organizing fantasies" (Nurnberg & Shapiro, 1983) or "archaic narcissistic fantasies." However, we now prefer the term "selfobject fantasies" because it emphasizes the centrality of selfobject experiences in subjective life. In the course of normal development selfobject fantasies undergo a process of developmental transformation that roughly corresponds to the maturation of primary process cognition described by Noy (1980). He argued that all areas of cognitive functioning, including thinking, perception, and communication, operate according to two different organizational modes: the primary process and the secondary process. In contrast to earlier analysts who believed primary process to be nothing more than a primitive discharge system (e.g., Kligerman, 1972), Noy viewed the two organizational modes as forming "two developmental lines whose courses of development are determined by the same intrinsic maturational factors" (p. 177). The two modes differ only in their function: The secondary process deals with reality orientation, whereas the primary process deals with "the regulation, maintenance and development of the self" (p. 172). Moreover, normal, healthy cognition depends on a sound balance between the reality-oriented mode and the self-centered mode.

It is my contention that the self-centered mode is employed in the unconscious selfobject fantasies that organize self-experience, whereas the reality-oriented mode is employed in experiences of subjective reality. In normal experience both modes of organization function side by side. As we shall see in Chapter 3, trauma profoundly affects their development and functioning.

Ulman and I (1988) described only those selfobject fantasies in which self is represented as the recipient of selfobject experiences provided by others. In recent years, I (1990, 1992) have discovered other selfobject fantasies in which self is represented as the provider of selfobject experiences for others. Relations between self and others in both types of selfobject fantasies include the three main types of selfobject experiences identified by Kohut (1971, 1977, 1984): mirroring, idealized merger, and twinship. Despite many recent suggestions for new categories of selfobject experience, no comprehensive list has been compiled to date (Bacal, 1990). Wolf (1980, 1988), for example, refers to efficacy and adversarial selfobject experiences; Ulman and Paul (1992) refer to pacifying and humanizing selfobject experiences; I (1992) distinguish between twinship and alter ego selfobject experiences; and Stolorow and Atwood (1992) mention self-delineating selfobject experiences. Thus, with the term *selfobject experiences* I include all those experiences essential for the establishment, preservation, and restoration of self-experience. As long as our selfobject fantasies remain intact, we experience ourselves as cohesive initiators of activity, existing over time, and worthy of esteem.

The following text will be concerned with trust that operates in the shadowy region between the world of subjective reality and the world of selfobject fantasy. In this "intermediate area of experiencing, to which inner reality and external life both contribute," Winnicott (1951, p. 2) located transitional phenomena (see Chapter 1). "Self-trust" is the name I have given to the dimension of trust that operates in this intermediate area (1989, 1990, 1992); it is broadly defined as *the hope or wishful expectation of obtaining and providing the selfobject experiences necessary for the development, maintenance, and restoration of cohesive selfhood.*

Self psychologists focus primarily on that which is observable via introspection and empathy, that is, on self-experience and the world of selfobject fantasy. Anything else, as Kohut (1959, 1981) cogently argued, belongs to the domain of the natural sciences and not to psychoanalysis. Nevertheless, Kohut has persuasively demonstrated that self-experience is determined by what actually transpires between children and their caretakers in the world of subjective reality. Children develop a sense of cohesive, stable, vital selfhood only if caretakers respond empathically to their selfobject needs. What is more, Kohut's (1971, 1977, 1984) case studies demonstrate his conviction that the restoration of self-experience is determined by what actually happens between therapists and their patients in the world of subjective reality. The patients' arrested self-experience will resume development only if therapists address failures in their empathic responsiveness to the patients' selfobject needs.

Kohut's (1971, 1977, 1984) concept of "transmuting internalization" has served as a bridge between the world of selfobject fantasy and the world of subjective reality. Transmuting internalization is a process by which the self-object experiences provided by a caretaker or therapist (events occurring in the world of subjective reality) are thought to be transformed into a child's or patient's psychic structure (the world of selfobject fantasy) as a result of "optimal frustration." This term refers to tolerable, that is, nontraumatic, disappointments in those required to provide selfobject experiences.

In recent years the validity and usefulness of the concepts of optimal frustration and transmuting internalization have been questioned. For example, Bacal (1985) asserted, "It has never been our intention, as analysts, to either traumatize or frustrate our patients, however optimally, but to understand them. Consequently, the notion of optimal frustration is not tenable as a working clinical concept" (p. 207). Assuming a "basic tendency toward growth and development," Bacal suggested that optimal frustration should be replaced by the concept of "optimal responsiveness." Stolorow, Brandchaft, & Atwood (1987) objected to the concept of optimal frustration because it retains the economic and quantitative metaphors of drive theory. They suggest "shifting the emphasis from optimal frustration to the centrality of affect attunement" (pp. 75–76). Stolorow and Atwood (1992) found fault with the notion of transmuting internalization on the grounds that it emphasizes autonomy as a successful outcome. They observed that it "elevates a variant of the isolated mind to an ideal goal of development" (p. 13).

The concept of self-trust, I believe, serves as a useful replacement for the problematic notion of transmuting internalization.[1] Insofar as self-trust is determined by our interactions with others but is accessible only via introspection and empathy, it spans the chasm between the world of subjective reality and the world of selfobject fantasy. That is to say, we place trust in ourselves and in others as participants in selfobject relationships on the basis of interpersonal interactions which are evaluated according to highly idiosyncratic criteria (I develop this idea more fully on p. 37). Only those who meet our self-trust criteria will be represented in selfobject fantasies. The developmental

[1]Emde's (1990) formulation of fundamental modes of development mobilized by empathy provides an alternative to Kohut's notion that psychic structure is laid down through transmuting internalization (see pp. 44–45, this chapter).

transformation of self-experience as well as its cohesiveness and vitality depend on the trustworthiness of our selfobject connections with others. As long as self-trust binds us to others in the world of subjective reality, our selfobject fantasies remain intact and we are likely to enjoy a sense of comfort, familiarity, safety, and general well-being in our lives. Self-trust, therefore, may be thought of as the "glue" of self-experience. Once the bonds of self-trust connectedness are severed, we are likely to descend, like Alice down the rabbit hole, into a terrifying and surreal world in which self-experience seems to fragment or disintegrate. As we shall see in Chapter 3, this is precisely what happens in psychic trauma.

FOUR SELF-TRUST DIMENSIONS

Self-trust is itself multidimensional. I have identified four major dimensions of self-trust: trust-in-others, trust-in-self, self-as-trustworthy, and others-as-self-trusting. Trust-in-others involves a tendency to view others as trustworthy providers of selfobject experiences; trust-in-self involves a tendency to view oneself as capable of eliciting selfobject experiences from others; self-as-trustworthy involves a tendency to view oneself as a trustworthy provider of selfobject experiences for others; and others-as-self-trusting involves a tendency to view others as trusting of their capacities to obtain and provide selfobject experiences.

These dimensions of self-trust refer to generalized tendencies of an individual. They may be considered psychic structures in that they organize experience and have a relatively slow rate of change (Rapaport, 1960). However, it must be stressed that self-trust dimensions are not invariant rules that govern relationships inflexibly. While a woman may be said to have little trust-in-others, for example, this does not rule out the possibility of her placing trust in specific people who demonstrate their trustworthiness under certain circumstances. Moreover, she may, based on her interactions with specific people, trust them to provide only certain selfobject experiences and not others. As we shall see in the next chapter, trauma affects the generalizability of self-trust.

Preliminary statistical analyses (Brothers, 1982)[2] indicate that no linear relationships exist among the four self-trust dimensions. Therefore, the degree of trust experienced will vary in each dimension. So, for example, a man

---

[2]When this statistical analysis was performed (Brothers, 1982), I had identified only three of the four self-trust dimensions: trust-in-others, trust-in-self, and self-as-trustworthy. I had not yet identified others-as-self-trusting.

might feel highly trusting of himself as a provider of selfobject experiences for others, but distrustful of others as providers of selfobject experiences for him. He may be extremely doubtful about his own capacity to elicit selfobject experiences from others but he may view others as highly trusting of their capacities to obtain and provide selfobject experiences.

Despite their separateness, the four self-trust dimensions are complexly interrelated. Changes that occur in one self-trust dimension often lead to changes in the other dimensions. Consider what is likely to happen, for example, when someone you deem trustworthy meets your selfobject needs by responding to you in ways that are predictable, reliable, and consistent. This behavior tends to confirm that your trust was well placed; trust-in-others is likely to be strengthened. Indeed, you may even represent this person in your selfobject fantasies as merged with you or as an extension of yourself. Kohut (1977) suggested that in "archaic" selfobject relations, selfobjects may be regarded more as limbs on our own bodies than as separate people. Since a predictable, reliable, consistently responsive person may give us the illusion of being under our control, our trust in our capacity to elicit selfobject experiences from others (trust-in-self) is also likely to be greatly strengthened. So it seems that when trust-in-others is confirmed by our experiences with trustworthy people, trust-in-self is concomitantly strengthened. Conversely, as a consequence of interactions with others who disconfirm our trust-in-others by behaving unpredictably, unreliably, and inconsistently, trust-in-self is likely to suffer.

SELF-TRUST AND AFFECTS

Socarides and Stolorow (1985) and Stolorow et al., (1987) call attention to the close relationship between selfobject experiences and affects: "selfobject functions pertain fundamentally to the affective dimension of self-experience, and . . . the need for selfobject ties pertains to the need for specific, requisite responsiveness to varying affect states throughout development" (p. 67). A person represented in selfobject fantasies as a mirroring selfobject is likely to be someone experienced as responding affirmatively to affect states such as those involving pride, expansiveness, efficacy, and pleasurable excitement. A person represented as an idealized selfobject is likely to offer calming and soothing responses to affect states involving anxiety, vulnerability, and distress. And, a person represented as a twin selfobject is likely to be experienced as assuaging affect states involving loneliness (Ulman & Paul, 1990) and fears about loss of humanness (Kohut, 1984).

This conceptualization helps to clarify the nature of self-trust. To say, for example, that a woman has strong trust-in-others implies that she strongly expects other people to provide attuned responsiveness to her affective experience. To say that she has weak trust-in-self implies that she has a poor estimation of her capacity to elicit attuned responses to her affective experience. In other words, the aspects of self-experience most relevant to the concept of self-trust involve responsiveness to affects.

SELF-TRUST CRITERIA

How do our interactions with other people in the world of subjective reality determine whether or not they will be represented in selfobject fantasies? How do we determine our own trustworthiness in providing for the selfobject needs of others? Whether or not we trust ourselves and others as providers of selfobject experiences depends on highly individual criteria arrived at as a consequence of our history of selfobject relationships (see Chapter 3). One person may evaluate the trustworthiness of others largely on the basis of such external characteristics as their physical size, beauty, and ethnicity whereas another person evaluates trustworthiness on the basis of such psychological qualities as decency, integrity, and moral rectitude. As we shall see, self-trust criteria in the various dimensions typically undergo a process of maturation over the course of development.

The criteria we use to evaluate self-trust are not the same for all self-trust dimensions. Imagine, for example, discovering that someone you depend upon as a source of affirmation and praise has lied to you. If you anticipate that your trust in that person as a provider of mirroring selfobject experiences would diminish, it is probable that one of your criteria for trust-in-others is truthfulness. However, truthfulness is not a typical criterion for trust-in-self. You are more likely to evaluate your capacity to elicit selfobject experiences from others on the basis of your personal strengths. Trust-in-self typically depends on such criteria as lovableness, intelligence, sexual and physical attractiveness, success in work and in relationships, and ability to control emotional expression. There is very little overlap in the criteria used to evaluate trust in these two self-trust dimensions.

Despite the fact that self-trust criteria in each dimension vary from person to person, research has shown that certain personality qualities commonly engender trust. For example, Rempel and Holmes (1986) found that people are likely to be trusted if they are perceived as predictable, reliable, and consistent. We have already seen that such qualities are likely to promote trust-in-others and trust-in-self insofar as they permit an experience of control over those desired as selfobjects. Recent findings about mother-infant mutual regulation (e.g., Beebe, Jaffe, & Lachmann, 1994) suggest that contingencies in the coordination of such areas of mutual regulation as facial mirroring and conversational timing involve predictability, reliability, and consistency. Hence, it is probable that these qualities play a role in the earliest development of selfobject experience.

To the extent that selfobject experiences involve affect states, a perception of self or other as empathic is a key determinant of self-trust. Kohut (1959, 1971, 1977, 1981, 1984) placed empathy, which he defined as "vicarious introspection," at the center of the psychoanalytic enterprise. From an experience-distant, epistemological standpoint, he (1981) described empathy as "a mode of observation attuned to the inner life of man" (p. 542). Viewed within an experience-near context, he proposed that it serves both as an "information-gathering activity" and as a "powerful emotional bond between people." Self psychologists tend to blame faulty empathic responsiveness of childhood caretakers for their patients' psychological disorders. Moreover, a self-psychological treatment approach involves, to a large degree, the working through of perceived failures in the therapist's empathic responsiveness as a means of facilitating the resumption of the patient's thwarted developmental strivings. The essential element in the process of cure, according to Kohut (1984), "is the opening of a path of empathy between self and selfobject, specifically the establishment of empathic in-tuneness between self and selfobject on mature adult levels" (p. 66).

Until shortly before his death, Kohut insisted that empathy is never by itself supportive or therapeutic; it is not the parent's empathy that satisfies the child's selfobject needs. In his posthumously published 1981 paper, however, he stated: "[E]mpathy per se, the mere presence of empathy, has also a beneficial, in a broad sense a therapeutic effect—both in the clinical setting and in human life, in general" (p. 544). It is my contention that a major beneficial effect of empathy is that it promotes self-trust. One is likely to place great trust in others as selfobjects after they have demonstrated affectively attuned responsiveness to one's experience through vicarious introspection. And, one is likely to perceive oneself as a trustworthy provider of selfobject experiences for others after one has responded empathically to another person's affect state.

SELF-TRUST IN THE CRADLE

If, as I propose, self-trust is essential for one's sense of cohesive selfhood, it should be experienced, at least in nascent form, at a time when self-experience is forming, that is, very early in life. Self-psychological theory supports this assumption. Taking exception to Benedek's (1938) assertion that the baby *develops* confidence in his or her environment, Kohut (1977) said, "[Benedek's statement] is inexact because it leaves out of consideration the critical fact that the baby's confidence is innate, that it was there from the start" (p. 119). M. Tolpin (1980) elaborated on Kohut's position in her description of "Kohut's baby": "Fitted together with its human environment from the start this is an active, vigorous baby . . . with an inherent 'feeling of obviousness and sure expectation'[3] that it has the 'power' to succeed in reaching and getting what it goes after" (p. 55). What is more, according to Tolpin, the baby's trusting expectations "are not extinguished by the inevitable small-scale anxieties, depressions, and rages accompanying frustration which are the lot of the human child, and of all human beings throughout life" (p. 55). Using the language of self-trust, we might say that Kohut's baby is born with a rudimentary sense of trust-in-others and trust-in-self. And, growing up with reasonably responsive care it will not, under normal circumstances (i.e., those that are not traumatic), lose the self-trust with which it is born.

Recent advances in the study of infant development verify the Kohut-Tolpin view of infants as born with trust. Innovative research techniques reveal the newborn as far more competent, active, and related to his or her caretakers than was imagined possible only a quarter century ago. Although no studies of trust in infancy *per se* have been attempted to date, some of the findings by "baby-watchers" seem to lend credence to the idea that rudiments of self-trust exist in very young infants.

By means of "inferential leaps" from the data of developmental psychology, Stern (1985), a psychoanalyst as well as a developmental psychologist, has traced the "developmental progression of the sense of self." His conceptualization of an emergent, a core, a subjective, and a verbal sense of self has been embraced by many self psychologists as highly congruent with Kohutian theory. As compared to the view of infants held by classical analysts and those influenced by the separation-individuation theory of Mahler (1979), Stern contemplated a very competent newborn, capable of amazing feats of discrimination and of experiencing itself as separate from others early in life.

Let us now examine some findings by Stern and others that support the hypothesis that self-trust exists in early life. To begin, there is considerable evidence that human adults are "pre-designed" to provide their infants with just the kinds of experiences they in turn are "pre-designed" to need and enjoy

---

[3]Ferenczi, 1913, p. 213.

(Stern, 1985). For example, the human voice is the auditory stimulus most likely to capture the infant's attention (Condon & Sandler, 1974). People, including quite young children, automatically adjust their voices when speaking to infants, providing the high-pitched, sing-song rhythms infants have been found to prefer. Fantz (1963) discovered that, given a choice of visual stimuli, neonates prefer looking at the human face. Conveniently, as Stern (1977) observed, the mother's face is exactly the right distance away during breast feeding for the infant's optimal focus. M. Tolpin (1986) noted, "Mothers . . . unconsciously match their 'multiple functions' with their babies' maturing perceptual capabilities."

This felicitous synchrony of infant demand and caretaker supply makes it likely that from the very first days of life most healthy infants are likely to experience the caretaking environment as predictably, reliably, and consistently satisfying. On the basis of such experiences infants appear to develop expectations that their physiological and psychological needs will be met. Stern (1985) called these expectations "representations of interactions that have been generalized (RIGs)." RIGs that involve the infant's experiences of being with others are "evoked companions." According to Stern:

> This view of being almost continuously with real or evoked companions encompasses what is generally meant when one says that the infant has learned to be trustful or secure in exploring the surrounding world. . . . The infant is, in subjective fact, not alone but accompanied by evoked companions, drawn from several RIGs, who operate at various levels of activations and awareness. *The infant is therefore trustful* [italics added]. (p. 118)

It would appear that only a small step in development is needed to transform evoked companions into selfobjects. And, it requires only a small conceptual leap to transform the infant's expectations with respect to evoked companions into trust that others will provide needed selfobject experiences (trust-in-others) and trust in oneself as capable of eliciting these experiences (trust-in-self).

According to M. Tolpin (1986), the mother who provides successfully for her baby's physiological needs is also performing selfobject functions: "picking up the baby, talking to him, soothing and holding him in such a way that he stops screaming and calms down enough to be able to nurse are selfobject functions" (p. 118). She observed that from birth on, the baby demonstrates a capacity to "get the selfobject to 'act right'":

His [the baby's] physically and gesturally conveyed expectations act as signals that reasonably attuned parents come to understand as "telling" them whether or not they are on the baby's "wavelength." Mothers usually respond automatically to these signals. Babies whose mothers fail to respond appropriately redouble their efforts to convey their expectations. Only after repeated failures of ever more insistent attempts at guiding their mothers, do the infants sag and collapse. However, after a short time, even without intervention, these babies are apt to "self-right" and begin anew to convey their expectations." (p. 120)

In a similar vein, Beebe and Lachmann (1988a) propose a "mutual influence model" in which the organization of experience takes place within the infant-caretaker system. They see this model as congruent with Sander's (1977, 1983) notion of a basic regulatory core that derives from regularities in sleep-wake and feeding states. Such regularities are established over the course of the first days and weeks of life as mother and infant mutually influence each other to establish predictable sequences. Furthermore, according to Beebe and Lachmann, "mutual influence structures organize infant experience through expectancies" (p. 6). Ingenious experiments indicate that very young infants can detect a predictable relationship between their own behavior and the environment's response. For example, DeCasper and Carstens (1980) taught infants to turn on music by either slowing down or speeding up the rate of their sucking, what Watson (1985) called a "contingent response." The confirmation of their expectations led to positive affect among the infants. When, in a second experiment, the researchers stopped giving music contingent on the responses of infants whose expectations had previously been confirmed, the infants whimpered, grimaced, cried, and some even stopped sucking. In a third experiment, infants who had first been exposed to music at random were unable to learn the contingent response. As Beebe and Lachmann suggest, if the environment were noncontingent, "the infant's very capacity to organize its experience within a dyadic relationship would be interfered with." Fortunately, however, infants are usually provided an abundance of contingent stimulation, which appears to offer them a superb opportunity for experiencing their caretakers as reliable, predictable, and consistent—experiences that undoubtedly contribute to a rudimentary sense of trust-in-others and trust-in-self.

Another indication that young infants experience the beginnings of trust-in-others and trust-in-self is the enormous distress they exhibit during the "still-face procedure" invented by Tronick, Als, Adamson, Wise, and Brazelton (1978). In this procedure, a mother who has been interacting with her infant suddenly makes her face impassive and expressionless and fixes her gaze above the infant's eyes. The infant first attempts to recapture the mother's expected response by trying to meet her eyes and moving its body. When these efforts fail, the infant collapses into an attitude of withdrawal (Beebe & Stern, 1977). Since selfobject experiences fundamentally involve affect attunement, it is little wonder that infants become agitated and withdrawn when signs of the mother's affective responsiveness (her facial expressions) are removed: The baby's expectation that mother will provide selfobject experiences (trust-in-others) is disappointed along with its expectation of eliciting these experiences (trust-in-self).

By the time babies reach one year, trust-in-others appears to be fairly well-established. One indication is Emde's (1981) finding that infants will overcome their fear of crossing a "visual cliff" (a glass apparatus that simulates the appearance of a steep drop) if they receive a silent smile of encouragement from their mothers, but will refuse to cross if the mothers give a look of fear. One-year-olds, therefore, appear to trust their mothers to provide the protective, reassuring experiences associated with idealized selfobjects.

The very notion of mutual influence structures, which have been observed in virtually every aspect of infant-caretaker interactions (Beebe & Lachmann, 1988b), suggests the beginnings of self-as-trustworthy. Infants as young as two months old exert a high degree of control over the "initiation, maintenance, termination and avoidance of social contact with mothers" (Stern, 1985). Beebe et al. (1994) describe the bidirectional coordination of facial mirroring and conversational timing. Even the act of smiling contributes to the infant's experience of itself as active in regulating social interaction. The infant's smile, as Lichtenberg (1983) observed, "turns on" the mother who is then likely to respond enthusiastically. Infants also exert a great deal of control over eye contact with caretakers. To judge from the great lengths to which infants will go to avoid eye contact with mothers who unempathically try to force the issue (Beebe & Stern, 1977), it appears that they expect to be able to elicit just the right sort of responsiveness from their caretakers and feel very distressed when they are unable to do so.

The infant's expectation of influencing the behavior and the affective responses of caretakers may also be viewed as a precursor to an expectation of being trusted to provide selfobject experiences for others (self-as-trustworthy). One of the means by which infants begin to provide these experiences is through imitation. Within the first month of life, newborns can imitate the facial expressions of their mothers clearly enough so that an observer can identify the expression without seeing the mothers' face (Meltzoff & Moore,

1977). Lichtenberg (1983) noted that this kind of imitation begins a complex process in which the infant becomes "the particular baby of its particular parents." This shaping, he added, is a reciprocal one in that the baby activates and alters the mother's reactions. The caretaker whose expression has been imitated by an infant can have little doubt that he or she has been influential in shaping the infant's behavior. Feeling proud and competent, the caretaker is likely to experience the infant as providing mirroring selfobject experiences; delighting in the infant as like himself or herself, the caretaker may experience the infant as providing twin selfobject experiences; and, pleased with the infant's competence, the caretaker may experience the infant as providing idealized selfobject experiences.

We have already observed that empathy is intimately connected with self-trust. In order to be experienced as a trustworthy provider of the selfobject needs of others, infants should demonstrate some nascent capacity for empathy. One of the earliest indicators of this capacity is the tendency of day-old infants to become distressed when they hear another infant crying (Sagi & Hoffman, 1976). Beebe and Lachmann (1988a, 1988b) have investigated the precursors of empathy through their focus on patterns of mutual influence in the first six months of life. They present data documenting the "matching of temporal and affective patterns of mother and infant" that demonstrate how the sharing of subjective states occurs. It is in the moment-to-moment mutual influence in matching and tracking the other's behavior that they find the "resonance" or "state sharing" which, in their opinion, marks the beginning of empathy.

> Empirical studies have shown mutual influences in infant-caretaker matching of affect and timing. These matching experiences provide each partner with a behavioral basis for knowing and entering the other's perception, temporal world, and feeling state, and may contribute to later experiences of being attuned, known, tracked, or "on the same wavelength." (1988a, p. 331)

These patterns of mutual influence, according to Beebe and Lachmann, provide an important basis for emerging self and object representations. It seems likely that they also contribute to an emerging sense of self-as-trustworthy. In other words, on the basis of experiencing themselves as "on the same wavelength" as their parents, infants form a rudimentary expectation of providing psychological experiences for others.

Around the first birthday, babies have been found to react to the pain of others as though it were their own (Goleman, 1989), an indication that they are developing a greater capacity for empathy and thereby consolidating a sense of self-as-trustworthy. Further evidence of the maturation of self-as-trustworthy is provided by research on children between nine months and two years, which found a high degree of "helping behavior" (Hoffman, 1981; Zahn-Wexler, Radke-Yarrow, Wagner, & Pyle, 1988).

As Goldberg (1988) pointed out, "every parent uses the child as selfobject, just as every mother needs the baby's responsiveness to continue the feeding, the cooing, and the dialogue" (p. 123). It is my contention that infants are not just passive recipients of their parents' selfobject longings; they come into the world with a nascent expectation of serving as selfobjects for their parents.

The existence of the dimension others-as-self-trusting, which refers to a view of others as trusting of their capacities to obtain and provide selfobject experiences, is difficult to discern in early life. Nevertheless, a number of theorists have alluded to the importance of the mother's "confidence" (Benedek, 1938; Erikson, 1968; Mahler, 1979) in her motherliness as a necessary ingredient for the development of the infant's sense of confidence or basic trust (see Chapter 1). Beebe and Stern (1977) described the intensely agitated reaction of infants whose mothers would not allow them to experience control over their interactions. It seems likely that mothers who trust themselves to obtain and provide selfobject experiences, that is, those who are confident, would not impose themselves on their infants so unempathically. Self-trusting mothers are also less likely to ignore or neglect their children. Thus the maturity of a caretaker's self-trust contributes to his or her ability to serve the psychological needs of the infant. Moreover, infants appear to be extremely sensitive to indications that their caretaker's self-trust is deficient.

THE DEVELOPMENTAL TRANSFORMATION
OF SELF-TRUST

Self-trust changes continually over the course of development. The transformation of self-trust occurs in two main ways: (1) at a slow rate, through maturational processes that occur in normal development, and (2) abruptly, as a result of traumas at any point in life. The remainder of this chapter is devoted to a consideration of self-trust in normal (nontraumatic) development. The effect of trauma on self-trust will be examined in detail in Chapter 3.

Emde (1990), a psychoanalyst who has contributed extensively to the literature on child development, observed that "certain early-appearing motivational structures are strongly biologically prepared, necessary for development, and persist throughout life. Developing in the specific context of the

infant-caregiver relationship, these structures can also be regarded as fundamental modes of development. As such, they can be mobilized through
empathy" (p. 898). It is my contention that the dimensions of self-trust,
insofar as they fit Emde's description of "fundamental modes of development,"
are also mobilized by empathy. Self-psychological theory supports this view.
M. Tolpin (1980) pointed out that if, as infants, we are responded to with a
reasonable degree of empathy, we will continue to expect that our needs
for selfobject experience will be met unless gross disappointments teach us
otherwise. In her words, "Reasonably attuned selfobject responses [empathic
responses] *preserve* the feelings of expectation which are already present in the
child (it is inherent in a normal infant born into a normal human environment)" (p. 49). The "feelings of expectation" Tolpin described are, in my
view, the precursors of self-trust. The empathic responsiveness of others not
only preserves self-trust, but also promotes its maturation throughout the life
span.

In order to appreciate the development-enhancing effect of empathy on
self-trust, it is necessary first to consider the means by which self-trust matures. As I noted earlier, we place trust in self and in others as providers of
selfobject experience to the extent that various criteria, which may or may
not be conscious, are met. It stands to reason that the criteria that guide
self-trust among adults differ to some extent from the criteria used by adolescents and more radically from those used by young children. It is probably
stretching matters too far to speak about the self-trust criteria of infants. Yet,
an infant's preference for the smell of its own mother's milk and the look of
her features might be said to constitute the beginnings of a criterion for
trust-in-others. If the infant could speak it might say, "I trust others to serve
my selfobject needs to the extent that they smell and look like mother."

There is little consensus among developmental psychologists about the
mechanisms of developmental transformation. One approach to understanding changes in self-trust development involves the idea that development
occurs in stages over the life cycle. Selman, Jaquette, and Lavin (1977)
attempted to study the development of trust in friendship from such a perspective. They identified five stages that correspond to increments in chrono-
logical age. Thus, for example, in Stage 0, ages 3 to 5, trust criteria involve
physical attributes. For children at this stage, someone who appears big,
strong, or good-looking is likely to be considered trustworthy. In Stage 1,
ages 5 to 11, the person's intentions are also considered. However, trust is
still a "one-way street" and an important criterion for trust is the person's
willingness to comply with the child's demands. In Stage 2, ages 7 to 14, trust
is based on the anticipation of an equalizing reciprocity between self and

others, for example, "If I do something for you, you will do something for me." Trust criteria in this period are likely to involve the other person's similarity to oneself. Trust in Stage 3, age 12 to adulthood, is experienced as a sharing in and supporting of each other's intimate and personal concerns "through thick and thin." Stage 3 criteria presumably would include loyalty, consistency, and dependability. In Stage 4, reached by some adolescents and adults, trust criteria include an openness to change and the capacity to maintain stability in relationships.

The research of Selman et al. (1977) examines a very narrow aspect of trust: trust in friendship. Since their findings are limited to trust between self and others in the world of subjective reality, it is difficult to know if they can be generalized to self-trust. Moreover, the very premise that any aspect of development follows an invariant sequence of stages has increasingly been questioned by contemporary theorists (Franklin, 1981; Kohlberg, Yaeger, & Hjertholm, 1968). Even the cognitive-adaptive theory of the preeminent stage theorist, Jean Piaget, has been widely criticized. For example, Watkins (1986) finds fault with "the theme of the inadequacy of the child's thought" inherent in Piaget's work. Moreover, she criticized his tendency to view imagination as inferior to reason.

Watkins (1986) also challenged a view of development common among many theorists (e.g., Piaget, Vigotsky, and Freud), in which thought increasingly reflects material reality. An alternative to this perspective is offered by Werner (1948) who emphasized the multiplicity of possible worlds and realities. In striking contrast to those who argue that fantasy gives way to reality as development proceeds, Stern (1985) argues that reality comes first and the capacity for fantasy, later. In a similar vein, Franklin (1981) wrote,

> development is not seen as a linear (or spiralling) progression directed toward a pre-existing "external reality" or (alternatively) towards the construction of a psychological reality dominated by a given mode of thought (such as the "scientific") but is a differentiation, progressive construction and integration of spheres within psychological reality. (pp. 2–3)

The traditional psychoanalytic stages of libidinal development—oral, anal, phallic, etc.—have also been criticized. Stern (1985), for example, questioned the notion of phases of development devoted to specific clinical issues. Stern does not view his four different senses of self as successive phases that replace one another. Once formed, each sense of self remains fully functioning and active throughout life; all continue to grow and coexist. Noy's (1980) criticisms of psychoanalytic thinking on secondary and primary processes are similar. Challenging the notion that secondary process replaces primary process thought, he argued that both function together in every cognitive act and that there is as much developmental change in the capacity for primary process thought as there is in the capacity for secondary thought (see above, pp. 32–33).

In keeping with the developmental perspectives of Werner, Stern, Franklin, and Noy, I propose that the maturation of self-trust criteria should also be viewed in nonlinear terms. That is to say, although the criteria upon which we base our trust in self and in others as receiving and providing selfobject functions tend to change in predictable ways over the course of development, they do not necessarily change according to an invariant sequence of stages. Moreover, self-trust criteria used early in development may be retained or reinstated later on. Self-trust criteria may be evaluated in terms of the following four attributes:

1. *Realism.* To say that self-trust criteria are unrealistic implies that they involve phantasmagorical and perfectionistic notions about self and others (see Chapter 3; also Ulman & Brothers, 1988). Thus, a person whose self-trust criteria are relatively unrealistic may invest trust in someone as a potential selfobject to the extent that the person is perceived as omnipotent, omniscient, and indestructible or possessing magical or supernatural powers, whereas someone whose self-trust criteria are more realistic may invest trust in potential selfobjects even if they are perceived as having more modest qualities.

2. *Abstractness.* Criteria for self-trust may be said to be concrete if they involve characteristics about self and others that include such physical, external, and superficial attributes as size, attractiveness, and material possessions. Abstract criteria are those that cannot be experienced directly, such as truthfulness, sophistication, integrity, or the adherence to valued principles.

3. *Complexity.* Self-trust criteria are considered simple if they involve "black or white" determinations about self and others (e.g. the belief that someone is "totally reliable" or "always a liar"). Self-trust criteria that take into account the multifaceted nature of human personality may be said to be complex. A person may be unreliable in providing only certain selfobject functions, or reliable only under certain conditions. Complexity also refers to the ability to be mistrustful when appropriate. Healthy self-trust does not imply unqualified trustfulness; it does imply a complex mix of skepticism and doubt along with wishful expectation.[4]

---

[4]See Rotter (1980) for a discussion of gullibility.

4. *Differentiation.* The ability to discriminate between qualities of self and qualities of others determines the extent to which self-trust criteria may be said to be differentiated. Differentiation also refers to the ability to discriminate among other people. Sweeping generalizations about the trustworthiness of others based, for example, on their inclusion in some ethnic or religious group or because they physically resemble someone who proved untrustworthy in the past are likely to occur among those for whom self-trust criteria are undifferentiated.

As development advances, we tend to rely upon self-trust criteria that are more realistic, abstract, complex, and differentiated than we did earlier in life. However, phantasmagorical, concrete, simple, and undifferentiated criteria are not entirely relinquished. It is the empathic responsiveness of those who constitute the selfobject milieu that facilitates the maturation of self-trust. To begin to understand the role of empathy in mobilizing self-trust transformation, let us examine the vicissitudes of one criterion for trust-in-self that assumed great importance in the development of a man I call Steven.

Fascinated by the cartoon superheroes he watched on TV, Steven, at the age of five, often pretended that, like them, he was magically invulnerable to harm. In his play he repeatedly enacted his imperviousness to injury by pretending to survive unscathed the villainous attacks of hordes of "bad guys." Since he unconsciously experienced his ability to elicit selfobject experiences from others as dependent on this criterion, he would object strenuously when another child insisted that Steven had been "shot dead" in play. Clearly, as a criterion for trust-in-self, invincibility is highly unrealistic (phantasmagorical), concrete (based on physical characteristics), simple (all or none), and undifferentiated (he experienced himself as having the same qualities as his heroes).

Empathically grasping the importance of his illusion of invulnerability, Steven's parents neither interfered with his play enactments nor challenged his highly unrealistic pronouncements about his imperviousness to harm. Instead, they became aware that serious illnesses Steven had sustained as an infant had caused them to assume a hovering, anxious posture whenever he fell or bumped into objects while learning to walk. They had come to regard even minor colds with alarm. Conjecturing that their inordinate fearfulness had in some way contributed to Steven's preoccupation with superheroes, they responded by adopting a more matter-of-fact attitude toward his injuries and illnesses. Moreover, they spoke reassuringly to him of his growing strength and ability to recover from disease.

When Steven reached adolescence, the criterion of magical invulnerability for his trust-in-self became somewhat less prominent. Nevertheless, Steven still evaluated his ability to elicit selfobject experiences from others, most notably his peers, according to his illusion of invulnerability. No longer pretending to possess the super powers of his cartoon heroes, his daydreams centered around becoming a heroic soldier like his father who had fought in Vietnam. His father, empathizing with Steven's need to envision himself as an invincible marine, spared his son the frightening and gory details of his combat duty.

All during his teen years, Steven still tested his criterion of physical invulnerability to some extent by performing daredevil stunts on his skateboard and by joining the high school wrestling team. However, Steven's adolescent trust-in-self was also based on less phantasmagorical, more abstract and complex criteria such as his ability to excel in sports and to earn high grades in school, and, most importantly, his popularity with his age-mates.

Now, as an adult, Steven tests his criterion of magical invulnerability by engaging in somewhat risky business deals. Since his judgment in these matters is quite good, he has gained considerable success and his daring as a businessman has won him the respect of his peers. In certain respects, the sphere of imagined invulnerability has shifted to his professional life and away from his physical being. However, he occasionally eats rich foods, smokes, and drinks to excess—behaviors that seem to suggest his belief in his imperviousness to bodily illness and aging. Other criteria that have become important for his trust-in-self are his ability to sustain love relationships, to realize his professional goals, to act like a patriotic citizen, and to uphold the teachings of his religion.

Thus, while Steven's criterion of physical invulnerability assumed less importance in his self-trust organization, he still used it to some extent. What if Steven's parents had responded less empathically, perhaps challenging and ridiculing his illusion of physical imperviousness or continuing to show an inappropriate concern for his health? It is probable that Steven's trust-in-self would have continued to center around this relatively immature criterion or others equally phantasmagorical, concrete, simple, and undifferentiated. For example, he might well have chosen even more dangerous enactments in adolescence, perhaps actually joining the armed services or choosing to experiment with delinquency. As an adult, he might have taken risks by breaking laws in business or even by choosing a career that involved physical danger. Moreover, it is unlikely that other more developmentally mature criteria for trust-in-self would have gained prominence in the organization of his self-trust.

Self-Trust Development and the Story of Pinocchio

Bruno Bettelheim (1976) observed that the enchantment of fairy tales for children, as well as for adults, resides in their unique capacity to deal with the most profound issues of psychological development. Moreover, stories beloved by children seem to provide "empathic penetration into the mental life of childhood itself" (Kohut, 1974). *Pinocchio*, the charming story of the puppet who becomes a little boy, is no exception.

Pinocchio has achieved a remarkable degree of popularity since its publication in Italy in 1883. Yet, Bettelheim did not include it in his widely read psychoanalytic study of fairy tales, *The Uses of Enchantment* (1976). Unlike the fairy tales with primarily oedipal themes that Bettelheim so skillfully interpreted, *Pinocchio* can not easily be understood in terms of Freudian drive theory. Rather, it may be read as an allegorical account of the problems and pitfalls that attend the emergence of selfhood. As such, it has a great deal to tell us about self-trust in early childhood.

Freud (1914a) observed that the attitude of fond parents toward their children is often a revival of the parents' "long since abandoned narcissism." Since, from the perspective of self psychology, narcissism is *never* abandoned, parents inevitably experience their children as selfobjects. Kohut's case descriptions abound with references to self-disordered parents whose use of their children as selfobjects hampered rather than promoted their development. Moreover, as Kohut (1972) noted, "even healthy parents relate at times to the child in empathic narcissistic merger and look upon the psychic organization of the child as part of their own" (pp. 617–618). Yet Kohut (1974) has also suggested that from the earliest moments of parent-child interaction, there may exist "the beginning of an attitude that involves the parent's relinquishment of the child, the precursor of that attitude of ultimate distance which acknowledges the new, separate individual, a new, independent, creative self in the next generation" (pp. 768–769).

Of all our selfobject needs as children, the most fundamental, perhaps, is our need for parents to respond with joy and pride to those unique aspects of ourselves that distinguish us from them. Children whose parents cannot be trusted to provide such responsiveness enter life with a severe handicap. They are in great danger of failing to develop a sense of themselves as unique and authentic.

Carlo Collodi,[5] the author of *Pinocchio*, appears to have been highly sensitive to these issues. The very notion of puppet as child or child as puppet,

[5]Carlo Collodi is the pen name of Carlo Lorenzini (1826–1890).

suggests the dangers that may befall children should their parents "pull the strings" in accordance with their own needs. In the opening chapter of Pinocchio, Gepetto is introduced as a highly self-involved man with a fiery temper, primarily concerned with his own comfort. Clearly intending to use the puppet for his self-aggrandizement, Gepetto indicates his wish for "a wonderful puppet that should know how to dance, to fence, and to leap like an acrobat. With this puppet I would travel about the world to earn a piece of bread and a glass of wine" (Collodi, 1987).

It can be no oversight on Collodi's part that Gepetto has no wife and Pinocchio is brought into the world without a mother. Here is the grandiose male fantasy par excellence: to reproduce (himself) without a woman. By creating a puppet/child on his own, Gepetto is enabled to deny any flaws in his perfection. Pinocchio acknowledges his longing for a mother later in the story, when he tells the Fairy with the Blue Hair, "I have wished for such a long time to have a mamma like other boys!"

Apparently subscribing to the notion that, in a sense, the child creates its parents (Spruiell, 1975) because the parents' feelings of self-esteem and confidence (Benedek, 1938, 1959) are so intimately connected to the child's development, Collodi quickly transforms Gepetto into a paragon of trustworthiness. His own needs forgotten, Gepetto sells his overcoat to buy Pinocchio a spelling book. When Pinocchio runs off, Gepetto searches the world for him at great risk to himself. Fathers are trustworthy, Collodi seems to assure children. They will not abandon you, no matter how naughty you are.

The Fairy with the Blue Hair also undergoes a similar process of transformation. She is first introduced as a "lovely little girl." When she mysteriously grows up after demonstrating her omniscience and other magical powers, Pinocchio says, "instead of calling you little sister, I will call you mamma." His trust has transformed her from a child to a woman.

Collodi appears to see children as well-equipped to withstand the threat posed by the narcissistic needs of their caretakers. By emphasizing that Pinocchio was fashioned from no ordinary piece of wood, but one that could talk and engage in mischief even before it had been fully carved, Collodi seems to convey his belief that children are born with the potential to develop selves that are not mere reflections of their parents' expectations. Pinocchio consistently foils Gepetto's attempts to use him for his own fulfillment. He is no obedient little doll—as soon as Gepetto carves his features, Pinocchio impudently stares and mocks Gepetto; when given feet and taught to talk, he runs away.

For all his mischief, Pinocchio is generously endowed with self-trust. In the beginning of the story, his trust-in-self and self-as-trustworthy appear to depend on many of the highly unrealistic, concrete, simple, and undifferentiated criteria typical of young children. These are Pinocchio's thoughts as he sets off to begin his education:

> Today at school I will learn to read at once, then tomorrow I will begin to write, and the day after tomorrow to cipher. Then with my acquirements I will earn a great deal of money, and with the first money I have in my pocket I will immediately buy for my papa a beautiful new cloth coat. But what am I saying? Cloth indeed! It shall have to be made of gold and silver, and it shall have diamond buttons. (Collodi, 1987, p. 51)

Imbedded within Pinocchio's grandiose fantasy are hints of realistic ambitions and idealized goals, which, according to Kohut, form the two poles of a cohesive self. Considered from this perspective, by joining the puppet theater and later choosing to go to Boobyland where it is "games and fun from morning till night," Pinocchio betrays himself as well as Gepetto's trust in him.

Loss of trust-in-self is frequently accompanied by searing shame. By turning Pinocchio into a donkey who must perform by jumping through hoops in a circus, Collodi gave Pinocchio's shame a form easily comprehended by children. But his representation of Pinocchio's betrayal of self-as-trustworthy was an even greater triumph: the famous nose that grew with every lie! Here Collodi empathically grasped the child's predicament. Children are constantly reminded that those upon whom they depend for psychological and physiological survival require them to be trustworthy. To a large extent children enjoy experiencing themselves as the trustworthy providers of their caretakers' needs (see Chapter 8). However, parents' excessive demands for compliance interfere with their children's self-development. One solution is to lie. By lying children pretend to conform to parental demands while protecting their sense of differentiated selfhood.

Heinz Kohut (1984) addressed the significance of the undetected lie in the child's efforts to establish a cohesive self: "A child's lie remains undetected and thus one aspect of the omniscient idealized object is lost. But omniscience is introjected as a minute aspect of . . . the all-seeing eye, the omniscience of the superego" (p. 71). Thus, according to Kohut's theory of transmuting internalization, the child who gets away with a lie must suffer some disappointment in the parents as omniscient idealized selfobjects. However, the child also benefits insofar as he or she now takes over a bit of the parents' function as conscience. In classical terms, the superego becomes more internalized.

What, then, are we to make of the fact that Pinocchio's lies do not go undetected—his nose always gives him away? Although Collodi was very much concerned with the child's moral development, he saw the issue of lying quite differently from Kohut. When Pinocchio lies to the Fairy about having the gold pieces Gepetto gave him (the means by which he hopes to realize his grandiose fantasies), his nose begins to grow. With each lying elaboration, his nose becomes longer and longer until the Fairy takes pity on him and orders a flock of woodpeckers to reduce it to its usual size. Instead of reacting with terror, Pinocchio is relieved and grateful. (Clearly, in this instance, a growing nose is not the symbolic equivalent of an erecting penis; the episode does not deal with the castration anxiety of the oedipal child.) Collodi apparently means to illustrate how empathic parents convince children that their desperate efforts to hide their uniqueness are unnecessary. As soon as Pinocchio's lies are discovered, he is forgiven. Moreover, the empathic Fairy does not demand that Pinocchio relinquish his coins or his dreams; she immediately places trust in him once again.

Not only do the grownups in *Pinocchio* "keep the faith" in the little puppet by continuing to reinvest their trust in him, he holds on to his trust in them despite their schemes to exploit him. His trust survives the attempts by the fox and his friend the cat to steal his money, the doctors who are so fearful of having a diagnosis disconfirmed they will not even say if Pinocchio is alive or dead, and the treachery of the coachman who plots to sell him as a donkey. Collodi, much like Tolpin (1980), well understood that the self-trust of children is strong enough to survive all but the most fierce disappointments in those on whom they depend.

Collodi is equally convinced that children must demonstrate their trustworthiness to those around them. If they fail in this their consciences will torment them. Collodi deals with the increasing structuralization of the child's conscience by means of the talking cricket. Near the beginning of the story, the cricket warns Pinocchio that if he fails to reward his parents' trust by going to school or learning a trade he will grow up "a perfect donkey," shamed by everyone. Pinocchio becomes so enraged by his moralizing that he kills him with a hammer. At a later point in the story, the cricket's ghost appears, this time warning him not to place his trust in others who might betray him. It has become less substantial, less external. Finally, at the end of the story, Pinocchio heeds the advice of the cricket, who has been magically restored to life; it is only after doing so that Pinocchio is allowed to become a child.

Ultimately, for Collodi, the most important feature of human interaction is reciprocal trust. When, near the end of the story, Pinocchio behaves in a trustworthy fashion, others come through for him. For example, after Pinocchio saves a dog from drowning, it rescues him from the hungry fisherman's frying pan. Collodi does not place much emphasis on children's longings for strong, self-trusting caretakers, although he certainly recognized the horror children feel when their parents seem vulnerable to illness and death. The parental figures in *Pinocchio* are hardly towers of confident strength. When Gepetto and the Fairy come close to death, it is Pinocchio who saves them. In fact, it is these acts of reciprocated trust that transform Pinocchio from puppet to child. Significantly, it is Pinocchio who helps Gepetto emerge from the belly of the monstrous Dog-fish; parent and child are born at the same moment. There can be little doubt that Collodi deeply understood the importance of trust in the psychological development of children. Without it, he plainly tells us, we would be no more than puppets.

Chapter 3

BETRAYED SELF-TRUST:

THE HEART OF TRAUMA

Albany: Well, you may fear too far.
Goneril: Safer than trust too far.

> *William Shakespeare*, King Lear, *I:4*

Marguerite: We have to distrust each other. It's our only defence against betrayal.

> *Tennessee Williams*, Camino Real, *Block 10*

That trust disturbances figure importantly in the symptomatology and treatment of trauma is hardly news to most experienced clinicians. As far back as 1932, Ferenczi recognized that one of the most damaging effects of sexual abuse in children was the destruction of their trust in themselves (see Chapter 1). More recent investigators, such as Herman (1992), have discovered not only that traumatic events "violate the victim's faith in a natural or divine order and cast the victim into a state of existential crisis" (p. 51), but also that trust disturbances associated with trauma profoundly affect the survivor's self-experience.

In this chapter I hope to show that trust disturbances are not merely *caused* by traumatic experiences, but rather that trauma and trust disturbance are fundamentally interrelated; indeed, in my view, psychic trauma can only be fully understood as *the betrayal of trust in the selfobject relationships on which selfhood depends*. My understanding of the nature of trauma derives primarily from my collaboration with Richard Ulman on a self-psychological study of incest, rape, and combat trauma (Ulman & Brothers, 1988). We defined trauma as "a real occurrence, the unconscious meaning of which so shatters (selfobject) fantasies that self-restitution is impossible" (p. 3). A distinguishing feature of this definition is that trauma is not seen as residing in the event. It is the unconscious *meaning* of the event and not the event itself that causes trauma. Because the need to preserve a sense of self always assumes motivational priority in human life (Atwood & Stolorow, 1984; Kohut, 1971, 1984; P. Tolpin, 1985), efforts to restore selfobject fantasies shattered by the traumatic meaning of some occurrence is seen as inevitable.

Both the shattering of selfobject fantasies and faulty efforts at their restoration find expression in a condition classified in DSM-IV (American Psychiatric Association, 1994) as posttraumatic stress disorder (PTSD). Although it is listed as an anxiety disorder, the reexperiencing and numbing symptoms of PTSD appear to be dissociative phenomena that reflect desperate attempts by trauma survivors to disavow the unconscious meaning of their traumatic experiences. What meanings are so powerfully destructive that they must be disavowed lest the very structures of self-experience disintegrate? I have come to believe that the shattering import of trauma resides in the discovery that self-trust has been betrayed. That is to say, trauma results when the experiencing of a real occurrence persuades us that others cannot be trusted to provide needed selfobject experiences, that we cannot trust ourselves to elicit selfobject experiences from others, that we cannot be trusted to provide selfobject experiences for others, or that others cannot be trusted to satisfy their own selfobject needs. The idea that the discovery of the untrustworthiness of self or other constitutes a betrayal is predicated on the assumption that self-trust is a given of human endowment. If, as Tolpin and Kohut (1980) contend, babies have trusting expectations that withstand the usual and inevitable frustrations and disappointments of life, an experience that damages this trust must be considered a betrayal.

In the previous chapter I alluded to self-trust as the glue of self-experience. Now it can be understood as a sort of psychic adhesive that holds selfobject fantasies together. Trauma loosens this glue, crippling psychological life. With the disintegration of the bonds of trust that connect trauma survivors to the principal figures represented in their selfobject fantasies, self-experience breaks down. Survivors are plunged into a nightmare world of self-fragmentation in which sanity, indeed the very continuity of existence, can no longer be taken for granted. This, I believe, is what Kohut (1984) meant when he referred to disintegration anxiety as the "deepest anxiety" humans can experience (p. 18). Disintegration anxiety is so unbearable that strenuous efforts must be made to reconnect the bonds of trust between self and others, and, concomitantly, to restore shattered selfobject fantasies.

The idea that trauma is experienced as a betrayal of self-trust refines the shattered-fantasy theory of trauma. The loss of selfobject connections per se does not cause disintegration anxiety—many people have endured long periods of actual separation from those represented in their selfobject fantasies without undergoing mental breakdown—it is the loss of trust in these selfobject relations that is intolerable. This helps to explain why the same event, say a specific battle in a war, may be traumatic for one soldier and not another. Only the soldier who experiences the battle as a betrayal of trust in vitally needed selfobject relationships is traumatized. In early life, it should be noted, the abrupt disappearance of caretakers functioning as selfobjects may be equivalent to self-trust betrayals because their trustworthiness for infants is conveyed largely by their physical proximity.

Betrayals of self-trust are associated with two extremely intense affects: shame and rage. Shame is likely to predominate when one can no longer experience oneself as providing for the selfobject needs of others or capable of eliciting selfobject experiences from others, that is, trust-in-self or self-as-trustworthy is betrayed. Rage is likely to predominate when others prove untrustworthy in providing selfobject experiences, that is, trust-in-others or others-as-self-trusting is betrayed. Shame and rage have been viewed primarily as "disintegration products" of a fragmenting self (Kohut, 1971). Narcissistic rage has also been understood as an aspect of self-restoration (Tolpin & Kohut, 1980, Ulman & Brothers, 1988). In the context of self-trust betrayal, it seems likely that one purpose of dissociation is that it enables the betrayed person to avoid experiencing shame and rage, the emotional correlates of trauma.

THE DISSOCIATIVE ALTERATION
OF SUBJECTIVE REALITY

No consensus exists as to the exact nature of dissociation (Yates & Nasby, 1990). According to the authors of DSM-IV (American Psychiatric Association, 1994), the essential feature of the dissociative disorders is "a disturbance or alteration in the normally integrated functions of consciousness, memory, identity, or perception of the environment" (p. 477). However, they do not attempt to explain how or why it occurs. A self-trust perspective helps to shed light on the bases of dissociation.

From the perspective of self-trust, dissociation can be understood as an alteration in self-experience resulting from the traumatic betrayal of self-trust and the changes that inevitably occur both in the world of selfobject fantasies and in the world of subjective reality. Remember that healthy self-experience depends on there being a sound balance between the self-centered (primary process) and the reality-oriented (secondary process) organizational modes and on both modes reaching optimal levels of development and maturation (Noy, 1980; also see Chapter 2, pp. 32–33). The shattering of selfobject fantasies and attempts at their restoration not only interfere with the developmental transformation of these fantasies (Ulman & Brothers, 1988), but insofar as trauma profoundly affects the experience and development of subjective reality, it also creates imbalances between the two organizational modes. These imbalances are primarily responsible for dissociative phenomena (Noy, 1980).

Selfobject fantasies shattered by self-trust betrayals can be restored only when trust in selfobject relationships is reestablished. Because those experienced as betrayers will not be represented in selfobject fantasies, survivors[1] must alter their experience of subjective reality so that self and/or others are experienced as trustworthy despite evidence to the contrary. While this alteration is necessary to avoid overwhelming disintegration and depletion anxiety and the looming menace of catastrophic retraumatization, it has many psychological drawbacks. The experience of subjective reality loses its clarity and distinctness as the meanings of traumatizing betrayals are disavowed (Basch, 1983) and the maturation of thought processes on which this experience depends is arrested. According to Noy (1980), depersonalization is created by imbalances in the representation of self, specifically between what he calls the "experiential self" (self-centered mode) and the "conceptual self" (reality-oriented mode) (p. 188). Similarly, derealization is created by imbalances in the representation of reality, specifically between "the experiential

---

[1]In deciding whether to use the term *victim* or *survivor* to describe a sufferer of traumatizing self-trust betrayals, I was influenced by Patricia Walter's suggestion (personal communication, 1993) that my choice should reflect the meaning of the experience for the person described. She observed that the same person may perceive himself or herself both as a victim and as a survivor. Which perception predominates at any given moment depends on a variety of factors including the trustworthiness of the environment. As a general term I prefer *survivor* because it reflects my belief that self-restitutive efforts are inevitably undertaken as a consequence of "the primacy of self-preservation" (Kohut, 1971, 1977, 1984).

representation of reality" and the "conceptual representation of reality" (p. 190).

The dissociative alteration of subjective reality results from changes that occur in the organization of the trauma survivor's self-trust as well as a variety of psychological and behavioral measures taken to support or confirm these changes. Let us consider the components of a dissociatively altered subjective reality in greater detail. There are two main ways in which the organization of the survivor's self-trust is affected by traumatizing betrayals: (1) trust in affected dimensions is either diminished or intensified; and (2) immature criteria for placing trust in self and others are retained or reinstated. Although, experientially, these two effects of trauma are inseparable, they are easier to understand if considered one at a time.

In the clinical literature, disturbances in trust are often equated with diminished or lost trust. While a lack of trust in others, and insufficient self-confidence are often cited as indicators of psychopathology, heightened or intensified trust in self or others is rarely mentioned. Nevertheless, an empirical research study conducted with rape and incest survivors found that trust disturbance resulting from trauma is bidirectional (Brothers, 1982). A traumatizing betrayal is as likely to result in the intensification of a self-trust dimension as in its diminution. In fact, since only those deemed trustworthy are represented in selfobject fantasies, the intensification of self-trust is often essential to a trauma survivor's efforts to allay disintegration anxiety and to restore shattered selfobject fantasies.

Intensifications and diminutions of trust have very different consequences depending upon which of the four self-trust dimensions is affected. A person whose trust-in-others is traumatically betrayed may become suspicious, hypervigilant, secretive, and withdrawn, or so unswervingly trustful that even blatant signs of another person's untrustworthiness are overlooked. Disturbed trust-in-self may be expressed either as insecurity, indecisiveness, and self-doubt, or as blind self-confidence and, thus, in the performance of acts of great risk and daring. A person for whom self-as-trustworthy is disturbed may become indifferent to the psychological needs of others or, as in the case of certain members of the helping professions, so dedicated to providing trustworthy care that the satisfaction of his or her own needs is neglected. Disturbed others-as-self-trusting may result in disillusionment and cynicism in authority figures or lead one to join a cult or other organization in which allegiance to a self-trusting leader is stressed.

In Chapter 2 I suggested that self-trust criteria tend to become increasingly realistic, abstract, complex, and differentiated over the course of development, but that less mature criteria may be employed under certain conditions. Following a shattering betrayal, when the need to combat disintegration anxiety is most urgent, survivors tend to employ self-trust criteria used in early development. Moreover, traumatic betrayals that occur early in life tend to impede the developmental shift toward the employment of more mature criteria. Thus, the self-trust criteria used by people severely and repeatedly traumatized in childhood usually remain quite immature.

The maturity of self-trust criteria is not determined by the intensification or the diminution of a self-trust dimension following trauma. However, diminutions or intensifications of self-trust do affect the extent to which one experiences self and other as meeting any given criterion. A person is unlikely to experience self or other as measuring up to a self-trust criterion if trust in that dimension has been diminished, whereas there is a greater likelihood that he or she will experience self or other as meeting the criterion if trust in that dimension has been intensified. Suppose, for example, that a criterion employed by a trauma survivor for trusting others to serve as her selfobjects is that they must always behave altruistically. If this survivor's trust-in-others has been traumatically intensified, she is likely to interpret the behavior of others as motivated by concern for the welfare of others. If her trust-in-others has been traumatically diminished, she is likely to interpret the same behavior as motivated by self-interest.

Among adults whose self-trust criteria have undergone normal developmental transformation, a disappointment in someone trusted to provide selfobject experiences might be expected to lead to a diminution of trust only in that person. However, among people who rely on immature self-trust criteria as a result of repeated self-trust betrayals, a disappointment in a trusted person may lead to the diminution or intensification of trust in all other people. Moreover, using mature self-trust criteria, distinctions can be made about which selfobject experiences a given person can be trusted to provide. A reliance on immature criteria may make such distinctions impossible. Thus, repeated traumatizations and the concomitant use of immature self-trust criteria tend to produce more dramatic changes in self-experience than would otherwise be true.

Over the course of normal development, everyone develops a unique self-trust organization. The self-trust organizations of people who have not been severely traumatized tend to be marked by only minor variations in the various dimensions of self trust. If we picture their self-trust dimensions as lines connecting points on a graph, the peaks and valleys representing the intensifications and diminutions of their four self-trust dimensions would be fairly shallow. In contrast, the self-trust graphs of victims of severely traumatizing betrayals would be marked by very high peaks and very deep valleys.

When a self-trust dimension is highly intensified or greatly diminished it is usually unstable. So, for example, a trauma victim's intense trust in a particular person as a provider of selfobject experiences may rapidly be replaced by a conviction of that person's untrustworthiness for reasons that may be hard for an observer to comprehend. Highly mistrustful people sometimes report having unexpectedly and suddenly "found faith" in a cause, a religion, or a charismatic leader. These rapid, sudden, and dramatic changes are usually the consequence of the survivor's desperate efforts to avoid retraumatization.

EXPERIENTIAL "BLACK HOLES"

In order to maintain highly intensified or diminished trust in self or others as providers of selfobject experience, it is often necessary for survivors to eliminate memories of the traumatizing betrayal from conscious awareness by means of repression. (See Chapter 6, pp. 149–151, for a discussion of the relationship between repression and dissociation.) I refer to these gaps in memory as "black holes," since affects associated with memories of betrayal are likely to be sucked into the void in self-experience created by these memory gaps.

This conceptualization is similar to that of Cohen and Kinston (1984); Kinston & Cohen, (1986). These authors understand trauma as resulting from an absence of emotional understanding which leads to a fault or defect in psychic structure—metaphorically, a "hole." Instead of dissociation they refer to "primal repression" as "the hole in the mind" and claim that psychoanalysis is the study of the hole in the mind.

Similarly, Laub and Auerhahn (1993) refer to trauma as "an event that defies representation and instead is experienced as an absence" (p. 289). The self-experience of many child incest survivors is illustrative. Children whose psychological survival depends on selfobject relations with the very relatives who betrayed them are likely to intensify trust-in-others and diminish trust-in-self (see Brothers, 1992). As part of this effort, memories of their abusive sexual experiences must be eliminated from consciousness along with the affects associated with their reactions to the abuse, such as fear or rage. Even when memories of incestuous betrayals are retained or recovered, the affects connected to the memories may remain inaccessible. This disconnection of affects permits the meaning of the trauma to be disavowed.

Clearly it is impossible for survivors to experience a sense of cohesive well-being without access to these dissociated aspects of self-experience. Insofar as PTSD symptoms symbolically represent or concretize the traumatizing betrayal and "give symbolic voice to the dissociated unconscious meanings of trauma" (Ulman & Brothers, 1988, p. 23), they function to fill in the black holes in survivors' self-experience. However, they are far from the only means by which survivors attempt to regain a sense of self-cohesion; a wide variety of psychological and behavioral strategies are also employed. Certain survivors retain access to that which has been eliminated from awareness by experiencing alternating states of consciousness. At certain times, these survivors may experience themselves as having one sort of personality organization with a corresponding range of affects, and at other times as having another, often quite opposite, sort of personality organization with its corresponding affects. For example, they may alternate between experiencing themselves as vulnerable, needy victims and invulnerable, aggressive survivors. Kernberg's (1966) description of the alternations in self-experience among patients diagnosed as "borderline" suggests they may have employed this psychological stratagem.[2]

An extreme form of this phenomenon is manifested by those who suffer from multiple personality disorder (MPD). When horrendously traumatizing betrayals are suffered repeatedly in early life, intolerable memories of these betrayals along with associated affects and meanings will create numerous black holes in the child-survivor's self-experience. The alter personalities not only concretize or reify the memories, affects, and meanings associated with the betrayals thereby filling in the black holes in the survivor's self-experience, they also serve as replacements for the selfobject fantasies that have been shattered. Lunt (1993), for example, conceptualized an alter personality as a "dissociatively split-off narcissistic fantasy."

ALTER EGO SELFOBJECTS

A much more common strategy for regaining a sense of cohesion following traumatizing betrayals is the search for others in whom the disavowed or hidden parts of self-experience are located. In recent papers (Brothers, 1993, 1994) I proposed that many survivors who develop dissociative black holes in self-experience following traumatizing self-trust betrayals require a specific type of selfobject experience—alter ego selfobject experiences. Despite the fact that Kohut used the terms "twin" and "alter ego" interchangeably, I suggested

---

[2]See Herman & van der Kolk (1987) and Herman, Perry, & van der Kolk (1989) for a discussion of the role of childhood abuse in patients diagnosed as borderline.

that significant differences are to be found between these two selfobject experiences (see also Detrick, 1985, 1986). I strongly endorsed Kohut's (1984) view of twin selfobjects as fulfilling the need for experiences of essential alikeness with another person as a means of confirming that one is "a human being among other human beings" (p. 200); however, I suggested that alter ego selfobjects should be reconceptualized as fulfilling "the need to experience the presence of essential sameness or alikeness with disavowed or hidden aspects of self" (Brothers, 1993, p. 195). Patients may use the therapeutic relationship as a means of obtaining alter ego selfobject experiences. They find embodied in the therapist hidden or disavowed aspects of themselves as a means of experiencing a sense of self-cohesion that would otherwise be impossible to attain. I suggest that the establishment of others as alter ego selfobjects has previously been referred to as projective identification.

To illustrate the search for alter ego selfobjects, consider the case of Lena.[3] When the bonds of self-trust connecting her to her father were severed by his brutal physical abuse of her in early adolescence, Lena sought to establish a selfobject relationship with her sickly, self-involved mother. She realized that such a tie could only be achieved if she presented herself to her mother as a strong, fearless, giving caretaker who would not make demands of her own. With the intensification of self-as-trustworthy, her own experiences of herself as needy, fearful, entitled, and ambitious were eliminated from conscious experience. In the initial stages of her treatment Lena related to me as an alter ego selfobject who embodied these disavowed characteristics. By criticizing what she perceived as my weakness, passivity, and cowardice as well as my exploitiveness and self-indulgence she was enabled to reconnect with these hidden aspects of herself and to temporarily attain a sense of cohesive selfhood.

Ironically, the very person who betrays a trauma survivor's self-trust often serves as his or her alter-ego selfobject. In other words, the survivor is likely to find embodied in the betrayer those aspects of self-experience that were dissociated as a means of restoring trusting bonds following a traumatizing betrayal. Earlier I indicated that self-trust operates at the boundary of fantasy and reality. It should now be apparent that when self-trust is damaged by traumatizing betrayals, the struggle to regain trust in self and/or others as providers of selfobject experience blurs the edges of reality; dissociation is likely to become a way of life.

---

[3]See Brothers (1993) for a detailed discussion of this case.

STUDIES IN SELF-TRUST BETRAYAL

To illustrate the devastating effects of self-trust betrayals that lie at the heart of trauma, I turn to my clinical practice. In reviewing the lives of two of my patients, Stuart and Nancy, my intention is not to describe a self-trust perspective on treatment—Chapter 6 outlines this perspective and Chapter 7 provides clinical examples—rather, I hope to show how these patients dissociatively altered subjective reality in the aftermath of traumatizing self-trust betrayals. In these clinical studies, as in all that follow, I have taken pains to protect the identity of my patients by changing their names and details of their histories.

Stuart

"Remember something from my childhood."

"Oh?"

"Tough for me to get out of my bed, especially in the middle of the night."

"What made it tough?"

"Afraid to let my feet touch down on the floor near the bed—had to swing them way out."

"What were you afraid of?"

"Demons."

"Demons?"

"The demons that lived under the bed and always tried to grab me."

In the early stages of Stuart's eight-year course of intensive self-psychological psychotherapy, he presented fiendish monsters, ferocious "boy-eating" animals, and other gruesome inhabitants of his imaginary childhood universe far more vividly than the humans who shared his real world. As Stuart described them, the members of his household seemed as lifeless and stereotyped as a family in a 1950s television comedy. He portrayed his father as a successful businessman, his mother as a pretty housewife, and his younger sister as a mischievous playmate. His account of his adult life and his relationships with his wife and three young children was equally lackluster.

Stuart himself at age 32 struck me as someone I would have difficulty recognizing outside my office. His regular features were usually arranged in a mild, gentle smile, and he dressed in drab, nondescript business clothes. He spoke as if dictating impersonal messages to a telegraph operator. Along with all extraneous pronouns and adjectives, Stuart seemed to eliminate emotional expressiveness from his staccato utterances. "Parents divorced when I was 10," he remarked in an early session. "How was it for you?" I asked. "Hard" was his complete response.

Very gradually over several years in treatment, as Stuart's dissociative disturbances in memory lessened and he recaptured details of his early life, it became increasingly clear to both of us that his horde of fantasy fiends gave concrete expression to the uncertainty and danger that attended all of his formative relationships. Although Stuart's mother stayed at home during his childhood, her unheralded bursts of anger and inexplicable crying jags lasting hours at a time made her an extremely unpredictable source of selfobject satisfaction. In a good mood, she might praise Stuart's accomplishments, tell him how good-looking and kindhearted he was, and otherwise provide mirroring selfobject experiences. A short time later, as her characteristic gloom descended, she found fault with virtually everything about him. "Never believed the good stuff," Stuart said, "Convinced I was just a bad, mean, selfish kid. Only virtue was my skill at outwitting the creatures."

Stuart is still uncertain if his father's alcoholism and affairs with other women exacerbated his mother's psychological problems or resulted from them. In any case, Stuart remembered that his father spent little time with the family and, on the rare occasions when he was at home, he often banished Stuart to his room in compliance with his wife's directives. She would insist that he punish Stuart for offenses purportedly committed in his absence. Despite his limited contact with his father, Stuart maintained a highly ideal-ized view of him. He cited the many "rescue missions" his father had under-taken on his behalf as evidence of his goodness and caring. When Stuart flunked out of several schools, broke bones in accidents, and landed in jail after "borrowing" a car for a joy ride, his father bailed him out of trouble.

Stuart's relationship with his sister was also unpredictable. Although she provided much needed companionship in the long, lonely days that filled his childhood, Stuart remembered that often, without warning, she would turn into a diabolical rival for the scant attention their parents seemed able to provide. He never knew when she would suddenly become "the enemy," a scheming brat who got him into "hot water."

The year that followed his parents' divorce was undoubtedly the most har-rowing of Stuart's life. As soon as the divorce was final, Stuart's father all but disappeared from his life. Although he showed up from time to time with tickets to sporting events, these infrequent and unscheduled outings usually proved cruelly disappointing for Stuart. He felt that his father attended only to the game they were watching and that any unrelated conversation would have violated an unspoken pact between them. Stuart's hope of eliciting his father's assistance in solving the problems that confronted him was invariably dashed.

His most urgent problems centered around his relationship with his mother. With the breakup of her marriage, Stuart's mother appears to have suffered a full-blown psychotic episode. She stopped bathing and grooming herself, and allowed trash to accumulate throughout the house. She rarely bought fresh food and would serve disgusting "stews" of moldy leftovers. Stuart recalled living with constant hunger and developing the habit of eating until he felt sick whenever tasty food was available. For weeks at a time Stuart's mother would keep him at home after school as punishment for breaking rules that changed daily. Between these periods of confinement, she seemed indifferent to his comings and goings, even if he stayed out with friends until late at night. Stuart also recalled feeling appalled by her graphic descriptions of her unsatisfactory sex life with his father. Nevertheless, Stuart devoted himself to tending to his mother's needs. "Tried to cheer her up and to act as if she were a terrific mother," he said. Until well into his treatment, Stuart continued to look after his mother, providing financial assistance and managing her affairs.

On top of all this, Stuart was sexually abused by a man he encountered during his after-school wanderings. The man had intrigued Stuart with fascinating stories and clever magic tricks. He seemed to Stuart a wizard who could teach him new ways to defeat the demons. Stuart recalled that on the afternoon of their first sexual contact, he had doubted the wisdom of accompanying the man to his trailer on the outskirts of town. "Finally just told myself it would be all right," he said to explain why he had consented.

"He didn't have to make me promise never to tell anyone what had gone on, felt so ashamed and guilty. Thought it was all my fault, that I must have wanted it or it wouldn't have happened," Stuart confided. His memories for what he believed were fairly frequent meetings with the pedophile over a period of about six months remain hazy. Yet, he distinctly recalled feeling a sickening mixture of dread and excitement each time he became aware that the man was waiting for him at the end of the schoolyard.

Several years after the man abruptly vanished, Stuart was shocked to see his photograph on the front page of the local newspaper above an article describing his arrest for killing a young man he had also abused. When Stuart told his mother that the killer had molested him, she expressed no concern for the anguish he felt and made no attempt to secure psychological treatment for him. Instead, Stuart reported, "She pumped me for details. Had this awful feeling that she was getting off on it."

"I watched my life play out like a horror movie," Stuart said, recalling the weeks following this shocking discovery. His concentration and memory were so impaired, he went from being a straight "A" student to the bottom of his class. He withdrew from his friends and lost all interest in after-school activities. Intrusive memories of his sexual experiences haunted his days and his sleep was disturbed by terrifying recurrent nightmares such as one he recounted in treatment:

I am in the movie, *The Wizard of Oz*. On the way to the castle some creatures, half men and half monsters, swoop down and take me to the witch's cave. She locks me in a cage but I find a way to escape down some dark and twisting tunnel. An evil wizard lives in the tunnel and he makes me evil like him. I somehow get back to my town but monsters have taken the place of the people.

Stuart's associations revealed that like Dorothy and her friends in the movie who turn to an impotent fraud for fulfilment of their psychological needs, the adults to whom Stuart turned in his longing for protection, support, and approval all betrayed his trust. His father abandoned Stuart to his treacherous mother (the enslaving witch in his nightmare); and the molester took brutal advantage of his neediness and vulnerability. The nightmare also reveals Stuart's sense of having been "contaminated" by his experiences. He described tormenting urges to sexually abuse his own children and fantasies of violently abusing women. The image of monsters replacing people reflects Stuart's fear that no one can be trusted and that underneath every kindly exterior an evil demon lurks. Stuart's representation of himself as escaping from the witch down a dark tunnel reflects his effort at self-restoration through his psychological withdrawal from others into the dark world of his fantasy life.

Despite the devastating effects of his traumas, Stuart managed to complete college and to attend graduate school, to marry and have children, and to find a well-paying job with a large company. He sought therapy after suddenly finding himself immobilized at work, unable to complete tasks he usually accomplished with a minimum of effort. I discovered that his symptoms had begun with his discovery that his father had sold the family business. For as long as Stuart could remember, his hopes and dreams had been pinned on eventually running the company that had been passed from father to son for several generations. He had been certain of his future. "Thought I stood on firm ground" he said sadly, "now all is shifting sand." Surprisingly, Stuart did not blame his father for his monumental disappointment. "Poor guy," he said, "must have been conned by lawyers and financial advisors."

In the early years of Stuart's treatment much time was devoted to his largely unsuccessful crusade to establish a close and meaningful relationship with his father and to wrest from him some provision of financial security for Stuart's mother as well as for himself and his own family. Although his father made it clear that he was content with his new wife and stepfamily and wished to keep contacts with Stuart to a minimum, Stuart plied him with phone calls, letters, and gifts. Stuart would meet him at airports for a few hurried moments between flights and arrive early for family celebrations in the hope that he could squeeze in some "quality time" before the effects of his father's heavy alcohol consumption made coherent conversation impossible.

Stuart never seemed to question the value of these efforts, nor that his father was worthy of them. He seemed equally convinced of his own worthlessness. Deriding his hopes to run the family business, for example, he referred to himself as "a stupid jerk for putting all my eggs in one basket." He mentioned feeling disgusted with himself for wasting time at work despite the fact that he found his job at once boring and stressful. He also attacked himself for keeping his office in a state of disorganization, for procrastinating about learning the computer system his company used, and for failing to complete a thesis for his masters degree.

I learned that as an adult Stuart had often chosen as mentors and guides men who exploited him psychologically and financially. One of these men, a clergyman terminally ill with AIDS, persuaded Stuart to act as his personal attendant during the final stages of his illness. Claiming that he could not afford his "cancer" treatments, he borrowed a great deal of money from Stuart. When the priest was near death, Stuart asked him to arrange for posthumous repayment of the loan. To Stuart's enormous distress, the clergyman insisted that the money had been a gift. Stuart realized that he had ignored early signs of the man's deceitfulness believing instead that he had finally found a worthy guide.

In his fourth year of therapy Stuart announced that he had begun a love affair after realizing that his wife had neglected and exploited him. She had always been cold and demanding toward him and had required that he make huge sacrifices for the good of her own career. Torn by his love for his children, Stuart found himself unable to end his marriage. He told his wife about his affair and urged her to join him in marriage counseling. In the course of their counseling sessions, Stuart learned that for years his wife had had affairs with men he had considered his friends. One of these men had often dined and slept at his home and borrowed money without repaying him. In retrospect Stuart realized that he had known all along that his wife had been adulterous. "Just couldn't let it be real," he said.

Case Summary

The diabolical imaginary creatures against whom Stuart matched wits and wiles for so much of his childhood served functions crucial to his psychological survival. By attributing to them all the danger and uncertainty that surrounded him, Stuart was able to maintain a much needed illusion that his family were trustworthy providers of his psychological needs. In addition, the creatures served as alter ego selfobjects[4] who embodied all the aggression and rage Stuart disavowed in himself. To the extent that he always triumphed over their fiendish schemes, Stuart experienced himself as a strong, fearless boy worthy of admiration, support, and protection from his family. Consequently Stuart was able to construct fairly cohesive selfobject fantasies that organized his life before age 10.

Stuart experienced the events surrounding his parents' divorce, including his father's disappearance and his mother's breakdown, as traumatic betrayals of his self-trust. With the dissolution of the bonds of trust between Stuart and his parents, his selfobject fantasies shattered and he was overwhelmed with the dissociative numbing and reexperiencing symptoms of PTSD. His effort to alter subjective reality involved the intensification of trust in the unpredictable, exploitative adults on whom he was forced to depend for the satisfaction of his selfobject needs. As I attempt to demonstrate in the next chapter, it is often a trauma survivor's very efforts at self-restoration that lead to his or her retraumatization. Stuart's intensification of trust-in-others and the immature criteria he employed for evaluating their trustworthiness may well have led to his sexual abuse. Stuart mistook the molester's magic tricks and storytelling ability as proof that he was a powerful, wise, and supremely self-confident man who would fulfill his selfobject longings. As a consequence of his intensified trust, Stuart was enabled to ignore all awareness of the danger and discomfort he may have experienced.

Stuart's exoneration of the molester by accepting blame himself represents another of his self-restorative efforts. By taking responsibility for the abuse, Stuart not only attempted to preserve his experience of others as trustworthy, he also tried to bolster his damaged trust-in-self. As one who caused his own abuse, Stuart could avoid feeling like a helpless victim without any control over those needed as selfobjects. Stuart reacted similarly after his father sold the family business. In addition to blaming his father's advisors and lawyers, Stuart castigated himself for hoping to inherit the business and for being an inadequate worker. If only he had been wiser and more competent, he

---

[4]See Bacal (1990) for a discussion of fantasy selfobjects.

seemed to say, he would not be in this shameful predicament. In this way, Stuart retained a sense of control over his fate.

Stuart's sense of himself as a trustworthy provider of the selfobject needs of others (self-as-trustworthy) was also greatly intensified following his traumas. His own trustworthiness became his only certainty in a dangerously unpredictable world. On a conscious level Stuart believed that he had dedicated himself to the well-being of others, sacrificing his own needs for the good of his parents, his wife, his friends, and all those whose selfobject functioning he wished to have. He had disavowed all feelings of rage and need for revenge. However, in his unconscious fantasies, Stuart experienced himself as betrayer as well as betrayed. He was overcome with guilt, shame, and crippling anxiety whenever fantasies of sexually abusing women and his children entered his conscious awareness. In the next chapter I explain how sadomasochistic fantasies frequently found among trauma survivors may represent restorative efforts and a desperate unconscious strategy for avoiding retraumatization.

The intensification of Stuart's need to experience others as self-trusting also affected his adult life. The immature criteria he used to evaluate those who seemed like self-confident guides and mentors often put him at the mercy of unscrupulous exploiters. Only the depth of his dissociation allowed him to function without conscious awareness of their treachery. However, when his father sold the business he so dearly longed to run as a means of anchoring himself to the man in a fantasy of idealized merger, his customary restorative efforts were no longer effective. Stuart experienced such a strong resurgence of PTSD that he was almost completely immobilized. Fortunately, Stuart entered therapy and by working through his traumas in the context of a therapeutic relationship, he has begun to establish trustworthy selfobject connections.

Nancy

"Here's an old picture of my parents," Nancy said, handing me a somewhat creased photograph of a handsome couple in their mid-forties. Posed cheek to smiling cheek with their arms wrapped tightly around each other, they had the look of honeymooners. "Don't they seem happy together?" she asked. When I nodded in agreement, Nancy's expression darkened and tears filled her eyes. "It was all an act," she said. "A week after this picture was taken my mother asked for a divorce and my father killed himself. In his suicide note he said he couldn't face life without her." Despite the grief and pain she still felt, Nancy had not connected her complaints on entering individual and group therapy with the traumas she experienced at age 16. She wanted treatment, she said, because she felt stymied by her failure to sustain relationships with men and by her inability to find a satisfying career. She also mentioned a dread of public speaking and inexplicable fainting episodes for which no physiological explanation had been found.

Nancy, a strikingly beautiful woman, was 29 when we first met. Although her large dark eyes seemed perpetually focused on some tragic inner scene, she presented herself as a competent and confident woman. She dressed in tasteful clothes that enhanced her slender figure. Initially, the other members of her therapy group were mystified about her reasons for joining. She seemed to have all a happy life requires: beauty, intelligence, a lively wit, and a well-developed capacity for empathic responsiveness. However, it was not long before they discovered that Nancy could not bear to be the focus of the group's attention. Any attempt to describe her painful past left her sweating, trembling, and overwhelmed by excruciating feelings of humiliation.

In her individual sessions Nancy would writhe in her chair whenever she exhausted her detailed account of current situations and concerns in her life. As soon as a few moments of silence opened between us she would complain of pains in her arms and legs and an urge to run out of my office. It was only after months of sessions that we discovered that Nancy's predicament in therapy reflected a central problem in her childhood. She had unconsciously joined her family in a pretense that theirs was a perfectly happy and wholesome household. Being scrutinized by me or members of the group aroused her dread of exposing dark family secrets she had gone to such great lengths to hide. For Nancy, even the spontaneous expression of anger or pain was tantamount to an open declaration of her family's failings.

Nancy described growing up in what she believed to be a "model" family: Her father had been a highly respected lawyer, her mother had been president of the PTA, and her bright, talented, athletic brothers were "the most popular kids in town." She wondered how she could have failed to realize that her father was addicted to drugs and had indulged in numerous extramarital affairs. She recalled childhood evenings when she thought she heard her parents fighting in the kitchen beneath her room. Since nothing amiss could be detected in their interactions at the breakfast table the following morning, she would doubt her perceptions and wonder if what she heard took place in her dreams.

To explain her husband's suicide, Nancy's mother fabricated a story about an accidental drowning and urged her children to be "strong and brave." "I guess that meant not showing unhappy feelings or asking a lot of questions," Nancy said. On the day Nancy learned of her father's death she locked herself in her room and stayed there for most of the following week. She left her self-imposed confinement only to join the family for the funeral. Although she desperately longed to be comforted and consoled, Nancy worried that family members would recoil from her intense grief. She recalled many instances in which her feelings had been ignored or minimized and she had been reprimanded for being overly dramatic and emotional. "My parents seemed to find tears and raised voices embarrassing. They tried to cure me of my 'Sarah Bernhardt' tendencies by making light of whatever was bothering me." If, for example, Nancy complained that a teacher had treated her unfairly or that she had been bullied by an older child, her parents chided her for being overly sensitive and urged her to "stop making such a big deal out of everything." On one occasion her mother told her that she was being a baby about pain in her arm after a skating accident. Many days went by before she was allowed to visit a doctor who found that she had broken a bone.

It seemed natural for Nancy to conceal the symptoms of dissociation she suffered following her father's death. She told no one about terrifying feelings of depersonalization and derealization that plagued her for years. "I lived alone in a twilight zone where nothing seemed the same as before," she said. Nancy also recalled that during the next few years her sleep was often interrupted by terrifying recurrent nightmares that involved falling from very high and exposed places. In one nightmare she is alone in a glass-enclosed elevator attached to the outside of a tall building. The elevator goes up hundreds of stories when suddenly the building starts to sway. She is thrown out of the elevator and wakes up screaming as she falls to the ground. Associating to the nightmare, Nancy said, "My father was very tall. I remember how much I loved it when he hoisted me up on his shoulders to 'touch the sky.' Maybe with him dead I can't climb up in my life without feeling endangered and precarious."

Nancy did not learn the true circumstances of her father's death until a close friend of her mother's inadvertently referred to his suicide during her first visit home from college. When confronted by Nancy, her mother indicated that she had "glossed the truth" at the time of her husband's death out of a wish to spare her children pain. They were not "ready" to know at the time, she explained. "Didn't she understand that I would be ready to know when she was ready to deal with my feelings?" Nancy asked. "I guess I always suspected that Dad had killed himself, but I just couldn't let on."

Nancy's fainting episodes, which began around the time she discovered the truth about her father's death, can be understood as dissociative phenomena related to her self-trust disturbances. They usually occurred when Nancy found herself in a situation in which knowing what was going on would have confronted her with knowledge of some potentially hurtful, exploitative, or otherwise untrustworthy behavior by others. For example, Nancy once fainted on a crowded bus on the way to my office. At first Nancy could find no reason for the first warning signals that generally heralded these episodes: a queasy feeling in her stomach and lightheadedness. Then she recalled that a man standing behind her had repeatedly jabbed his briefcase into her back despite her efforts to reposition herself. "Maybe I didn't want to know what he was doing because I would have had to make a scene. I didn't want everyone on the bus to get upset." Further exploration connected Nancy's reaction on the bus to her efforts "not to know" what was going on at home for fear that her reactions would not be validated by others. She worried about the consequences of loudly accusing the man of jabbing her with his briefcase, certain that he would have denied it. "The other passengers would have thought that I was creating a fuss over nothing," she said. "I would have embarrassed the man and myself." Having little hope that she would be supported, Nancy fainted as a means of blotting out all awareness of her circumstances.

Nancy's efforts to hide awareness of disappointments in others took myriad forms and affected many of her adult relationships. For example, after several years in treatment, Nancy realized that the woman she considered her best friend had never supported her in times of need. In her relationships with men she also frequently failed to pay attention to "fatal flaws" in their characters, such as their abusiveness, their instability, or their loyalty to other women. In time, a pattern could be discerned in Nancy's usually short-lived love affairs. She often chose men who were unhappily but securely connected to other women. Even those who projected an initial image of confidence and strength were perceived as extremely vulnerable and needy "deep-down," much like her father. Despite her wholehearted efforts to "rescue" these men by devoting herself to the fulfillment of their needs, they invariably left her heartbroken. After mistreating her, they would return to their old girlfriends or find someone new. A similar pattern could be discerned in her work relationships as well. She would fiercely devote herself to a strong-appearing but insecure boss hoping to be rewarded with choice assignments and praise. Instead, she was often passed over in favor of someone who had made comparatively few sacrifices for the company.

The meaning of these patterns of relating became clear only when Nancy became aware of tormenting feelings of guilt and shame associated with her father's death. "Down-deep I always felt responsible," she said. "I knew my father was depressed and that my parents' marriage was troubled. Maybe if I'd had the guts to say I knew what was going on, they would have faced facts and he would have gotten the psychiatric help he needed." We discovered that Nancy had been placed in an insoluble dilemma. How could she "blow the whistle" on her family and call attention to their defects without betraying their trust in her as someone who protected their idealized facade?

Nancy realized that her involvement with men like her father, beneath whose strong appearances she detected weakness and vulnerability, gave her an opportunity to enact a restorative fantasy: She would be rewarded with undying love for "rescuing" a needy man. However, her immature criteria for trusting others led her to choose potentially abusive men. Unable to attend to their exploitiveness or abusiveness, she would invariably suffer retraumatizing betrayals. This sort of restorative enactment as a prelude to retraumatization is discussed in detail in the next chapter.

Case Summary

All of the complaints that led Nancy to seek therapy—her inability to establish satisfying love and work relationships, her public-speaking phobia, and her fainting spells—become understandable when viewed in terms of a dissociative alteration of subjective reality in the aftermath of betrayals of her self-trust in childhood. As a child, Nancy's trust in her parents as selfobjects was greatly disturbed by their failure to validate her affective experiences. Her hopes of eliciting selfobject experiences from her parents (trust-in-self) turned on her efforts to corroborate their belief that theirs was a model family. To do so, Nancy had learned to disavow any perceptions that contradicted this image.

Even before her father's death Nancy had responded to her family's failure to provide a trustworthy selfobject milieu by intensifying trust-in-others and self-as-trustworthy. She attempted to prove herself a trustworthy provider of her family's selfobject needs by avoiding scrutiny by others that might reveal her pain over their shortcomings. Consequently she was overcome by anxiety when all eyes were on her as they often were at a business meeting or in group therapy. In any situation that put her in the position of "blowing the whistle" on potential betrayers of her trust, Nancy went to great lengths to protect herself and others from her awareness even if this entailed the loss of consciousness.

Her father's suicide placed Nancy in a "no-win" situation. On the one hand, she felt that, as the trustworthy provider of her family's needs, she should have blown the whistle on her father's drug abuse and extramarital affairs. On the other hand, she felt that their trust in her depended on the extent to which she went along with their pretense at perfection. Her effort at self-trust restoration involved finding love and work relationships in which she experienced herself as "rescuing" others, a means by which she confirmed her intensified self-as-trustworthy. In the next chapter I shall attempt to explain experiences of this kind as efforts to rescript trauma scenarios.

Chapter 4

RESCRIPTING THE TRAUMA

SCENARIO: BETRAYAL,

SADOMASOCHISM, AND

RETRAUMATIZATION

When I ask myself why I have always behaved honourably, ready to spare others and to be kind wherever possible, and why I did not give up doing so when I observed that in that way one harms oneself and becomes an anvil because other people are brutal and untrustworthy, then, it is true, I have no answer.

Sigmund Freud, Letter to J. J. Putman, July 8, 1915 *(cited in Jones, 1955)*

The notion that surviving a trauma provides immunity against future suffering appears to be little more than wishful thinking. Recent studies suggest it is far more common for a survivor's trust in self and in others, like Job's faith in God, to be tested by one ordeal after another. For example, 82% of the women in Russell's (1986) interview study who were traumatized by incest also reported having been raped or subjected to other forms of sexual victimization by nonrelatives. A number of other researchers, including Herman and Hirshman (1981), Frieze (1983), and Browne and Finkelhor (1986), report significant correlations between sexual abuse in childhood and sexual abuse in later life (see Brothers, 1992).

In the Old Testament story, Job's so-called "comforters" added weight to his sorrow by suggesting that his torments were punishment for his sins. They regarded the recurrences of misfortune in his life as evidence that he had brought it on himself—an early but excellent example of "blaming the victim" (Ryan, 1971). Unfortunately, psychoanalysis has offered survivors little more than did Job's comforters in its reliance on the notion of a "repetition compulsion." Many who have sought relief from the devastating effects of multiple traumas have been led to believe that their suffering was caused by a destructive force within themselves. Since, as we shall see, a great number of survivors are only too willing to blame themselves for the catastrophes that befall them, clinicians who believe in an instinctual need to repeat trauma may, inadvertently, reinforce and perpetuate what often represents a faulty effort at self-restitution.

Although Freud outlined his understanding of the "compulsion to repeat" in a paragraph of his 1919 paper, "The Uncanny" (Freud, 1919a) the concept was not fully developed until the publication of "Beyond the Pleasure Principle" the following year (Freud, 1920). The idea of a repetition compulsion endowed with all the attributes of an instinct appears to have grown out of his effort to explain aspects of trauma that violate the pleasure principle. According to this principle, human behavior is motivated by the quest for pleasure, which is attained when excitation in the mental apparatus is reduced or maintained at a constant level. Freud initially proposed that repetitions such as those occurring in children's play and in the treatment situation arise from the need to transform experiences of passive traumatization into active mastery. This explanation, variations of which have been offered by many contemporary analysts (see below), poses no threat to the pleasure principle. However, "an instinct for mastery," in Freud's view, is inadequate to explain other repetitions of trauma such as those seeming to involve no active effort on the part of the traumatized individual. Freud cited as an example the case of the woman who married three successive husbands, each of whom fell ill soon afterward, and had to be nursed by her on their death beds.

Freud also mentioned dreams in traumatic neuroses (those that modern clinicians would probably identify as recurrent traumatic nightmares) that "override" the pleasure principle by repeatedly bringing dreamers back to their traumas and causing them to wake up in fright. In light of these common experiences, Freud (1920) concluded, "we come now to a new and remarkable fact, namely that the compulsion to repeat also recalls from the past experiences which include no possibility of pleasure" (p. 20). To explain this state of affairs Freud invoked an instinct that seeks to restore an earlier state of things, a death instinct. The repetition compulsion, he therefore concluded, is a manifestation of Thanatos, the death instinct.

In light of recent understanding, Freud's distinction between the active recreation of a traumatic experience by a trauma survivor as opposed to passive retraumatization is problematic. Did the unfortunate woman in Freud's example truly play no part in the disasters that befell her, or did some unconscious motive affect her choice of illness-prone husbands? Ulman and Brothers (1988) found that recurrent traumatic nightmares not only contain symbolic representations of passively experienced traumas, but representations of active, albeit faulty, efforts at restoration as well. Another example of the blurriness between active and passive retraumatization is to be found among incest survivors. As Russell (1986) pointed out, the mere knowledge that a child or woman has already been sexually abused may rouse some potential abusers to acts of sexual violence. Such cases seem to involve no active recreation of trauma on the part of the survivor. But, it has also been found that many sexually abused children compulsively masturbate or engage in sexual play—behaviors that, frequently, are mistaken for seductive invitations to sexual relations. Although few children who engage in these behaviors actually desire more sexual contact with adults, they may unwittingly contribute to its recurrence.

Psychoanalysts have tended to regard as "masochistic" patients whose behavior they interpret as actively recreating past traumas within present relationships. In a 1921 revision of "Beyond the Pleasure Principle," Freud hinted that the function of recurrent traumatic nightmares relates to "the mysterious masochistic trends of the ego" (1920, p. 14n). Although Freud (1905) had originally argued that masochism is "sadism turned round upon the subject's own ego," he now suggested the possibility of "primary masochism." In this and in subsequent writings, Freud explained the essence of masochistic phenomena in terms reminiscent of his explanation of the repetition compulsion in that both derive from the death instinct (e.g., Freud, 1937). However, as Freud developed his understanding of masochism he increasingly downplayed its roots in trauma and emphasized instead its relationship to the psychological development of women.

In "A Child is Being Beaten" (Freud, 1919b), written during the same year as "Beyond the Pleasure Principle," Freud linked masochism and femininity for the first time. He observed that, for a girl, the essential meaning of a pleasurable recurrent fantasy that a child is being beaten, which often accompanies masturbation, concerns her sense of guilt over incestuous wishes toward her father and the conversion of her sadism, which he assumed was primary, into masochism. For a boy, the fantasy expresses a wish to be put in a feminine, passive relationship with a punishing father. Masochism, then, is "feminine" whatever the sex of the person in which it is found.

In the "Economic Problem in Masochism," Freud (1924) distinguished among three types of masochism: an erotogenic type based on lust in pain from which the other types derive, a feminine type, and a moral type. Freud observed that feminine masochism is the form most accessible to observation. Again, Freud argued that when this form of masochism occurs in men it involves fantasies characteristic of "womanhood," such as giving birth, assuming a passive position in intercourse, and castration. In moral masochism, punishment does not come from a loved one but rather from the individual's own superego and is characterized by an unconscious sense of guilt.

In his 1925 paper, "Some Psychical Consequences of the Anatomical Distinction Between the Sexes," Freud developed the idea that women are, by nature, masochistic. He explained that in the phallic phase of development little girls recognize the penis of a brother or playmate as the superior genital and become consumed with envy. Noticing that the mother does not possess a penis they assume she deprived them of theirs. Consequently, they renounce her as primary love object and turn to the father. If development proceeds optimally, the girl gives up her wish for a penis and replaces it with a wish to have a child by her father. From this point on, the girl's personality develops a masochistic character.

Many theorists have taken strong exception to Freud's understanding of masochism. That women are fundamentally masochistic, an idea most energetically propounded by H. Deutsch (1944), was challenged by such analysts of Freud's time as Adler (1927) and Horney (1924, 1926, 1933) and by such recent writers as Schad-Somers (1982) and Shainess (1984), who attributed masochism in women to their experiences of growing up in a patriarchal society. Caplan (1985) argued that behavior typically construed as masochistic in women often has other meanings, such as the attempt to put the needs of others ahead of one's own and the attempt to avoid punishment, rejection, or guilt.

A number of contemporary analysts have sought to reestablish the connection between masochism and trauma and have emphasized its self-restitutive function. Menaker (1953), for example, suggested that masochistic self-hatred, self-devaluation, and feelings of worthlessness are the outcome of traumatic deprivation and serve self-preservation insofar as they are "a means of perpetuating whatever bond there is to the mother" (p. 224). Stoller (1975, 1979) viewed sadomasochism and other "perversions" as fantasies that revive traumatic childhood experiences of victimization in order that these humiliating experiences may be transformed into triumphant victories. Similarly, Bach and Schwartz (1972) interpreted the sadistic and masochistic fantasies of the Marquis de Sade as functioning to stave off narcisistic decompensation. Ornstein (1991) noted that the complex defense organizations associated with "self-defeating" behavior are likely to result when caretakers fail to provide phase-appropriate selfobject functions "responsible for the transformation of the infantile narcissistic structures" (p. 395).

Ornstein's formulations derive from Kohut's (1977) view of masochism as resulting from traumatic disappointment in those experienced as selfobjects and the consequent need for self-restoration:

> The puzzling nature of sexual masochism . . . is broadly illuminated if examined in the light of the explanation that, after the child's healthy merger wishes with the idealized selfobject have remained unresponded to, the idealized imago breaks into fragments and the merger needs are sexualized and directed toward these fragments. The masochist attempts to fill in the defect in the part of the self that should provide him with enriching ideals through a sexualized merger with the rejecting (punishing, demeaning, belittling) features of the omnipotent parental imago. (p. 127)

Kohut's famous case study, "The Two Analyses of Mr. Z" (Kohut, 1979), illustrates the dramatic differences between a traditional psychoanalytic understanding of masochism and a self-psychological approach. In his first analysis of Mr. Z, which was conducted in accordance with classical theory, Kohut viewed Mr. Z's masochistic fantasies as resulting from his presumed oedipal victory over his absent father. He believed that Mr. Z's guilt over this victory was sexualized and expressed in the form of fantasies of sexual enslavement to a dominating woman. In other words, Mr. Z's masochism was blamed on intrapsychic processes involving a pathological fantasy of defeating the father.

Following Mr. Z's second analysis, which was informed by his theoretical shift to self psychology, Kohut explained the same masochistic sexual fantasies in terms of traumas Mr. Z incurred in his relationship with his mother. Kohut realized that Mr. Z's fantasies of being forced to perform sexually by a strong, demanding, insatiable woman were reflections of actual experiences of psychological enslavement by his mother.

Concomitant with Kohut's changed understanding of the meaning of Mr. Z's masochistic fantasies was his changed view of their function. In keeping with classical theory, Kohut originally thought they operated as unconscious protection against castration. That is, by imagining himself to be enslaved by the woman, Mr. Z no longer posed a threat to the retributive father. From a self-psychological vantage point, Kohut viewed their function, particularly insofar as they accompanied masturbation, as enabling him to experience "the reassurance of being alive, of existing." In other words, they served self-restorative functions.

Implicit in Kohut's revised conceptualization of masochism is the idea that it must be understood within a relational context; masochism cannot be understood as an intrapsychic phenomenon. The meaning and function of Mr. Z's masochistic fantasies are comprehensible only within the intersubjective field created by him and his mother. Jones (1989) supported this position as follows: "Masochistic experience always involves two persons: the subject who suffers for and at the hands of the desired other and thus is forever restituting and recreating the other" (p. 19).

It appears that masochism cannot exist outside of relationships with others experienced as sadistic, or as Stekel (1929) expressed it: "There is no sadism without masochism, and no masochism without sadism" (p. 138). Moreover, many theorists such as Brenner (1959) and researchers such as Weinberg and Levi Kamel (1986) believe that masochism and sadism are always to be found within the same individual. There is still much disagreement about which is primary. Baumeister (1989), for example, argued that masochism is more important and prevalent, while many support Brenner's (1959) observation that masochism invariably involves both sadistic and masochistic aims.

Stolorow (1975) and Stolorow and Lachmann (1980) agree that sadistic and masochistic tendencies are usually intermingled. Like Kohut, they concern themselves with what they term the "narcissistic function" of masochism and sadism, or the extent to which these activities serve to restore and maintain self-experience. They suggest that a preponderance of masochism over sadism usually results among those who seek narcissistic reparation by resurrecting the idealized parent imago, while the preponderance of sadism over masochism "suggests an early massive disappointment by or absence of idealized selfobjects and a resultant reliance on the primitive grandiose self" (Stolorow & Lachmann, 1980, p. 40). Ornstein (1991) associated masochism with childhood trauma caused by an emotionally indifferent environment, whereas sadism results when the child experiences the emotional environment as "unpredictable, volatile, and violent" (p. 396).

Ulman and I (1988) used Kohut's and Stolorow's insights into sadomasochism in an effort to understand women's beating and rape fantasies. We concluded that they are best conceptualized as symbolic expressions of experiences that disturb or shatter selfobject fantasies as well as faulty efforts at

restoration. Rape fantasies from this perspective may be viewed as the consequence of growing up in a society in which male power and female subordination are blatantly manifested; beating fantasies may reflect actual traumas
suffered at the hands of the father.[1]

The idea that trauma survivors are driven to repeat their traumas has won
widespread acceptance. It is as basic to Freudian theory as it is to modern-day
conceptualizations of PTSD (e.g., van der Kolk, 1987). And, indeed, repetition is ubiquitous in human experience. From birth to death, from waking to
sleeping, our lives are replete with recurrences. Only a moment's reflection
reveals that repetition is an indispensable ingredient of trust. Indeed, our trust
in ourselves, in others, and in the world is confirmed and reconfirmed
through repetition. From earliest infancy we gain trust in our capacity to
perform new tasks by repeating them over and over. Throughout our lives
we crave the reassurance of ritual, the comfort of regularity, and the ease of
familiar companionship. All of these experiences promote trust. Perhaps the
most "addicting" aspect of repeated alcohol and drug use is the trust-
promoting repetition of experience they predictably provide. Given these
considerations it may seem to follow that the repetition of trauma would
somehow provide solace following the betrayal of trust in self or in others.

However, the notion of trauma repetition flies in the face of the need
for self-preservation as the supraordinate motivational striving in human life
(Atwood & Stolorow, 1984; Kohut 1971, 1977, 1984; Tolpin, 1985). The
shattering of selfobject fantasies as a result of self-trust betrayal is accompanied
by the most excruciating affective state imaginable—disintegration anxiety
(Kohut, 1971). Without recourse to Freud's death instinct, there is no way
to understand why anyone might seek to reexperience the terror of self-
dissolution. Yet, the reexperiencing symptoms of PTSD do contain symbolic
representations of traumatic experiences and many masochistic and sadistic
enactments do closely mimic past traumas. How can this apparent paradox
be explained?

It is my contention that trauma survivors are *not* driven to reexperience
self-dissolution, nor do they unconsciously wish to. Although they may,
through intrusive recollections in the form of nightmares and flashbacks,
reexperience some aspects of traumatic experience, *trauma is not compulsively
repeated.* As Ulman and I (1988) pointed out, the dissociative symptoms of
PTSD give symbolic expressions to both the shattering *and the faulty restora-*

---

[1]Greif (1989) also suggested that these fantasies may represent actual experiences of the
father's cruelty.

tion of selfobject fantasies. Even the feeblest effort to restore selfobject fantasies changes the traumatic experience to some degree. In other words, what
appear to be efforts to recreate trauma as it originally occurred turns out, on
closer examination, to be efforts to revise it, or as I think of this now, to
rescript the original trauma scenario. In other words, in order to avoid reexperiencing actual betrayals of self-trust, trauma survivors may attempt to
change the meaning of the old trauma through enactments in their present
lives. These enactments are intended to confirm their altered versions of
subjective reality.

While it is true, as van der Kolk (1987) reminded us, that some Vietnam
vets enlist as mercenaries, some victims of sexual abuse become prostitutes,
and some physically abused children expose themselves to constant danger,
these enactments are not undertaken for the purpose of replicating trauma.
They are born of a desperate need for self-restitution and undertaken in the
hope of altering the experience of victimization. Retraumatizations occurring
in the course of these enactments, while common, are usually inadvertent.
My effort to refine the shattered-fantasy theory of trauma by proposing that
selfobject fantasies shatter in the context of self-trust betrayal (see Chapter 3)
now leads me to attempt to explain how the rescripting of trauma scenarios,
sadomasochism, and retraumatization are interrelated.

THE SADOMASOCHISTIC RESCRIPTING
OF TRAUMA SCENARIOS

The bewilderingly complex nature of sadomasochistic phenomena has been
widely acknowledged (see, e.g., Stolorow & Lachmann, 1980). Moreover,
the terms "masochism" and "sadism" have been assigned many different meanings by various theorists. To explain the relationship between sadomasochism
and self-trust betrayal, I find it necessary to limit the meaning of these terms
by redefining them from the perspective of self-trust.

*Masochism from this perspective refers to experiences of being betrayed or of being
vulnerable to betrayal by those needed as providers of selfobject experience.* Broadly
speaking, it refers to the experience of being a victim. Masochistic experience
may be limited to fantasy or may be expressed in a wide variety of activities
that derive from such fantasies. A posture of inferiority or subordination to
another person, for example, takes on masochistic meaning to the extent that
such a posture contributes to an experience of victimization.

*Sadism refers to fantasies of betraying others who are dependent upon one for the
provision of selfobject experiences, or any activity that reflects such fantasies.* A sadist,

therefore, is a victimizer. Sadistic activities often entail revenge, a shift from betrayed to betrayer. Thus, a stance of superiority with respect to another person or persons has sadistic meaning when it signifies a betrayal.

In the last chapter I tried to show that, in the aftermath of a shattering betrayal, subjective reality is dissociatively altered as one or more of the survivor's self-trust dimensions is intensified. Because intensifications of self-trust represent desperate attempts to restore the bonds of trust connecting self to those represented in selfobject fantasies, they must be confirmed and validated at all cost, especially when self-cohesion is once again threatened. I now propose that efforts to confirm intensified self-trust dimensions often take the form of rescriptings of trauma through sadistic and masochistic enactments.

A person who symbolically attempts to rescript a childhood trauma by adopting a stance of vulnerability to betrayal in relation to someone experienced as a potential betrayer engages in this masochistic enactment in the hope that this time things will come out differently. For example, the survivor may attempt to prove that intensified trust in another person needed to provide selfobject experiences, especially those related to idealization, is warranted. This conceptualization is congruent with Benjamin's (1988) assertion that the crucial point of masochism is not "pleasure in pain," but rather submission to an idealized other. It is also consistent with the following summary of research findings by Stolorow and Lachmann (1980):

> [T]he masochistic character stunts his own independent development, sacrifices his competence, and creates a debased and depreciated perception of his own self in order to sustain the image of an idealized, all-good, all-powerful . . . object on whom he can depend for nurture and protection. (p. 35)

Masochistic enactments may also be undertaken to confirm intensified trust-in-self. Many writers (e.g., Benjamin, 1988) have remarked upon the high degree of control exerted by masochists over those who are supposed to dominate them. In sexual contacts they often orchestrate the specific nature of sadomasochistic scenarios and limit the degree of pain or humiliation involved (Baumeister, 1989). Demonstrating this sort of control enables survivors to rescript a childhood situation in which they were utterly at the mercy of those who betrayed them. Calling the shots in their masochistic scenarios confirms their trust in their ability to extract requisite selfobject experiences from their betrayers.

A person who engages in a sadistic enactment also hopes for an outcome that is different from the original trauma. The experience of betraying others often represents an attempt to confirm intensified trust-in-self and thereby to reverse an experience of oneself as lacking the power to obtain urgently needed selfobject experiences from others. Sadistic enactments may also be undertaken in the hope of confirming intensified others-as-self-trusting. For example, Benjamin (1988) observed that "the adult sadist . . . is searching for a surviving other, but his search is already prejudiced by his childhood disappointment with an other who did not survive (p. 68)." Hence, the purpose of certain sadistic enactments is to prove that, unlike a disappointing caretaker who exploited the survivor out of weakness, the new "victim" will not be done in. It can be assumed that one of the sadist's immature criteria for others-as-self-trusting is that the other person demonstrate imperviousness to destruction.[2]

The temptation to engage in sadistic rescriptings of trauma appears to be very great among parents who were traumatized as children. For example, many investigators report that child abusers are themselves likely to be survivors of incest and other forms of severe abuse within their own families (Bowlby, 1973, 1984; Elder, 1985; Herman & Hirshman, 1981). While a multitude of factors contributes to the generational transmission of trauma (see Krugman, 1987), the "flipping of identification" (Steele, 1970) found to occur among survivors who abuse their own children is well-explained in terms of their need to confirm intensified trust-in-self. Attempting to avert retraumatizing betrayals, and reminded by their children of the helpless vulnerability that led to their own victimization, survivors often feel compelled to adopt the role of betrayer.

Sadomasochistic enactments undertaken in the hope of rescripting trauma are usually doomed to failure and lead to retraumatization for a number of reasons. First, the rescripting of trauma requires a situation that closely resembles the original trauma scenario, and individuals chosen by survivors for roles in their enactments often resemble the original betrayers in many respects. Second, the immature criteria used by survivors for placing trust in self and others often blind them to the possibility of additional betrayal. Thus, instead of achieving a new outcome the survivor is likely to experience a repetition of the old trauma. One might think that repeated retraumatizations would lead to a cessation of sadomasochistic enactments, but unfortunately the reverse is likely to be true. The more times a survivor is retraumatized, the

---

[2]Winnicott (1954) suggested that the mother is "used" psychologically only after surviving a child's fantasized and actual attacks on her without retaliation of any kind.

more desperate his or her efforts to corroborate intensified self-trust dimensions are likely to be. Moreover, survivors who repeatedly attempt to rescript trauma do not reduce the risk of retraumatization; in fact, the risk may be greater with each succeeding attempt.

SADOMASOCHISM AND ALTER EGO SELFOBJECTS

In the previous chapter, I suggested that the dissociative alteration of subjective reality following traumatizing betrayals often leads to the creation of black holes in the survivor's self-experience. I further suggested that for some survivors the only means available for experiencing self-cohesion and filling in these holes is through their relations with others experienced as alter ego selfobjects, that is, others perceived as embodying the disavowed and hidden aspects of themselves. It is often the case that survivors who attempt to rescript their traumas through sadomasochistic enactments also seek alterego selfobjects. For example, survivors who adopt a masochistic posture as a means of rescripting traumatic betrayal frequently repudiate their rage and aggressivity. Because their sadistic partners may give full expression to rage and aggression, they may be experienced as alter ego selfobjects. Similarly, survivors who adopt a sadistic posture frequently disavow their vulnerability and fearfulness. They may experience their masochistic partners as alter ego selfobjects in contact with whom they are enabled to achieve an experience of self-cohesion.

Maggie

The rescripting of trauma takes on either masochistic or sadistic character depending on the overall self-trust organization of the person involved, the specific self-trust dimension requiring confirmation, and the specific qualities sought in an alter ego selfobject. By way of illustration, let us follow the story of Maggie, an attractive Black woman in her early twenties, following a traumatic rape.[3]

A handsome emergency-room doctor asked Maggie out on a date after treating her for a minor injury. Instead of escorting her to dinner as he had initially proposed, he lured her to his apartment where he violently raped her. Maggie experienced the rape primarily as a betrayal of her trust-in-self.

[3]This case was first presented in Ulman & Brothers (1988, pp. 142–151), and excerpted in Brothers (1992, pp. 78–79).

As a result of earlier traumas incurred in growing up with a neglectful mother and an abusive, alcoholic father, intensified trust-in-self had dominated her self-trust organization. Until the rape, she had prided herself on possessing extraordinary powers to size up other people and to predict the outcome of events and situations, one of her highly immature criteria for trust-in-self. The rape confronted Maggie with unassailable evidence that she had been deceived; her belief in her omniscience and prescience was thoroughly shaken. Failing to live up to her criterion for trust-in-self, Maggie's wishful expectation of receiving admiration from those needed as mirroring selfobjects was destroyed and a central selfobject fantasy of mirrored grandiosity was shattered. In a desperate effort to ward off encroaching disintegration anxiety, Maggie further intensified her trust-in-self.

She sought confirmation of this precariously maintained intensification through sadistic fantasies, the enactment of which involved "turning the tables" on men. She would first seduce a man and persuade him to provide her with money and drugs. Then, as soon as she had convinced him of her fidelity, she would suddenly end the relationship only to repeat this scenario with someone new. Like the rapist, she betrayed her victim's trust through deception. As the betrayer instead of the betrayed, Maggie recaptured, at least temporarily, an experience of herself as powerfully in control of the outcome of events and, therefore, as capable of eliciting the selfobject experiences she needed from others. Her sadistic enactments resemble those that Freud (1920) described as the turning of passive into active, and have the character of what Ferenczi (1933) termed "identification with the aggressor."

As part of her effort to intensify trust-in-self, Maggie dissociatively repudiated those aspects of her self-experience involving her neediness, vulnerability, fearfulness, and gullibility. Her doomed lovers also functioned as alter ego selfobjects who embodied these disavowed and hidden aspects of herself.

In the course of Maggie's sadistic rescriptings of her trauma scenario she was repeatedly retraumatized. A number of the men she betrayed became enraged and retaliated with violence. In addition she contracted a variety of venereal diseases and underwent numerous abortions. In recounting these episodes, Maggie often represented herself as a victim. In other words, these experiences also took on masochistic coloring as well. We have already seen that highly intensified self-trust dimensions tend to be unstable. This instability accounts for much of the shifting between masochistic and sadistic activity that has led many observers to conclude that masochism and sadism are two sides of the same coin.

Another function of sadomasochistic rescriptings of trauma scenarios is that they serve to concretize (Atwood & Stolorow, 1984; Stolorow et al., 1987) or "give symbolic voice" (Ulman & Brothers, 1988) to traumatizing betrayals. In other words, in the very act of rescripting a trauma scenario, a survivor who disavowed the traumatic meaning of some occurrence unconsciously confirms the reality of the self-trust betrayal.

FREUD, THE TRAUMA SURVIVOR

As Freud's patients chronicled their childhood sexual traumas, they often described devastating betrayals at the hands of those entrusted with their psychological survival. Yet Freud's theories fail to take this aspect of their experience into account. In Chapter 1 I suggested that Freud could not examine the role of trust betrayal in trauma and psychopathology without compromising the self-restitutive efforts he initiated in the aftermath of his own childhood traumas. Applied to Freud's life, the foregoing discussion of sadomasochistic enactments and the rescripting of trauma brings the reasons for his neglect of trust and betrayal into sharper focus. Indeed, Freud's adult relationships illustrate only too well how efforts to confirm a dissociatively altered subjective reality by means of such enactments can lead to retraumatization.

The remainder of this chapter is devoted to Freud as a trauma survivor. I first review evidence that early betrayals of Freud's self-trust resulted in posttraumatic symptomatology and profoundly affected his self-experience. Next, I examine his relationships with Fliess, Adler, and Jung in an attempt to show that through his interactions with each of these powerful figures, Freud, as betrayed and betrayer, sought to rescript painful trauma scenarios of his early life. Finally, I discuss the part Freud's theories played in his self-restorative efforts, particularly his concepts of the death instinct, the repetition compulsion, and sadomasochism.

Kohut (1976) warned that the psychoanalyst who attempts to investigate Freud's life and personality is faced by the following "uncertainties and difficulties":

> first, by those which in all areas of applied analysis arise because we are not participating in a living clinical situation; second, by those that arise because we might not be objective about Freud, who is for us a transference figure par excellence — we are prone to establish an idealizing transference toward him or to defend ourselves against it by reaction formations; and third, by those that arise because Freud's self-analysis is a unique event in the history of human thought. (p. 171)

In addition to Kohut's excellent points, I realize that it is one thing to try to understand Freud's life from the vantage point of the theory he developed through his self-analysis and quite another to apply a theory that reflects the organization of one's own self-experience (Stolorow & Atwood, 1979). Even more than is true of material I may present from recent or ongoing therapeutic relationships, my speculations about a man whose life and times were radically different from mine are bound to reveal my own prejudices and values. It is my hope, therefore, that the illustrative value of what follows outweighs the consequences of misrepresenting any aspects of Freud's self-experience as a result of inevitable failures in my empathic understanding.

The Organization of Freud's Self-Trust

Biographies of Freud as well as his personal correspondence contain many references to dissociative posttraumatic symptomatology. Consider for example Jones's (1961) description of what appear to be his recurring dissociative states: "Sometimes there were spells where conciousness would be greatly narrowed, states, difficult to describe, with a veil that produced almost a twilight condition of mind" (p. 199). Jones also mentions periodic disturbances in Freud's mental functioning so severe he could neither write nor concentrate. In his letters to Fliess (see Masson, 1985) Freud repeatedly mentioned difficulties with memory and concentration, which are hallmarks of trauma. Moreover, Freud was plagued by a dread of dying (*Todesangst*), a symptom Kohut (1981) associated with disintegration anxiety. As we have seen, disintegration anxiety is most likely to occur when the glue of self-trust is loosened by betrayal and selfobject fantasies are endangered.

Bunselmeyer and Ellerby (1991) suggested that Freud developed PTSD following the near-tragic Emma Eckstein affair (see below), although he acknowledged that earlier traumas probably exerted a "cumulative effect." According to these authors, Freud experienced numbing symptoms, irritability, and melancholy along with mental hyperactivity. They cited Freud's use of cocaine and nicotine as part of his effort to "self-medicate," another common feature of PTSD. And, they suggested that instead of flashbacks, Freud's traumatic imagery is contained within the dreams he recorded in "The Interpretation of Dreams" (Freud, 1900). (Several of these dreams are reviewed as part of my discussion of Freud's relationship with Fliess, pp. 98–101) In Chapter 3 I proposed that these posttraumatic symptoms reflect, in part, the dissociative alteration of subject reality. Let us now imagine how Freud's traumas affected the organization of his self-trust, a major component of the experience of subjective reality.

Trust-in-Self

Referring to himself, Freud wrote, "A man who has been the indisputable favorite of his mother keeps for life the feeling of a conqueror, that confidence of success which often induces real success" (Jones, 1961, p. 6). Yet from the time he was a year and a half old, Freud's experience as his mother's indisputable favorite was repeatedly disrupted by the births of his siblings (see Chapter 1). The "feeling of a conqueror" Freud described, may well reflect intensified "trust-in-self," a response to repeated betrayals of this self-trust dimension. His "confidence of success" not only appears to have been exaggerated but also extremely precarious and his criteria for trust-in-self remained highly unrealistic and perfectionistic. One such criterion appears to have been imperviousness to the malevolence of others. He apparently attempted to live up to this criterion through defiant and risky confrontations with anyone who threatened or opposed him. Once, for example, armed only with a walking stick, he took on a gang of ten men who had shouted anti-Semitic epithets at his sons (Jones, 1961). It is also likely that his pride in having relinquished "the dubious privilege of belonging" to the Viennese medical establishment and the great delight he took in expounding the "minority opinion" (Gay, 1988, pp. 27–28) represent further efforts to confirm intensified trust-in-self.

Another immature criterion for Freud's trust-in-self appears to have been that he exercise absolute control over the thoughts and feelings of those he wished to experience as selfobjects. His efforts to wield this power were particularly evident in his relationship with his wife, Martha. Freud's letters to her reveal his insistence that she identify completely with him as well as with his opinions, feelings, and intentions. As Jones (1961) noted, Freud needed to "perceive his stamp" on her. When, before they married, Martha paid attention to other men, Freud flew into jealous rages. Later, he became furious when she failed to take his side against her brother and mother in a family dispute. Freud's rage-fueled outbursts when he could no longer "perceive his stamp" on disciples who strayed from strict adherence to his theories are further examples.

Self-as-Trustworthy

From the moment their son was born with a caul, Freud's parents appear to have entertained fantasies of his future greatness. The often-told story about an old woman in a pastry shop who assured Freud's mother she had brought a great man into the world, and the poet in the restaurant who foresaw Freud's becoming a "minister," (see Jones, 1961, pp. 5–6) must have deeply impressed Freud with the strength of his parents' idealizing selfobject needs and their wish to bask in his reflected glory. There is little doubt that Freud was singularly well-equipped to justify his parents' anticipation of his future greatness. We might conjecture that Freud's early sense of himself as the trustworthy provider of the selfobject needs of others was stimulated by his parents' expectations. However, even a budding genius can feel burdened by the need to realize the dreams of those upon whom he is dependent – especially when they produce rivals for his exalted place in the family. It is the very intensity of his mother's idealization of Freud as a young child that, in all likelihood, caused Freud to experience her withdrawal from him at the time of his siblings' births as traumatic betrayals.

That Freud's sense of self-as-trustworthy was highly unstable is reflected in his tendency to denigrate perceptions of him as a caring healer. Despite having chosen medicine over law as a profession, Freud denied ever having had "any craving to help suffering humanity." He insisted that he had "no particular partiality for the position and activity of a physician," and claimed, instead, to have chosen medicine because of his "greed for knowledge." Moreover, Freud argued that his patients did not suffer from his "lack of genuine medical temperament." As he expressed it, "it is not greatly to the advantage of patients if their physicians' therapeutic interest has too marked an emotional emphasis. They are best helped if he carries out his task cooly, and, so far as possible, with precision" (in Gay, 1988). Thus, it may be that Freud's suggestion that analysts adopt a stance of distant "neutrality," and his metaphor of the analyst as surgeon (Freud, 1908) were informed by the diminution of his self-as-trustworthy.

Others-as-Self-Trusting

Disappointment in his father as a model of self-trusting, competent masculinity appears to have contributed to his craving for contact with self-trusting mentors. The immaturity of his criteria for evaluating others in terms of this dimension often led to bruising injuries. In the case of Fliess for example, he appears to have mistaken a dogmatic refusal to consider criticism for justifiable self-confidence. Although Freud initially celebrated his friend's belief in his own worth, he eventually came to regard his posturings as pathetic and beneath contempt.

Trust-in-Others

Freud's need to confirm highly intensified trust-in others is probably the most outstanding feature of his self-trust organization. His disavowal of his mother's betrayals, his efforts to locate blame and badness in himself as a lusting and hating Oedipus, and his unswervingly positive regard for his mother throughout his life is the prime example (see Chapter 1, and Stolorow & Atwood, 1979). As is often true of adults traumatized as children, Freud tended to place his trust in many who ill deserved it. However, the instability of this intensified self-trust dimension is evidenced by the fact that the people he trusted most intensely frequently ended up as discredited enemies.

The Rescripting of Freud's Trauma Scenarios

A sizeable portion of the vast biographical literature on Freud has been devoted to his intense relationships with prominent men. (See for example Gay, 1988; Grosskurth, 1991; Jones, 1961; Schur, 1972). Although Freud regarded some predominantly as teachers, mentors, or guides (e.g., Breuer and Fliess), and others as students, disciples, or admirers (e.g., Adler and Jung), and the strength of his attachments varied considerably, his relationship with each of them followed a similar course. In the early stages, Freud would become keenly interested in, if not enthralled, with the man and accord him special status in his life. While hints of future discord were probably present from the start, Freud would ignore them or disavow their meaning. After a time Freud would seem to have flashes of awareness that his trust in the man had been misplaced and that betrayal was imminent and inevitable. For a while, however, even when disturbances in the relationship became too blatant for him to disregard, he would still make every effort to maintain the connection. At the same time, Freud would often behave sadistically toward the man. Finally, he would fully acknowledge that he had been betrayed and the relationship would end with brutal finality. It is my contention that the invariant pattern of these relationships is best explained in terms of Freud's doomed efforts to confirm his intensified and unstable self-trust dimensions through sadomasochistic rescriptings of trauma scenarios.

Freud and Wilhelm Fliess

Many Freud scholars have commented on the strange intensity of Freud's attachment to Wilhelm Fliess, a man deemed undeserving of it on many counts. Some have excused Freud's apparent lapse in social judgment on the grounds that the relationship, viewed as similar to a psychoanalytic transference, was necessary for the liberation of his creative genius (e.g., Gay, 1988; Jones, 1961; Schur, 1972). Jones, for example, observed that

> for a man of nearly middle age, happily married and having six children, to
> cherish a passionate friendship with someone intellectually his inferior, and for

him to subordinate for several years his judgment and opinions to those of that other man, this also is unusual, though not entirely unfamiliar. But for that man to free himself by following a path hitherto untrodden by any human being, by the heroic task of exploring his own unconscious mind: that is extraordinary in the highest degree. (p. 186)

In my view, Fliess's importance far transcended his tutelary role; he was a key actor in one of many dramas of trust and betrayal that were staged and restaged throughout Freud's life. Since the story of this relationship has been well-chronicled by others, I will retell it in only as much detail as is necessary to demonstrate its role in Freud's attempts to rescript trauma. In 1887, the year they met, Fliess, 29, was a successful otolaryngologist in Berlin, while Freud, 31, had just opened a medical practice in Vienna. Freud was also a lecturer in neurology at the University of Vienna. During a trip to Vienna to study with medical specialists there, Fliess attended one of Freud's lecturers on hysteria. Soon after Fliess returned home, Freud initiated a correspondence with him that lasted until 1904. The men also met periodically for what they came to call their "congresses."

The timing of Freud's meeting with Fliess had much to do with the strength of their mutual attraction (Schur, 1972). Freud had just begun to explore the psychological bases of hysteria, an undertaking he must already have suspected would, at least in the short run, damage his chances for selfobject connectedness to colleagues and superiors. He had recently married and taken on the burdens and responsibilities associated with supporting a wife and children. And, by the time he met Fliess, he had probably become aware of his wife's limitations as an intellectual companion (Gay, 1988). Adding to all this, he had begun to experience the frightening symptoms of a mysterious heart condition. If we are correct in assuming that Freud's sense of cohesive selfhood had been undermined by childhood traumas, these difficult circumstances may well have strained whatever restorative efforts he had made. His psychological well-being apparently turned on his finding a trustworthy companion to satisfy what could only have been urgent selfobject requirements. There is little doubt that Fliess must have appeared to Freud, perhaps from their first meeting, as the very embodiment of all his longings for selfobject fulfillment. Fliess could hardly have been more like Freud, at least superficially: He, too, was a Jew, close in age to Freud, a medical doctor, and soon to marry and become a father. A photograph taken in 1890 (see Gay, 1988) even reveals a striking physical similarity. Thus, he appears to have been well-suited to fulfill Freud's need for twinship selfobject experiences to ease the loneliness of his intellectual explorations.

By all accounts, Fliess was a brilliant conversationalist given to flamboyant and imaginative theorizing. He would set forth the most preposterous ideas with bold assurance and vigorously repudiate any criticism of them. Freud appears to have accorded Fliess the right to speculation he diffidently denied to himself (Jones, 1961). In this way, Fliess seems to have represented his hopes for an alter ego selfobject, an embodiment of disavowed aspects of his own self-experience. In fact, Freud occasionally addressed him in letters as "the other, the alter" (e.g., May 21, 1894, in Masson, 1985, p. 73).

Fliess's charisma and vitality, as well as the professional success he attained so early in life, must have convinced Freud that his search for a teacher, critic, and physician was over; in Fliess he found so much more than a friend—he found a man he could represent in selfobject fantasies as the quintessential idealized paternal selfobject. Moreover, Fliess's apparent generosity with praise and support in their early meetings must have excited Freud's hopes that his unique gifts would be appreciated and celebrated by Fliess as a perfectly attuned provider of mirroring selfobject experiences.

Let us keep in mind that Freud's criteria for evaluating the trustworthiness of a person needed as a selfobject were, in all likelihood, immature. Consequently, the immoderately grandiose, larger-than-life aspects of Fliess's character—cause, perhaps, for concern in those whose self-trust criteria were more mature—may well have enhanced his appeal for Freud. The extravagantly positive way Freud addressed Fliess in his earliest letters to him lends weight to my assertion that Freud's trust-in-others had already been greatly intensified as a result of earlier traumas. This is especially noteworthy considering that, as many of his biographers point out, Freud's enthusiasm for Fliess came on the heels of his disillusionment in Breuer, his former mentor and collaborator, for failing to support his sexual theories. Instead of becoming more cautious, Freud fairly leapt into this relationship without allowing the time necessary for even a moderately critical look. Consider the florid tone of the opening words of his first letter to Fliess on November 24, 1887: "I entertain hopes of continuing the relationship with you . . . you have left a deep impression on me which could easily lead me to tell you outright in what category of men I place you" (Masson, 1985, p. 15).

Much as Fliess represented the potential fulfillment of Freud's selfobject longings, it could not have been long before Freud was confronted with signs that in embracing Fliess with such unreserved enthusiasm he risked almost certain betrayal. To begin with, there were Fliess's bizarre theories, among which were his proposition that the nose is responsible for a wide variety of neurotic and physical ailments, and his scheme of periodicity in which the numbers 23 and 28 were held to organize much of human life. Not only were Fliess's ideas extreme and unsound, they were basically incompatible with Freud's growing belief in psychological determinism. Yet, it was not for many years (in a letter dated August 7, 1901) that Freud gave any sign of recognizing that a clash was inevitable (Schur, 1972). Moreover, he went to great lengths to demonstrate his adherence to Fliess's innovations by allowing him to operate on his own nose and on the noses of several patients, and by applying his number theory to predict critical events in his life and in his patients' and family members' lives.

It is my contention that despite all evidence to the contrary, Freud, on an unconscious level, was greatly affected by the dubiousness of Fliess's ideas as well as by obvious flaws in his character. However, in his urgent need for selfobject connectedness at the time he met Fliess, all conscious awareness of these threats to his trust in Fliess were dissociatively repudiated. In fact, it might well have been his potential for betrayal that made Fliess so attractive to Freud. He had all the qualifications required of a leading actor in Freud's sadomasochistic dramas.

Evidence that Freud initially adopted a predominantly masochistic stance in relation to Fliess abounds in the early letters. Interspersed among his fervid proclamations of admiration for Fliess are self-deprecating assessments of his own capacities and achievements as well as statements asserting his subordinate position in the relationship. Like so many survivors of childhood trauma who maintain idealizing ties to abusive partners through self-abasement, Freud repeatedly devalued himself and his own ideas as he elevated Fliess to Olympian heights. For example in his second letter to Fliess, dated December 28, 1887, Freud wrote, "I still do not know how I won you; the bit of speculative anatomy of the brain cannot have impressed your rigorous judgment for long" (Masson, 1985, p. 16). In a letter dated July 20, 1893, he wrote: "I hope that you will explain the physiological mechanism of my clinical findings by your approach. I still look to you as the messiah who by an improvement of technique will solve the problems I have pointed out" (Masson, 1985, pp. 50–51).

The early correspondence also reveals how, by means of his self denigrating posture, Freud adroitly avoided finding fault with Fliess's ideas. He repeatedly claimed that limitations in his own grasp of mathematics and biology rendered him incapable of comprehending them. By portraying himself as too ignorant to evaluate Fliess's work, he eliminated a significant threat to his experience of Fliess as an idealized selfobject and his intensified trust-in-others gained confirmation.

Freud's intensified experience of others-as-self-trusting also required confirmation. A letter of August 29, 1988 reveals his effort to confirm his experience of Fliess as self-trusting through masochistic depreciation that extended beyond himself to the city he lived in.

> The whole atmosphere of Vienna is such that it does little to steel one's will or to foster that confidence of success which is characteristic of you Berliners and without which a mature man cannot think of changing the basis of his existence. So it seems I must remain what I am, but I have no illusions about the inadequacy of this state of affairs. (Masson, 1985, p. 24)

I have argued that the need to confirm highly intensified self-trust dimensions is most keenly felt when the threat of betrayal is once again imminent. It is not surprising, therefore, that Freud's masochistic enactments crescendoed during the period of the Emma Ekstein affair, a time when his trust in Fliess was dealt its severest blow. Emma Eckstein was a patient of Freud's who complained of irregular and painful menstruation supposedly connected to masturbation. In February, 1895, Freud assisted Fliess in an operation on her nose after being assured it would cure her condition. There appears to have been no rational grounds for this operation and, to make matters worse, Fliess's negligence (he left a piece of gauze in the surgical wound) nearly caused Eckstein to die of hemorrhages and infections.

On learning of these complications, Fliess denied any misconduct and demanded an apology from the doctors Freud was forced to call in to save his patient's life. Freud repeatedly downplayed Fliess's culpability despite the fact that Fliess's nearly fatal negligence seems indefensible. Moreover, Freud strenuously reassured Fliess that his trust in him had not been in any way compromised. The following excerpts from their correspondence are illustrative:

> March 8, 1895: "no one is blaming you nor would I know why they should . . . rest assured it was not necessary for me to reaffirm my trust in you again." (Masson, 1985, p. 118)
>
> March 13–15–20, 1895: "It is now about time you forgave yourself the minimal oversight, as Breuer called it." (Masson, p. 120)
>
> April 20, 1895: "For me you remain the physician, the type of man into whose hands one confidently puts one's life and that of one's family . . . I wanted to pour forth my tale of woe and perhaps obtain your advice concerning E, not reproach you with anything. That would have been stupid, unjustified, and in clear contradiction to all my feelings." (Masson, p. 125).

Along with his assertions of trust in Fliess's blamelessness, the letters of this period also reveal Freud's efforts to assume responsibility for the fiasco. For example, on March 20 he wrote, "Poor Eckstein is doing less well. In my thoughts I have given up hope for the girl and am inconsolable that *I involved you and created such a distressing affair for you*" [italics added]. (Masson, 1985, p. 121)

That these efforts were insufficient to quell Freud's disintegration anxiety and to avert retraumatization is evidence by the enormous distress he consciously experienced. His letters reveal his genuine concern for Eckstein and his own considerable pain. On March 13 he wrote, "I have rarely felt so low down, almost melancholic, all my interests have lost their meaning," and on March 15, "How have I been? In a word, like a dog—infamously miserable" (Masson, 1985, pp. 119–120). On March 20 he revealed, "I also feel very sorry for her, I had become very fond of her" (Masson, p. 121).

In discussing Freud's reaction to the Eckstein episode, Schur (1972) noted, "We may state with certainty that Freud unconsciously knew very well that Fliess was responsible for the critical complications and blamed him for them, so that his trust in Fliess was deeply shaken" (p. 81). And, in fact, there are many indications that hard as Freud tried to confirm his intensified trust-in-others through these masochistic enactments, the struggle became increasingly unsuccessful. His conscious awareness of Fliess's betrayal seems to have broken through repeatedly. On April 11, 1895 for example, he wrote, "Am I really the same person who was overflowing with ideas and proposals as long as you were within reach? . . . I am really very stricken to think that such a mishap could have arisen from an operation that was purported to be harmless" (Masson, 1985, p. 124). And on April 20, he mentioned feeling "offended that you deem it necessary to have a testimonial certificate . . . for your rehabilitation" (Masson, 1985, p. 125).

Moreover, Freud subsequently lessened his dependence upon Fliess as his physician and, not surprisingly, his physical condition improved dramatically (Schur, 1972). Alternating with these indications of diminished trust in Fliess, however, were strenuous efforts to resurrect an image of Fliess as trustworthy. For example, after Eckstein recovered fully Freud even asserted that Fliess had been right after all, that her episodes of bleeding had been hysterical. As I see it, Freud could not sustain his dissociative disavowal of Fliess's betrayal. But awareness of Fliess's treachery proved so disorganizing to his self-experience, possibly because of his need for Fliess as an alter ego selfobject, that he quickly stepped up his efforts to maintain trust in him with ever more heroic enactments.

An intimate view of Freud's efforts to rescript his trauma scenarios through sadomasochistic enactments is furnished by his masterwork, "The Interpretation of Dreams" (Freud, 1900). Fortunately, because Freud worked on this book at the very time that his efforts to maintain his selfobject connectedness to Fliess were at their zenith, several of the dreams he included in the book are exquisitely revealing of these efforts. In reviewing the relevant aspects of three of these dreams I will rely chiefly on Schur's (1972) insightful analysis of them. To my mind, the dreams not only chart the gradual diminution of Freud's dissociative efforts to maintain his trust in Fliess as a selfobject, they also reveal a shift in the character of his self-trust confirming enactments from masochistic to sadistic.

Sometime in July of 1895, not long after Eckstein's recovery, Freud had the dream known as "Irma's injection" (Freud, 1900). In the dream, Irma, a young woman, visits his home during a party. She complains of pain in her throat. He calls in several physician friends as consultants. They all examine Irma and agree that one of the examining physicians is responsible for her pain insofar as he had given her an injection with a dirty needle. Despite the obvious parallels between the Eckstein fiasco and the dream, Freud never made the connection. Instead he interpreted the dream as expressing his wish to be freed of responsibility for his daughter's illness (see also Bunselmeyer & Ellerby, 1991). Associating to a dream of 1898 known as "Goethe's attack on Herr M," Freud mentioned having resigned from a journal on which he served as editor after it had published a scathing criticism of Fliess's work. Although Freud interpreted the dream as representing his attack on Fliess's critics, Schur's analysis revealed that it disguises his agreement with the criticisms.

Both of these dreams support my notion that trauma is not merely repeated as it originally occurred. In each dream Freud unconsciously rescripted his traumatic betrayals by Fliess such that Fliess's incompetence is revealed and punished. In his sleep, Freud transformed himself from betrayed to betrayer. However, his failure to interpret these meanings in his dreams suggest that on a conscious level, Freud still maintained his dissociatively intensified trust in Fliess.

The "Non Vixit" dream, which also occurred in 1898, is another story. In the dream Freud goes to Brucke's laboratory where a dead professor, Ernst Fleischl, enters. In a second dream, Freud encounters Fliess on the street while he is talking to a friend (Joseph Panef), who is also dead. Fliess speaks about his sister and says that "in three quarters of an hour she was dead" and adds something like "that was the threshold." I quote the remainder of the dream as Freud reported it.

As P. failed to understand him, Fl. turned to me and asked me how much I had told P. about his affairs. Whereupon, overcome with strange emotion, I tried to explain to Fl. that P. (could not understand anything at all, of course, because he) was not alive. But what I actually said—and I myself noticed the mistake was "NON VIXIT." I then gave P. a piercing look. Under my gaze he turned pale; his form grew indistinct and his eyes a sickly blue—and finally he melted away. I was highly delighted at this and I now realized that Ernst Fleishl, too, had been no more than an apparition, a "revenant" ["ghost"— literally, "one who returns"]; and it seemed to me quite possible that people of that kind only existed as long as one liked and could be got rid of if someone else wished it. (in Schur, 1972, p. 154)

According to Freud, the dream was triggered by Fliess's announcement that he intended to have an operation around the time of his 40th birthday. Freud claimed that he could not rush to his friend's bedside because he had a physical ailment that made moving painful (a furuncle on his scrotum). However, his correspondence with Fliess indicates that his illness did not coincide with Fliess's. Moreover, Freud sent a letter to Fliess congratulating him on his birthday without mentioning the operation. A week later he wrote chastising himself for not responding to the fact that Fliess planned "to let (himself) in for new experimental torments," a clear statement of his critical attitude toward Fliess's medical experiments as well as his need to have the operation during a supposedly critical period.

A key feature of the dream centers around Freud's having said "non vixit"— he did not live—instead of "non vivit"—he is not alive. Freud associated to words he had seen on the pedestal of a monument to Emperor Joseph II at the Imperial Palace in Vienna: "For the well-being of his country, he lived not long but wholly." The dream involved another Josef, Josef Paneth who had succeeded Freud in Brucke's laboratory and died early. In the dream, Freud annihilates a rival with a "piercing look," However, according to Freud, it had been Brucke, not Freud, who had done the annihilating when Freud had shown up late as demonstrator in the laboratory. Freud recalled "the terrible blue eyes with which he looked at me and before which I melted away." In other words the dream represented a turning of the tables on Brucke; Freud was now the annihilator. Freud also represented himself as the triumphant survivor of Josef Paneth.

Freud associated the dream, which occurred on the first anniversary of his father's death, with important figures of his childhood including his nephew John who was one year older than Freud, and with whom he had been inseparable until his third year. He wrote:

All my friends have in a certain sense been re-incarnations of this first figure . . . ; they have been revenants. My nephew himself re-appeared in my
boyhood, and at that time we acted the parts of Caesar and Brutus together.
My emotional life has always insisted that I should have an intimate friend and
a hated enemy. I have always been able to provide myself afresh with both,
and it has not infrequently happened that the ideal situation of childhood has
been so completely reproduced that friend and enemy have come together in a
single individual. (in Schur, 1972, p. 162)

Remarkably, Freud's associations also connected Fliess with Julius Caesar
and himself with Brutus. No longer was Freud merely disguising his own
betrayal by Fliess, Freud now represented himself as the betrayer in the
relationship. Interestingly, as Schur pointed out, Freud omits any reference
to his brother Julius whose birth and death had been severely traumatizing.
Since Fliess was born in 1858, the year Julius died, Fliess was a revenant of
Freud's younger brother. As Schur (1972) noted, "Freud was anticipating
that Fliess, too, would soon be left by the wayside to become a 'revenant'"
(p. 170).

Schur (1972) compared the three dreams as follows:

In the Irma dream the hostility to Fliess was disguised by being displaced onto
others. In the dream of Goethe's attack on Herr M., Freud's agreement with
the devastating criticism of Fliess's work was disguised as a derisive attack on
the critics themself. The conflict in the non vixit dream went much further, or,
to be more accurate, deeper. It was expressed in the most elementary terms:
who will survive whom? (p. 168)

Viewed in terms of Freud's experience of subjective reality, all three dreams
represent a shift in Freud's relationship with Fliess; the gradual relinquishment
of Freud's masochistic posture by means of which he had striven to confirm
his intensified trust-in-others and others-as-self-trusting. With increasingly
greater awareness, Freud represented himself in a sadistic posture toward
Fliess that centered around a retributive turning of the tables by means of
which Freud confirmed his intensified trust-in-self. Freud's associations to the
three dreams appear to reflect a gradual diminution of his dissociation. However, in spite of the apparent clarity with which the non vixit dream exposes
Freud's experience of himself as betraying Fliess, he clearly did not fully
integrate its meaning. After finishing "The Interpretation of Dreams," Freud
sent Fliess some galleys and wrote,

The principal part of my interpretive achievements comes in this installment. The absurd dreams! It is astonishing how often you appear in them. In the non vixit dream I am delighted to have survived you. Isn't it awful to have to hint at such things? (Masson, 1985, p. 374)

It seems unlikely that Freud would have displayed such naive pleasure if he had been fully conscious of all the implications of the dream.

Masson (1985) quoted from the unpublished notebook of Marie Bonaparte, one of Freud's students and analysands, on the deterioration of the relationship:

The friendship with Fliess began to decline as early as 1900 . . . when Freud published the book on dreams. Freud had not realized this! I taught it to him. His friendship with Fliess made him reluctant to impute envy to Fliess. Fliess could not bear the superiority of his friend. Nor could he tolerate, this time according to Freud, Freud's scientific criticisms. (p. 3)

By 1904 Freud appears to have been quite conscious of his disillusionment in Fliess. Their correspondence dwindled in frequency and depth. However, the actual ending of the friendship was precipitated by what appears to have been a "real-life" sadistic enactment by Freud as opposed to those that occurred in his dreams. The final break coincided with Fliess's accusation that Freud had plagiarized his theory of bisexuality. He reminded Freud that when he had first mentioned it to him, Freud had disputed it. In fact, Freud had revealed Fliess's theory of bisexuality to one of his patients, Hermann Swaboda, who transmitted it to Otto Weininger. Fliess discovered Freud's indiscretion on reading Weinberger's book, *Geschlect und Charakter [Sex and Character]* (1975) in which Weininger attributed the theory to Freud. Freud initially denied Fliess's accusation. However, in a letter dated July 27, 1904, he observed, "I suspected that one of us might come to regret our formerly unrestrained exchange of ideas" (Masson, 1985, p. 467).

Freud subsequently dismissed his intense attraction for Fliess by attributing it to some homosexual aspect of his character. From the standpoint of self psychology, the sexualization of Freud's relationship is an understandable disintegration product of his unmet selfobject longings. Despite Freud's protestation that by breaking with Fliess he "had succeeded where the paranoiac fails" and had withdrawn "a piece of homosexual charge" for the "enlargement" of his own ego (quoted in Gay, 1988, p. 275), there is much to suggest that Freud experienced a retraumatizing betrayal in this relationship. As Gay pointed out, "Freud saw Wilhelm Fliess everywhere, incorporated in others"

(p. 275). In fact, he confided to Jung that Adler "awakens in me the memory of Fliess, an octave lower. The same paranoia" (quoted in Gay, p. 275).

Freud and Alfred Adler

According to an unconfirmed account by Adler's biographer, Phyllis Bottome (1939), Freud invited Adler to the first meeting of his Wednesday evening discussion group in the autumn of 1902 shortly after a Viennese newspaper published Adler's defense of "The Interpretation of Dreams" (see Stepansky, 1983). Although Freud asked him to join "not as a 'pupil' but as an 'equal'" and Adlerians maintain that he entered Freud's circle as an independent thinker, Freud apparently mistook Adler's enthusiasm for his work on dreams for an oath of allegiance to psychoanalysis. With all the impetuousity born of his intensified trust-in-others, Freud once again welcomed to his home and heart a man he would later cast out as a betrayer. At the Wednesday night meetings, which subsequently became the Vienna Psychoanalytic Society, Adler was generally thought to be one of Freud's "reigning favorites" (Stepansky). In 1910, after Freud enraged the Viennese by announcing that Jung, an outsider, had been made permanent president of the International Psychoanalytic Association, Adler, one of their own, was elected President of the Vienna Society. Only a year later, on the heels of Freud's scathing criticism of his work, he left the Society with a group of supporters.

Writing to Ferenczi on April 6, 1911, Freud described Adler as "a little Fliess come to life again" (Stepansky, 1983, p. 183). And, in fact, striking similarities are to be found in Freud's relationship with the two men. Like Fliess, Adler strongly espoused theories that were basically incompatible with Freud's and which, curiously, resembled Fliess's in many respects. He, too, emphasized the physiological and the biological determinants of neuroses, (e.g., his theory of "organ inferiority"), and downplayed the role of the unconscious and the primacy of sexuality. His notion of "psychic hermaphroditism" paralleled Fliess's belief in human bisexuality. Both emphasized the masculine in women and the feminine in men. Adler even championed Fliess's theory of periodicity.

Just as Freud had ignored the inevitable clash of his ideas and Fliess's, so he failed to acknowledge that he and Adler were on a collision course from the outset. Moreover, Freud's seemingly uncritical acceptance of Adler's work in the early years of their acquaintance is highly reminiscent of his initial attitude toward Fliess's work. Stepansky's (1983) examination of the Minutes of the Vienna Society, which were begun in 1907, show that initially and for some time, Freud fully approved of the biological viewpoint Adler brought to the psychoanalytic discussions. Even when Adler emphasized the importance of repressed aggression and the aggressive drive, Freud expressed full concurrence with his ideas. Moreover, he minimized the glaring disparities between his ideas and Adler's on this crucial point by suggesting that "what Adler calls aggressive drive is our libido" (Stepansky, p. 91). That is, he bent over backward to interpret Adlerian concepts in terms of Freudian ones as if the differences between them were merely semantic. He even praised Adler with the flowery extravagance he had once heaped on Fliess. As late as 1910, on hearing Adler's paper, "Hysterical Lying," he referred to Adler's "masterly skill."

However, Adler was no Fliess, and Freud's enthusiasm for him never approached the passionate zeal he displayed toward his former friend. As Gay (1988) observed, "Contemporary partisans—on both sides—testify that Freud's and Adler's sartorial habits, personal styles, and therapeutic manners could not have been more unlike: Freud neat, patrician, and striving for clinical distance; Adler careless, democratic, and intensely involved" (p. 220). Thus he was not a likely candidate to fulfill Freud's longings for twin selfobject experiences. Moreover, Adler did not have the flamboyance and charisma of Fliess. Jones (1961) described him as "a morose and cantankerous person, whose behavior oscillated between contentiousness and sulkiness" (p. 313)— qualities that do not easily lend themselves to idealization. Gay (1988) pointed out that although Adler was second only to Freud in the esteem of his colleagues, Freud did not consider Adler a threatening rival. Rather, he strained to view Adler as a loyal disciple who would help ground psychoanalysis in clinical medicine and biology. As such Adler would have provided him primarily with mirroring selfobject experiences.

Freud's posture in relation to Adler never appears to have assumed the self-denigrating masochistic character of his early interactions with Fliess. As Stolorow and Lachman (1980) pointed out, such a posture is usually adopted in the hope of establishing a connection to someone represented as providing idealized selfobject experiences, not mirroring ones. Hence, although Freud repeatedly attempted to prove, despite much evidence to the contrary, that his trust in Adler as a provider of mirroring selfobject experiences had been justified, the relationship was dominated by Freud's efforts to confirm his intensified trust-in-self. That is to say, Freud tried to demonstrate, primarily by means of sadistic enactments, his power over Adler. If he could not force from him the ardent loyalty he craved, he could at least force him out of his kingdom. In so doing, Freud appears to have rescripted the traumatic scenarios in which he had been the child dethroned from his position as favorite.

Considering Freud's conscious association of Adler and Fliess, it seems likely that in experiencing himself as Adler's betrayer, Freud also attempted to avenge Fliess's betrayals as well.

Clearly, the demise of the Freud-Adler relationship was not prompted by any reversal in Adler's behavior or attitude, but rather by dramatic changes in Freud as he increasingly recognized the irreconcilable nature of their differences. As Stepansky noted, "the quality and tenor of Adler's contributions after 1909 were substantially the same as his earlier presentations . . . Freud became disenchanted with Adler at the time he began to take Adler's language at theoretical face value and not as a gratuitously cryptic approximation of the language of psychoanalysis" (p. 105). It seems likely that Freud became aware of the negative implications of Adler's biological perspective only when he could no longer keep himself from consciously recognizing that Adler had betrayed his trust in him as a provider of mirroring selfobject experiences. Remember that one of Freud's criteria for trust-in-self was that the other person accepted without question his point of view. Adler could contribute to Freud's "confidence of success" only to the extent that Freud disavowed the essential incompatibility of their thinking.

In a February 3, 1909 lecture entitled, "A Case of Compulsive Blushing," Adler made the first recorded acknowledgment of his difficulty with the "sexual factor." According to Stepansky (1983) however, it was the paper he presented on June 2 of that year, "Oneness of the Neuroses," "that generated the first subterranean speculation about the compatibility of his work with Freud's and that prompted Freud to speculate on the direction Adler's work was following" (p. 95). Stepansky noted that from then on, Freud's attitude toward Adler showed "wildly erratic fluctuations." Just as his awareness of Fliess's betrayals seemed to be followed by intensified efforts at disavowal so it was in his dealings with Adler. Immediately after harshly criticizing one of Adler's presentations he would often find some opportunity to praise him. For example, in response to the "Oneness of the Neuroses," Freud took firm exception to the ego-psychological framework Adler was erecting and emphasized that his libido theory accounted for the oneness of the neuroses. Yet he still commended Adler's "unusually lucid and consistent train of thought."

Freud's struggle to maintain some connectedness with Adler in the face of his growing awareness of their differences is also reminiscent of his efforts to hold on to Fliess. For a time he continued to declare acceptance of Adler's contributions in public, while voicing his misgivings in private. For example, in response to a June 12, 1909 letter from Jung asking Freud to confirm reports that Adler was breaking away from psychoanalysis and going in his own direction, Freud wrote,

> He is a theorist, astute and original, but not attuned to psychology; he passes it by and concentrates on the biological aspect. A decent sort, though: he won't desert in the immediate future, but neither will he participate as we should like him to. We must hold him as long as possible. (McGuire, 1974, p. 235)

By November of the following year, Freud was much less inclined to be generous and tolerant. In fact, the harshness of the final rupture suggests that Freud, by this time, was fully committed to a sadistic scenario. On November 16, 1910, Hitschmann, a member of the Vienna group, proposed that Adler's theories should be reappraised. Adler apparently viewed this proposal as an honest invitation to reconsider the common ground between his views and Freud's. He complied by setting out his position so bluntly that Freud could not ignore his theoretical divergences. Freud responded by contemptuously demolishing the same Adlerian formulations he had once praised. "All these doctrines of Adler's will make a great impression and do psychoanalysis damage" he said (quoted in Gay, 1988, p. 222). Late in February Adler resigned. Freud then unleashed an unbridled attack on Adler by denouncing his personality as pathological, a weapon he would later use unsparingly against Jung. That Freud consciously experienced himself as turning the tables on someone who had already betrayed him is evident in this excerpt from a letter he wrote to Oskar Pfister in February of 1911: "Adler has created for himself a world system without love, and I am in the midst of carrying out revenge of the insulted goddess Libido on him" (quoted in Gay, 1988, p. 221).

Freud and Carl Jung

Freud's relationship with Jung, no less than with Fliess, was largely epistolary. Their correspondence began in April of 1906 with Freud's warm acknowl-edgement of having received *Diagnostic Association Studies*, a book Jung had sent to him. This book, which Freud had already bought, included studies by Jung and Bleuler demonstrating their acceptance of psychoanalysis through their application of it at the famous Burgholzli Mental Hospital in Zurich. However, the seeds of betrayal were quickly planted, for in Jung's first letter to Freud on October 5, 1906 Jung expressed serious reservations about the place of sexuality in Freud's work: "though the genesis of hysteria is predominantly, it is not exclusively sexual" (McGuire, 1974, pp. 4–5).

Despite the fact that Freud was at that very time, struggling with Adler's rejection of this cornerstone of his theory, his response, dated October 7, 1906, expressed hope that Jung would eventually see the light.

> Your writings have long led me to suspect that your appreciation of my psychology does not extend to all my views on hysteria and the problem of sexuality, but I venture to hope that in the course of years you will come much closer to me than you now think possible. (McGuire, 1974, p. 6)

Nevertheless, some months later Jung completed a monograph on "The Psychology of Dementia Praecox." In the foreword he acknowledged his debt to Freud's "brilliant discoveries," but added,

> If I . . . acknowledge the complex mechanisms of dreams and hysteria, this does not mean that I attribute to the infantile sexual trauma the exclusive importance that Freud apparently does. Still less does it mean that I place sexuality so predominantly in the foreground, or that I grant it the psychological universality which Freud, it seems, postulates. . . . As for Freud's therapy, it is at best but one of several possible methods, and perhaps does not always offer in practice what one expects from it in theory. (McGuire, 1974, p. xviii)

We have already noticed that in order for a trauma survivor to rescript a scenario of past betrayal, the present relationship must resemble it to some extent; retraumatization must lurk as a dangerous possibility. It seems likely that Jung's open declaration of his independence of mind evoked Freud's longing to rescript not only his childhood trauma scenarios but his traumatizing betrayal by Fliess as well. There can be little doubt that Freud's attachment to Jung, at least in its earliest stages, rivaled in passionate enthusiasm his earlier connection to Fliess. The selfobject longings this good-looking, forceful, vibrant man stirred in Freud must have been similar to those he once hoped Fliess would fulfill. Despite the fact that Jung was much younger than Freud and had explicitly requested of him: "Let me enjoy your friendship not as one between equals but as that of father and son" (February 20, 1908; McGuire, 1974, p. 122), Freud's laudatory comments both to Jung directly and in his letters to others about him leave little doubt that he was quickly represented in Freud's selfobject fantasies as an idealized figure.

Jung also appears to have represented the fulfillment of his longings for an alter ego selfobject who might embody qualities Freud did not perceive in himself. As Gay (1988) points out, "Jung was not Viennese, not old and, best of all, not Jewish, three negative assets that Freud found irresistible" (p. 202).

In fact, Freud fervently hoped that Jung would save psychoanalysis from being dismissed as a "Jewish science." Jung also figured importantly as the guarantor of Freud's most cherished grandiose fantasy: immortality. With Jung as proselyte and proselytist, Freud was convinced the impact of his discoveries would be felt by future generations. In a letter to Binswanger dated March 1911, Freud wrote, "When the empire I founded is orphaned, no one but Jung must inherit the whole thing" (Homans, 1988, p. 51).

From the outset Freud portrayed himself to Jung as the aging leader hoping to pass the torch. And Jung seemed eager to live up to the appellations of "crown prince" and "son and heir" that Freud bestowed on him. In August, 1907 Jung gave a lecture in Amsterdam advancing Freud's ideas. Freud's letter of August 18, 1907 reveals his selfobject fantasy of idealized merger with Jung as his ticket to immortality:

> Your lecture in Amsterdam will be a milestone in history and after all it is largely for history that we work. . . . And when you have injected your own personal leaven into the fermenting mass of my ideas in still more generous measure, there will be no further difference between your achievement and mine. (McGuire, 1974, p. 77)

Freud's belief that this time his intensified trust in a potential betrayer would result in a rescripting of trauma such that he would never again be psychologically abandoned is evident in this extract from a follow-up letter of September 2, 1907:

> but now of all times I wish I were with you, taking pleasure in no longer being alone and, if you are in need of encouragement, telling you about my long years of honorable but painful solitude, which began after I cast my first glance into the new world, about the indifference and incomprehension of my closest friends, about the terrifying moments when I myself thought I had gone astray and was wondering how I might make my misled life useful to my family, about my slowly growing conviction, which fastened itself to the interpretation of dreams as to a rock in a stormy sea, and about the serene certainty which finally took possession of me and bade me wait until a voice from the unknown multitude should answer mine. That voice was yours. (McGuire, 1974, p. 82)

Despite the fervor of Freud's selfobject longings, it seems that he was less successful in maintaining his intensified trust in Jung through disavowal and dissociation than he had been in the early stages of his relationships with Fliess and Adler. He consciously glimpsed portents of treachery much sooner, perhaps as early as their first meeting in March, 1907 when Jung, his wife, and a young colleague, Ludwig Binswanger, visited Freud's home in Vienna. During the visit Jung told Freud a dream that, according to Binswanger, Freud interpreted as signifying a wish to dethrone him. Although Freud wrote him: "Your person has filled me with confidence in the future. . . . I am sure that you will not leave the work in the lurch" (April 7, 1907; McGuire, 1974, pp. 18–19), it seems likely that the meaning of this dream alarmed him.

It also appears that Jung displayed his ambivalence toward Freud in rather crude ways. A far less shrewd student of human nature than Freud would have been alarmed by Jung's incessant protestations of his trustworthiness. In one letter of 1907 Jung wrote, "You may rest assured that I shall never abandon a piece of your theory essential to me—I am far too committed for that." In 1909 he claimed, "Not only for now but for all the future, nothing Fliess-like will happen." In 1910, after Freud's final break with Adler, he wrote, "I am not disposed to imitate Adler in the slightest."

In certain respects this relationship was a mirror image of Freud's early attachment to Fliess. Jung related to Freud with much of the masochistic self-devaluation that Freud had once shown in his dealings with Fliess. For example, Jung positioned his disagreements with Freudian theory in terms of his personal flaws. In his letters to Freud he mentioned "feelings of inferiority toward you which frequently overtake me" and spoke of being "very receptive to any recognition the father bestows." An explanation for Jung's attitude is suggested in a letter he wrote Freud on October 28, 1907:

> Actually—and I confess this to you with a struggle—I have a boundless admiration for you both as a man and a researcher . . . my veneration for you has something of the character of a "religious" crush. Though it does not really bother me, I still feel it is disgusting and ridiculous because of its undeniable erotic undertone. This abominable feeling comes from the fact that as a boy I was the victim of a sexual assault by a man I once worshipped. (McGuire, 1974, p. 95)

Jung frequently and explicitly cast Freud in the role of betrayer, perhaps as part of his own efforts to rescript trauma scenarios of sexual abuse in his early life. Excruciatingly vulnerable to insult, Jung frequently railed against what he took to be Freud's sadism. One such instance occurred when Freud expressed an interest in applying psychoanalysis to the cultural sciences and mentioned a longing for "students of mythology, linguistics and historians of religion to help in the work" and added, "otherwise we will have to do it all ourselves"

(December 19, 1909; McGuire, 1974, p. 276). Jung interpreted this as a criticism and wrote, "By this, I told myself, I am unfit for this work" (McGuire, 1974, p. 279) When Freud began work on *Totem and Taboo*, Jung wrote: "It is . . . very oppressive to me, if you too become involved in this area, the psychology of religion. You are a dangerous rival" (McGuire, 1974, p. 460).

In April of 1912, on learning that Binswanger had undergone an operation for a malignant tumor, Freud rushed to visit him in Kreuzlingen, Switzerland. Because of a busy schedule, Freud did not stop to visit Jung in Kusnacht, only 40 miles away. Jung, grievously offended, came to refer to this as the "Kreuzlingen gesture" which he attributed to Freud's displeasure over his theoretical differences.

Freud, for his part, seemed to enjoy experiencing himself in the Fliess-like position Jung assigned to him. In the role of potential betrayer, Freud could afford to be generous and reassuring. As Gay (1988) observed, "When Jung was touchy, Freud was soothing" (p. 227). In response to Jung's claiming to feel unfit to apply psychoanalysis to mythology, for example, Freud wrote, "Your displeasure at my longing for an army of philosophical collaborators is music to my ears. I am delighted that you yourself take this interest so seriously that you yourself wish to be in this army" (McGuire, 1974, p. 282).

At the same time, Freud went to great lengths to maintain his image of Jung as the loyal, loving son, whose occasional acts of disobedience were merely harmless "pranks." In June, 1909 Jung confided that he had been sexually involved with one of his young female patients, Sabina Spielrein. He complained that Spielrein planned his seduction. Just as Freud had once held Emma Eckstein responsible for Fliess's botched operation, he now took Jung's account at face value. Even after Jung guiltily admitted that he was to blame for actively seducing Speilrein, Freud repeated in a letter of June 30, 1909, "It was not your doing but hers" (McGuire, 1974, p. 238).

Freud's famous fainting spells in Jung's presence may be understood as desperate efforts to maintain his dissociatively intensified trust in Jung in the face of evidence that it was Jung and not he who was the more likely betrayer. The first episode occurred on August 20, 1909 in Bremen while Freud, Ferenczi, and Jung were waiting to set sail for Clark University in the United States where Freud would receive an honorary degree of Doctor of Laws and both he and Jung would lecture on their discoveries. At the end of their luncheon, Freud fainted after interpreting Jung's lengthy discussion about prehistoric remains that had been dug up in northern Germany as concealing a death wish against him.

As Homans (1988) pointed out, a turning point in the relationship occurred during January and February of 1910. Freud had suggested to Jung that psychoanalysts should associate themselves with a local ethical society. Jung, at the height of his idealization of Freud, wrote him on February 11,

> Religion can be replaced only by religion . . . I imagine a far finer and more comprehensive task for psychoanalysis than alliance with an ethical fraternity. I think we must give it time to infiltrate into people from many centers, to revivify among intellectuals a feeling for symbol and myth, ever so gently to transform Christ back into the soothsaying god of the vine. (McGuire, 1974, p. 294)

Freud quickly responded: "You mustn't regard me as the founder of a religion. My intentions are not so far-reaching. . . . I am not thinking of a substitute for religion; this need must be sublimated" (McGuire, p. 295).

Although he outwardly maintained his stance as favorite son, Jung apparently never recovered from his disappointment. He intermittently neglected his duties as president of the International Psychoanalytic Association, and more forcefully accused Freud of attempting to suppress his intellectual independence. Until 1912, Freud desperately warded off full recognition that his friendship with Jung was doomed (Gay, 1988). However, Jung's bitter accusations about his "Kreuzlingen gesture" must have gone a long way toward convincing him that Jung's defection was inevitable. In response, as he proudly informed Ferenczi, he become "emotionally quite detached and intellectually superior" (Gay, p. 231). It seems that Freud attempted to ward off retraumatization by refusing to play the role of the injured party, the betrayed.

In November, 1912, during a talk at Fordham University in New York, Jung dispelled all of Freud's remaining hope. There he summarized ideas contained in "Transformations and Symbols of the Libido" which repudiated almost all of Freud's most cherished ideas: childhood sexuality, the sexual etiology of neuroses, and the Oedipus complex. Afterward he audaciously wrote Freud (November 14, 1912) that he had managed to win over many who had been put off by "the problem of sexuality in neurosis" (McGuire, 1974, p. 515). Although Freud made no bones of his displeasure, he still spared Jung to some extent: "I greet you on your return home from America, no longer so affectionately as previously in Nurnberg—you have successfully weaned me of that—but with still enough sympathy, interest and satisfaction in your personal success" (November 14, 1912; McGuire, p. 324). He voiced concern that Jung's success had been gained at the expense of the most important insights of psychoanalysis. And, while he held open some hope for their personal relationship, he noted, "Your insistence on the 'Kreuzlingen gesture' is, to be sure, as incomprehensible as it is insulting, but there are things that cannot be settled in writing" (McGuire, p. 324).

The two faced each other one last time at a luncheon in Munich. At the end of the meal a discussion ensued about Ikhnaton, who had defamed his father by scrawling his name on a public monument. Freud then railed against the Swiss for publishing psychoanalytic articles without mentioning his name. Jung defensively insisted that Freud's name was well-known enough that it did not need to be cited. Just as in Bremen three years before, after interpreting Jung's remarks as unconscious wishes for his death, Freud fainted. On recovering in Jung's arms, he is reported to have murmured, "How sweet it must be to die." Did Freud mean that in death as in unconsciousness, he would not have to experience another retraumatizing betrayal of his self-trust?

The death throes of the relationship were marked by hostility, misunderstanding, and suspicion on the parts of both trauma survivors, each apparently experiencing the other now as the betrayer and now as the betrayed. For example, in a letter of November 29, 1912, Freud admitted that his fainting spell had contained "a piece of neurosis" and praised Jung for having "solved the puzzle of all mysticism" (McGuire, 1974, p. 524). Apparently unable to accept Freud's high praise, Jung believed this was a sarcastic comment. He attributed Freud's inability to value his work to his unanalyzed neurosis. In mid-December, Jung informed Freud that he was preparing a scathing review of one of Adler's books. However, instead of saying, "Even Adler's accomplices do not want to regard me as one of 'theirs,'" Jung slipped and wrote, "one of yours." When Freud disparagingly asked Jung whether he could mobilize enough objectivity to consider the slip without anger, he responded:

> May I say a few words to you in earnest? I admit the ambivalence of my feelings toward you, but am inclined to take an honest and absolutely straightforward view of your situation. If you doubt my word, so much the worse for you. I would, however, point out that your technique of treating your pupils like your patients is a *blunder*. In that way you produce slavish sons or impudent puppies (Adler-Stekel and the whole insolent gang now throwing their weight about in Vienna). I am objective enough to see through your trick. . . . Meanwhile you remain on top as the father, sitting pretty. (McGuire, pp. 534–535)

Freud's final sadistic enactment was memorialized in his "History of the Psycho-Analytic Movement" (1914b) in which he outspokenly criticized Adler and Jung. The "History" became known by those still loyal to him, such as Abraham, Eitingen, and Ferenczi, as the "bomb." On April 20, 1914, in the wake of the bomb's detonation, Jung resigned as president of the International Psychoanalytic Association. In June of 1914, Freud wrote to Abraham, "So we are rid of them at last . . . the brutal holy Jung and his pious parrots" (Gay, 1988, p. 241).

Freud's Theories as Rescriptings of Trauma

Despite Freud's celebrations after ridding himself of the contemptible likes of Fliess, Adler, and Jung, it is painfully obvious that he experienced retraumatizing betrayals by all three. The self-restitutive benefits he derived from rescripting his trauma scenarios through sadomasochistic enactments in relation to each of these men appear to have been meager. In the aftermath of each disastrous rupture, Freud was once again forced to represent himself as a victim, the betrayed. Grosskurth's (1991) account of the workings of his secret committee, the inner circle of adherents that formed around Freud as his relationship with Jung deteriorated, suggests that Freud did not abandon these restorative strategies; he merely found a new stage for their enactment.

Freud's continuing struggle to come to terms with his recurring personal catastrophes greatly affected his theory-building. Many of the fundamental tenets of psychoanalytic theory bear traces of his efforts to confirm intensified aspects of his self-trust and to rescript his childhood traumas. For example, it is tempting to view the concept of a repetition compulsion arising from the death instinct as his creative explanation for his own retraumatizations. The following paragraph in "Beyond the Pleasure Principle" (1920) is undoubtedly self-referential.

> Thus we have come across people all of whose human relationships have the same outcome: such as the benefactor who is abandoned in anger after a time by each of his *protégés*, however much they may otherwise differ from one another, and who thus seems doomed to taste all the bitterness of ingratitude; or the man whose friendships all end in betrayal by his friend; or the man who time after time in the course of his life raises someone else into a position of great private or public authority and then, after a certain interval, himself upsets that authority and replaces him by a new one. (p. 22)

Stolorow and Atwood (1979) stated, "Freud's (1920) postulation of an innate death instinct, through which hostility becomes an internal biological necessity rather than a reaction to betrayal and disappointment, may be viewed as the final triumph of his wish to absolve his mother" (p. 67). Not only did the repetition compulsion let his treacherous childhood betrayers off the hook and enable him to experience them as trustworthy selfobjects, it also enabled him to confirm his intensified trust-in-self. We have seen that at a certain point in his relationships with Fliess, Adler, and Jung, Freud's enactments assumed a sadistic character and the roles of betrayer and betrayed were reversed. In so doing he apparently reestablished himself as powerfully in charge of his psychological universe. Since the repetition compulsion locates the source of treachery within the psyche of those betrayed, it serves the same purpose: The victim becomes the ultimate cause of the victimization. Freud's use of the Oedipus myth, as I pointed out in Chapter 1, is another case in point, the ultimate transformation of betrayed into betrayer.

This restorative strategy also appears to inform Freud's theory of masochism. We have seen that Freud's close association of masochism with the psychological lives of women eclipsed his original thoughts about its origins in trauma. Stolorow and Atwood (1979), citing Tompkins (1963), argue that Freud's developmental scenario for girls reveals his own disavowed rage at his mother for her treacherous betrayals early in his life. Writing about the girl's renunciation of her mother as a love object in favor of her father, for example, Freud (1933[1932]) noted, "The turning away from the mother is accompanied by hostility; the attachment to the mother ends in hate" (p. 121). By associating masochism with femininity, Freud put women (mothers and potential mothers) in the position of those vulnerable to betrayal by sadistic others (men). Here, too, Freud's efforts to rescript his childhood trauma through a sadistic turning of the tables is encoded in theory.

In "Beyond the Pleasure Principle," Freud (1920) described the emergence of the repetition compulsion during psycho-analytic treatment in terms of the patient's need "to *repeat* the repressed material as a contemporary experience instead of, as the physician would prefer to see, *remembering* it as something belonging to the past" (p. 18). The occurrence of such repetitions, according to Freud, heralds the replacement of the earlier neurosis by a fresh, "transference neurosis." The working through of this transference neurosis became, for Freud, the cornerstone of psychoanalytic cure. I propose that although survivors often experience the treatment situation as fraught with the danger of retraumatization they use every means at their disposal to avert it. In Chapters 6 and 7 I attempt to demonstrate that efforts to rescript trauma scenarios, not to repeat them, may occur in the therapeutic situation.

THE PARANOID EXPERIENCE

> Every attempt at murdering my soul, or at emasculating me for purposes
> *contrary to the order of things* (that is, for the gratification of the sexual
> appetites of a human individual), or later at destroying my understanding—
> every such attempt has come to nothing. From this apparently unequal
> struggle between one weak man and God himself, I have emerged trium-
> phant—though not without undergoing much bitter suffering and privation—
> because the order of things stands upon my side.
>
> *Daniel Paul Schreber*, Memoirs of my Nervous Illness *(1988)*
>
> There are no acts of treachery more deeply concealed than those which lie
> under the pretence of duty, or under some profession of necessity.
>
> *Marcus Tullius Cicero*, In Verrem *(1966)*

Compared with the conspicuous scarcity of psychoanalytic writings on trust,
the amount of literature devoted to paranoia and its chief symptom, distrust,
is vast. There can be little doubt that Freud's example is largely responsible
for the proliferation of theoretical and clinical studies in this area. His efforts
to fathom the mysteries of paranoia began at least as early as 1895 with the
unpublished "Draft H" he sent to Fliess and continued into the last decade of
his life (Freud, 1933, 1938). For our purposes, his initial insights into the
nature of paranoia, guided as they were by his trauma model of pathogenesis,
provide the richest explanatory yield. In one of his earliest published papers
on the subject, for example, he conceptualized paranoia as a "defence-
psychosis," which he explained as follows: "[I]t results from the repression of
painful memories, as do hysteria and obsessions, and . . . the form of the
symptoms is determined by the content of the repressed memory" (1896, p.

169). He asserted that the painful memories necessitating repression were of childhood traumas often involving abusive sexual experiences. Whereas in hysteria the special path of repression is *conversion* into bodily symptoms, and in obsessional neurosis the path of repression is *substitution* whereby self-reproach is transformed into self-distrust, the path of repression peculiar to paranoia is *projection* whereby self-reproach is transformed into distrust directed against others. He held projection responsible for such paranoid symptoms as "delusions of distrust," "suspicion," and "persecution by others." Other paranoid symptoms, he suggested, involve a "return of the repressed" such that the self-reproaches reappear in hallucinations, delusions, etc.

Although in my view it is dissociation rather than repression that underlies paranoid symptomatology, these early Freudian formulations are still enormously helpful. Freud's understanding of paranoia changed radically with his revised theory of pathogenesis. Following his retraction of the "seduction theory," Freud downplayed the primacy of trauma as a causative factor. In a 1905 paper he discussed the paranoid's transformation of love into hate, and in 1908, he observed that paranoid delusions are basically sadomasochistic in composition. In his 1911 analysis of the Schreber case, he used these insights to develop his major thesis that the core conflict in paranoia involves a homosexual wish-fantasy. Delusions of persecution arise according to the following scenario:

> The proposition "I (a man) love him" is contradicted by: (a) Delusions of *persecution*; for they loudly assert: "I do not *love* him—I *hate* him." This contradiction, which must have run thus in the unconscious, cannot however, become conscious to a paranoiac in this form. The mechanism of symptom-formation in paranoia requires that internal perceptions—feelings—shall be replaced by external perceptions. Consequently the proposition "I hate him" becomes transformed by *projection* into another one: "*He hates* (persecutes) *me*, which will justify me in hating him." And thus the unconscious feeling makes its appearance as though it were the consequence of an external perception: "I do not *love* him—I *hate* him, because HE PERSECUTES ME." (Freud, 1911, p. 63)

As Meissner (1978) pointed out, Freud's subsequent elaborations of this theory of paranoia in his 1914 paper on narcissism, his 1922 paper on pathological forms of jealousy, and his 1923 analysis of the demonic possession of Chistoph Haizmann, a 17th century painter, do not represent significant changes from the position he formulated with respect to the Schreber case, except that he gave greater weight to the role of hostility. [1]

With Abraham's (1908) view of paranoia as involving regression to the phase of anal sadism and the partial introjection of the love object, and Klein's (1946, 1968, 1973) developmental perspective according to which the origin of paranoia is the "normal" oral sadistic phase of libidinal development, the role of childhood trauma in the etiology of paranoia was all but ignored. For many years, as MacAlpine and Hunter (1953) argued, the psychoanalytic literature on paranoia served to confirm Freud's theories. Despite the fact that case material offered in support of the formulations, such as that presented by Schmideberg (1931), frequently revealed childhood experiences of horrifying abuse, the role of instinctually derived hatred was emphasized over actual experience.

Beginning in the 1950s however, a number of developments paved the way for a reconsideration of Freud's original conceptualization of paranoia as related to trauma. First, new material came to light on the Schreber case suggesting that as a child Schreber had been cruelly abused by his father (Niederland, 1951, 1959a, 1959b, 1960, 1984). Many writers then began to appreciate the persistence of "the kernel of historical truth" (Freud, 1938) around which paranoid delusions are erected. The application of self-psychological theory to the problem of paranoia has also strengthened the case for its traumatogenic etiology. Challenging prevailing theories, Kohut (1960, 1971, 1976, 1977) suggested that paranoia is the result of traumatic failures in empathy by those required as selfobjects. It is an expression of the narcissistic rage that accompanies the disintegration of self-experience. Kohut (1977) observed:

> If the phase-appropriate need for omnipotent control over the self-object has been chronically and *traumatically frustrated* [italics added] in childhood, then chronic narcissistic rage, with all its deleterious consequences will be established. Destructiveness (rage) and its later ideation companion, the conviction that the environment is essentially inimical—M. Klein's "paranoid position"—do not therefore constitute the emergence of an elemental, primary psychological given, but despite the fact that they may, throughout a lifetime, influence an individual's mode of perceiving his world and determine his behavior, they are disintegration products—*reactions to failures of traumatic degree* [italics added]

[1]See Meissner (1978) for a detailed discussion of the evolution of Freud's understanding of paranoia, criticism of his formulations, as well as an excellent review of the general psychoanalytic literature on the topic.

in empathic responsiveness of the self-object vis-a-vis a self the child is beginning to experience. (p. 121)

A number of contemporary theorists such as Aronson (1989), Garfield and Havens (1991), Meares (1988), and Meissner (1978, 1986) have incorporated Kohut's views into their formulations on paranoid experience. For example, in reconceptualizing the Schreber case, Meissner (1986) noted:

> Schreber's persecution at the hands of his father constitute a continual undermining and attack on his burgeoning narcissism. Consequently, at the very roots of his development was a distortion and impairment of his basic sense of self-esteem . . . the childhood persecution was a persecution indeed but its dynamic impact was specifically rooted in the narcissistic deprivation and trauma associated with it. It is the deprived and pathologically distorted narcissism which provides the dynamic impulse and motivation for the defensive operation that gave rise to and determined Schreber's adult illness. (p. 96)

In this formulation, Freud's original insights about the role of childhood trauma in paranoia are combined with Kohut's discoveries about self-experience. Although I believe this represents a significant theoretical advance, a fundamental aspect of paranoid experience is still unaccounted for: the fact that it is primarily a trust disorder. Clinical descriptions of paranoid experience make this abundantly clear. For example, Meissner (1978) noted that paranoia as "a descriptive personality trait" is characterized by isolation, hypersensitivity, guardedness, suspiciousness, and the use of projection as a defense. The essential feature of paranoid personality disorder, according to DSM-IV (APA, 1994), is "a pervasive distrust and suspiciousness of others such that their motives are interpreted as malevolent" (p. 634). It cites the following as distinguishing characteristics of people with this disorder: a general expectation of being harmed or exploited, a tendency to question the loyalty or trustworthiness of others, a reluctance to confide in others for fear the information will be used against them, a tendency to bear grudges, and an unwillingness to forgive insults, injuries, or slights; pathological jealousy; and a wish to maintain complete control of intimate relationships to avoid being betrayed. Among the associated features of the disorder it lists argumentativeness, difficulty accepting criticism, rigidity and unwillingness to compromise, an excessive need to be self-sufficient, and an inordinate fear of losing independence or the power to shape events according to their own wishes (p. 635). As I hope to demonstrate in this chapter, all of these characteristics reflect profound disturbances in self-trust that result from traumatizing betrayals.

While stopping far short of conceptualizing paranoia primarily as a trust disorder, a number of writers with experience treating paranoid patients have intimated that betrayals of trust are to be found at the heart of paranoid pathology. For example, Searles (1965), reporting on his work with a deeply paranoid woman, wrote, "[I]t occurred to me that her seemingly limitless scorn, cynicism, and distrust were the qualities one would expect to find in a person who was fixed in a state of unresolved—that is, in complete—*disillusionment*" (p. 606). Garfield and Havens (1991) understand paranoid phenomena as occurring among those who have, in the past, "trusted too much" (p. 75); relying on Kohut's early formulations, they see the betrayals underlying paranoid symptomatology as involving failures in the formation of an "ego ideal" (pp. 75–76).

SELF-TRUST DISTURBANCE AND
PARANOID EXPERIENCE

It is my contention that a thorough understanding of paranoid experience is impossible without an appreciation of the relationship between what Kohut referred to as selfobject failures "to a traumatic degree" and self-trust disturbance. Indeed, the distinguishing characteristics of paranoid experience provide solid support for one of the central theses of this book, namely, that disturbances in self-trust resulting from traumatizing betrayals underlie all disorders of self-experience (see Chapter 6). Paranoid phenomena, I submit, are best understood both as attempts to establish the actuality of traumatic betrayals and as extreme measures taken to alter subjective reality in their aftermath. Much like the symptoms of PTSD, paranoid symptomatology both concretizes (Stolorow et al., 1987) or symbolically expresses (Ulman & Brothers, 1988) shattering self-trust betrayals and represents attempts at self-restoration. To the extent that these self-restorative measures create imbalances between the reality-oriented and self-centered organizational modes (Noy, 1980), they invariably result in massive dissociation.

Rather than viewing paranoia as a unified diagnostic category I follow Meissner (1978, 1986) and other contemporary writers in using the adjective, paranoid, to describe clinical phenomena traditionally associated with paranoia. Disorders warranting the designation of paranoid are found with varying degrees of severity among very diverse patient populations, including those with toxic and organic conditions. In what follows, I attempt to sketch my understanding of those manifestations of paranoid experience associated with traumatizing self-trust betrayals.

THE PARANOID PROCESS AND THE DISSOCIATIVE ALTERATION OF SUBJECTIVE REALITY

In Chapter 3 I proposed that traumatizing betrayals of self-trust result in dissociative phenomena caused by profound changes in survivors' selfobject fantasies and alterations in their experience of subjective reality. In Chapter 4 I described the sadomasochistic rescripting of trauma scenarios as a means of confirming a dissociatively altered subjective reality. To the extent that these efforts prove successful, disintegration anxiety is extinguished and the survivor feels protected against retraumatizing betrayals. However, as we discovered, rather than averting retraumatization, this dissociative alteration of subjective reality frequently leads to further self-trust betrayals and to ever more desperate rescripting efforts.

Paranoid experience may be understood as a byproduct of a specific means by which subjective reality is altered. It appears that this "paranoid process" (Meissner, 1978) begins early in life with brutal and repeated betrayals of a child's self-trust. I believe that Liotti (1992) may have discovered the roots of paranoid experience in the "disorganized/disoriented attachment" he holds to exist between children who develop dissociative disorders and their caretakers. Based on the findings of Main and Hesse (1990, 1992) and Ainsworth and Eichberg (1991), Liotti suggested that the parents of children who develop dissociative disorders themselves suffered "unresolved traumas" related to past abuse or to loss by death of significant others. He described how their infants stir frightening memories of unresolved traumas and cause them to "invert the normal attachment relationship." They act, he suggested, as if they unconsciously expect their children to soothe their discomfort. From a self-trust perspective we might say that parents who survived traumatizing betrayals experience resurgences of disintegration anxiety when interactions with their own children arouse traumatic memories. They then turn to their children as providers of selfobject experiences. Liotti (1992) observed:

> When the child fails to match the parent('s) unconscious expectations to be cared for (and it is obvious that a child will fail in such a task), the parent may become aggressive and therefore frightening to (the child). . . . A frightening parent presents a child (and an infant particularly so) with a paradox that cannot be solved—namely, to simultaneously flee from the parent as a source of danger, and to approach the parent as a haven of safety (Main, 1981). . . . A positive feedback loop of fear → avoidance → fear is thus created in infants dealing with a threatening attachment figure. A high intensity loop may lead to the collapse of behavioral and attentional strategies observed in disorganized/ disoriented attachment behavior (Main & Hesse, 1990). (p. 198)

Liotti identified a number of pathways for the development of dissociative disorders following these disorganized/disoriented attachments. One pathway typically associated with serious physical or sexual abuse leads to the development of multiple personality disorder. Another pathway, it seems to me, leads to the development of paranoid disorders. Extrapolating from Liotti's formulations, it seems probable that caretakers of the children who develop paranoid disorders were themselves horribly betrayed. Not only do they form disorganized/disorienting attachments with their children, they are also likely to involve them in sadomasochistic enactments as a means of rescripting their own trauma scenarios.

While children subjected to enactments of this sort experience betrayals that affect all four self-trust dimensions, trust-in-self is likely to be most damaged. Kohut's (1977) observation that paranoia results from traumatic frustration of the normal childhood need to experience "omnipotent control over selfobjects" (p. 121) supports this hypothesis. Such children suffer a devastating loss of trust in their ability to elicit the selfobject experiences they require for the development, maintenance, and restoration of self-experience. They become excruciatingly vulnerable to disintegration anxiety and fears of retraumatizing betrayal, and also, because of their highly unrealistic and perfectionistic self-trust criteria, to feeling worthless, powerless, fundamentally unlovable, and undesirable.

Many writers offer support for the hypothesis that a profound lack of trust-in-self underlies paranoid disorders. For example, Searles (1965) emphasized the tormenting "uncertainty" of the paranoid patient. Garfield and Havens (1991) find a preoccupation with "internal questions" that arise as a consequence of "mistrust of the self" such as: "Who am I? What do I stand for? Why would anyone want to be with me? What am I made of? How did I come to be the way I am now and feel the way I do?" (p. 161). They also suggest that the potential for homosexual panic among paranoid patients reflects their mistrust of such fundamental features of self-experience as gender and sexuality, that is, "Am I a man or a woman?"

In Chapter 3 I observed that betrayals of trust-in-self are often accompanied by feelings of inordinate shame. Shapiro's (1965) description of people with a "paranoid style" addressed this point.

They are ashamed, sometimes to the point of delusional preoccupation about body odor, weak muscles, the shape of their nose, the size of their genitals, their lack of "manliness," the softness of their hands, and so forth. Although this feeling attaches typically to some external feature, one can be sure that it is actually quite pervasive and continuous and reflects a general lack of self-respect. (p. 81)

Those who develop paranoid disorders respond to early, repeated traumatic betrayals with a massive alteration of subjective reality such that the intolerably painful affects associated with a loss of control over selfobject relations are eliminated. One means by which this dissociative feat is accomplished is the extreme intensification of trust-in-self. While others who intensify this dimension often have a heightened expectation of eliciting needed selfobject experiences from others, paranoid people develop the illusion of transcending all need for selfobject experience (which they presumably could elicit at will if they so chose). Because of their highly immature criteria for trust-in-self, they now perceive themselves as flawless and blameless, completely self-sufficient and independent of others—absolute masters of their own fate. As Freud (1896) first discovered, much paranoid symptomatology involves efforts to remove self-reproach from consciousness. To the extent that paranoid people permit themselves no self-reproachful ideation, they feel immune to disintegration anxiety associated with a loss of trust-in-self and invulnerable to further betrayal.

Intensified trust-in-self according to highly immature criteria also accounts for what Kohut (1971) characterized as the "cold and haughty grandiosity" often associated with paranoid disorders. Meissner (1978) noted, "[T]he intensity of the [paranoid's] grandiosity is obviously a function of the need to deny the underlying weakness and inadequacy that the patient senses. This can, and often does, reach delusional proportions" (p. 37). In other words, the arrogance and contemptuousness so typical of people with paranoid disorders cover crippling doubts about their psychological survival.

Another means by which such people attempt to recast themselves as transcending the need for selfobject relations is the diminution of trust-in-others. If others are perceived as absolutely untrustworthy in providing requisite selfobject experiences, one is protected against feeling shameful disappointment when such provision is not forthcoming. Diminished trust-in-others, therefore, guards against further proof of failure to exert control over selfobjects. It is the urgent and powerful need of the paranoid person to confirm this altered subjective reality that accounts for what has been called "paranoid cognition" or "paranoid construction." Meissner's (1978) description of paranoid suspiciousness is illustrative:

Paranoid suspiciousness, therefore, is almost scientific in its interest in assimilating the available data of reality to the paranoid construction. If the data do not fit the theoretical construction, however, the paranoid runs the risk not merely of the destruction of a theory, but of something more devastating and more personally threatening. The paranoid interest, therefore, in assimilating data to the construction is not merely one of curiosity but one of suspiciousness that is consistent with the implicit threat. . . . The overwhelming emphasis and the pressing need in the paranoid, in his constant testing of his construction of reality, is the preservation of threat construction. There is a constant pressure to reinterpret, to modify, and even to distort data that do not seem consistent with it. (pp. 36–37)

From the perspective of self-trust, we might say that paranoid suspiciousness functions to guard the paranoid person against anything that might disconfirm his or her intensified trust-in-self and diminished trust-in-others or that undermines his or her self-perception as omnipotently transcending any need for selfobject relations. Noy (1980) pointed out that the reality-oriented organizational mode loses autonomy and becomes subject to the dictates of the self-centered mode: "[T]he paranoid patient who may display the highest intellectual ability, but whose logic is totally enslaved in the service of the self . . . is no longer able to pay attention to any objective reality considerations." (p. 208).

Another important element in the paranoid process is frequently described as the employment of the defense mechanism of projection (e.g., Meissner, 1978, 1986; Shapiro, 1965). Despite the frequent usage of the term, there is little agreement about what projection is and how it operates. According to Anna Freud (1966), in projection "ideational representations of dangerous instinctual impulses are displaced into the outside world" as a means of protecting oneself against various kinds of anxiety. Kernberg (1987) viewed projection as having four components: "(a) repression of an unacceptable intrapsychic experience, (b) projection of that experience onto an object, (c) lack of empathy with what is projected, and (d) distancing or estrangement from the object as an effective completion of the defensive effort" (p. 94). Shapiro noted that projection substitutes an external threat for an internal one.

Many writers (e.g., Shapiro, 1965) have observed that projection is commonly used by nonparanoid people. In its benign form it can be understood merely as a heightening of one's "take" on subjective reality. Why then is projection so closely associated with paranoid processes? An answer to this question is suggested when what has been generally conceptualized as paranoid projection is thought of as a part of the dissociative reaction to traumatizing betrayals and a major aspect of the paranoid alteration of subjective reality. We have seen that black holes often develop in the self-experience of trauma survivors who desperately attempt to free themselves from the intolerable affects and meanings associated with memories of betrayal. All aspects of self-experience that would contradict their altered subjective reality and undermine the intensifications and diminutions of self-trust are eliminated from conscious awareness.

However, as we have already discovered, it is impossible to achieve a sense of cohesive selfhood when important parts of self-experience are irretrievably lost to consciousness. To restore a sense of self-cohesion, alter ego selfobjects who embody these lost or hidden self-perceptions are often sought. The paranoid experience of being perfect, above reproach, and transcending the need for selfobjects depends on such an extreme intensification of trust-in-self that huge regions of self-experience must be eliminated, including any thoughts or feelings of a self-critical, self-demeaning, or self-punitive nature. To restore a sense of cohesive selfhood, others who are experienced as critical, demeaning, and punishing are sought. Insofar as these others embody aspects of self-experience that have been repudiated, they function as alter ego selfobjects. Only by perpetually experiencing themselves as threatened by these hostile others against whom they must maintain a hypervigilent, suspicious, guarded stance, are paranoid people enable to attain a sense of cohesive selfhood. Should the threat posed by hostile others cease to exist, the entire structure of their altered subjective reality would collapse.

It is interesting to find that the predisposing factors for paranoid disorders listed in DSM-III (APA, 1980) include immigration, emigration, deafness, and other severe stressors. These events may well lead to acute paranoid episodes because they disrupt stable alter ego selfobject connections. It is when breaches occur in this alter ego selfobject surround that the paranoid process usually takes on a frankly psychotic character. Delusions of persecution and grandeur are elaborated in a desperate bid to reconfirm the reality of the traumatizing betrayals and to restore hopelessly shattered selfobject fantasies. Insofar as delusions represent sadomasochistic rescriptings of trauma, they reestablish lost alter ego selfobject connections. For example, persecutory delusions involving diabolic plots, conspiracies, and the like enable the paranoid person to experience himself or herself masochistically as the betrayed in relation to sadistic alter egos. Delusions of grandeur enable the paranoid person to maintain illusions of transcending the need for selfobjects and of achieving sadistic control over betrayers. A number of writers including Freud (1908), Bak (1946), and Nydes (1963) have emphasized the link between paranoia and sadomasochism.

THE SCHREBER CASE

In "Psycho-Analytic Notes upon an Autobiographical Account of a Case of Paranoia" (1911), Freud, following Abraham's (1908) lead, extended his libido theory to the psychoses. Departing boldly from the prevailing wisdom, Freud argued that paranoid hallucinations and delusions are comprehensible. Their meanings, he explained, reflect the paranoid patient's conflicts over disavowed homosexuality. Referring to Daniel Paul Schreber, the subject of the case, Freud stated confidently, "[T]he exciting cause of his illness was an outburst of homosexual libido" (p. 43).

Credit for the enormous amount of interest that continues to be generated by the Schreber case must be paid equally to Freud's work and the remarkable book on which it is based, *Denkwürdigkeiten eines Nervenkranken* (*Memoirs of My Nervous Illness*) (1903). Hailed as "a work of art, a uniquely crafted narrative . . . one of the most glorious books ever written by a psychiatric patient (Lothane, 1992), it was this book that Freud analysed; Schreber was never his patient.

Because the Schreber case so beautifully illustrates a self-trust perspective on paranoid disorders, I will add my own notes to the immense Schreber literature. My understanding rests chiefly on the heroic research efforts of Niederland (1984) and Lothane (1992), although I am also indebted to the findings and insights of many others including Baumeyer (1956), Israëls (1989), Meissner (1978, 1986), and Orange (1993). I do not intend what follows as a thorough examination of this complex and multifaceted case; my focus is limited to those aspects of Schreber's experience that, in my view, typify the reactions to self-trust betrayals associated with the development of paranoid disorders. After outlining what I see as the components of Schreber's dissociative reaction to these betrayals, I present my understanding of the cause of his breakdowns as well as my interpretation of the meanings of some of his delusions.

In 1884, at the age of 42, Schreber, a respected German jurist and politician, was first hospitalized for "severe hypochondriasis." After his discharge the following year, he functioned well for eight years. He was readmitted to the hospital and, after a worsening of his condition, was transferred to a state insane asylum. The *Memoirs* were written during his institutionalization and published in 1903 after Schreber's legal initiatives for release proved successful. As Orange (1993) noted, although Schreber avowedly wrote the *Memoirs* "to acquaint [his] wife with [his] personal experiences and religious ideals" and to explain "various oddities of behavior" to her, it became an increasingly ambitious enterprise. Its intended readers grew to include his psychiatrist, the courts, which he hoped to persuade of his sanity, and finally, an educated public whom he hoped to enlighten. Tragically, despite Freud's allusion to Schreber's having achieved "something approximating to a recovery," he was readmitted to the asylum four years after his release and died there only a few months after the publication of Freud's paper.

Childhood Betrayals

While there is considerable disagreement among those who have investigated the Schreber case[2] as to how his early experiences contributed to his psychological breakdowns in adulthood, few have rejected Freud's view that his relationship with his father was a prime factor. In recent years Freud's thesis about the homosexual etiology of Schreber's psychosis has been overshadowed by interpretations relying on the impact of his father's psychological disturbance, thanks largely to Niederland's (1951, 1959a, 1959b, 1960) findings about the coercive child-rearing practices his father advocated which included the use of bizarre posture-improving devices, contraptions to prevent masturbation, enemas, and other harsh physical manipulations. Even Lothane (1992), who strongly defended Schreber's father against charges of having sadistically abused his son, portrayed him as a man who suffered from severe depression and disappointments over "the discrepancy between high ambition and insufficient recognition."

Schreber's father, Dr. Daniel Gottlieb Moritz Schreber, was an orthopedist, lecturer, and writer, and a social, medical, and educational reformer. His fame as an educator was largely posthumous thanks to the association of his name with Schrebergärten (family gardens), and Schreberverein (educational associations) which, according to Israëls (1989), he never founded. Nevertheless, he was widely celebrated during Schreber's lifetime as an authority on medicine and child-rearing. Frail and sickly as a child, and diminutive in stature as an adult, he transformed himself through rigorous physical training into an accomplished athlete who excelled in swimming and gymnastics. On the basis of a case study by Dr. Schreber entitled "Confessions of One Who had Been Insane," Niederland (1960) inferred that he must have had a severely disturbed adolescence: "[T]he study is filled with vague allusions to attacks of melancholia, morbid brooding, and tormenting criminal impulses that in its veiled language reads like an autobiographical record" (p. 64). Although a sudden adult onset of depression, headaches, and personality

---

[2]See Israëls (1989) and Lothane (1992) for reviews of this literature.

change was attributed by family members to a ladder falling on his head in a gymnasium, one biographer (Ritter, 1936) suggested the possibility that his symptoms were actually the result of a "severe nervous breakdown." Niederland (1959a, 1959b, 1960) believed that this accident occurred only three years before his death when Schreber was 16, while Israëls (1989) and Lothane (1992) placed its occurrence 10 years before his death, when Schreber was only 9. Baumeyer (1956) discovered the following note in Schreber's chart at Sonnenstein asylum: "The father, founder of the Schreber gardens in Leipzig, suffered from compulsive manifestations with murderous impulses" (in Lothane, 1992, p. 470).

In Moritz Schreber's writings on child-rearing he advocated the application of pressure and coercion during early childhood strong enough to produce "blind," "unconditional," "unconscious" obedience. In *Kallipädie* (Schreber, 1858) he warned against giving children excessive attention, picking them up, or petting them. Children should be left to cry it out. If they showed "stubbornness," he advised "repeated threatening gestures, which a child already months old [4, 6, or 8] can understand, of if needed, dampen such small whims even by means of mild bodily punishments and persistent refusal to gratify them" (quoted in Lothane, 1992, p. 157). He regarded "groundless screaming and crying" as "the first manifestations of selfishness." The procedure he outlined, which included "repeated, of course, appropriately mild bodily admonitions, in small intervals," was designed to produce lasting results:

> Such a procedure is needed only once or at most twice—one is master of the child forever. From then on, one gaze, one word, one threatening mien will suffice to rule the chid. Think that with this you offer the child the greatest benefit . . . you free him from inner torment. (quoted in Lothane, p. 168)

In dealing with a child of 7 or older, he advised that efforts be made to inculcate "the steadfast habit of the good in feeling, thinking and acting" on the basis of the child's "own conviction." By 10 or 12 corporal punishment should be replaced by "rebuke and reprimand" (Lothane, 1992, p. 157). Dr. Schreber apparently found no irony or contradiction in suggesting that only if parents achieve complete domination over the child could they instill strong ethical values based on love, benevolence, and forgiveness.

His writings are also filled with admonitions about masturbation, "the secret plague of the young" (Schreber, 1858, p. 258) which if not strenuously combated, leads to all sorts of dire psychological and physical ills. He urged that children be subjected to a rigid system of vigorous physical training (a reflection, perhaps, of his own program of self-improvement), and the employment of physical and emotional restraint (Niederland, 1984). The orthopedic devices he designed were meant to enforce absolutely straight posture in children awake and asleep and to prevent masturbation. That he used these methods on Schreber and his older brother, Gustov, is strongly suggested by several references in his books to the success he achieved with his own children. Further support for this assumption is provided by Niederland (1951, 1959a, 1959b, 1960), who related the content of many of Schreber's delusions, particularly those he referred to as "miracles," to specific devices and manipulations employed by his father.

Kohut (1960) compared the father's pathology to Hitler's and suggested that it might be regarded as "a kind of healed-over psychosis":

> The absolute conviction father Schreber had toward his ideas, the unquestioning fanaticism with which he pursued them, betrays, I believe, their profoundly narcissistic character, and I would assume that a fear of hypochondriacal tensions lies behind the rather overt fight against masturbation. His fanatical activities, too, although lived out on the body of the son, belong to a hidden narcissistic delusional system. The son, in other words, is felt as part of the father's narcissistic system and not as separate. (p. 307)

Schreber's relationship with his mother appears to have been of major importance throughout his life (Israëls, 1989; Lothane, 1992). However, she does not appear to have provided him with much relief from his father's relentless control. If anything, Pauline Schreber appears to have been a staunch champion of her husband's ideas and methods. In light of his finding that Schreber's delusions contained a "condensed, archaically distorted fusion of both parental images," Niederland (1963, p. 96) concluded that Schreber perceived his mother as actively participating in his father's sadistic regime (see also White, 1961). Lothane describes her as "a person of high culture, a patron of humanities and the arts" who very likely became "the power behind the throne" during the days of her husband's decline. Niederland obtained a letter written by Schreber's eldest sister, Anna, which contains the following remarks: "Father discussed with our mother everything and anything, she took part in all his ideas, plans and projects; she read the galley proofs of his writings with him, and was his faithful, close companion in everything" (p. 96). A note in Schreber's hospital chart that reads, "Mother with mood swings and nervous" raises the possibility that, she, like her husband, suffered a self-disorder (Baumeyer, 1956).

Schreber's parents appear to have demanded the renunciation of behaviors and attitudes traditionally associated with active masculinity. They discouraged his self-differentiation, independence, assertiveness, and oppositionalism and trained him to actively suppress such "negative" affects as anger and rage. At the same time any hint of effeminacy including the expression of sensuality, self-indulgence, and "softness" was strongly opposed (Lothane, 1992). In fact there appears to have been little room in Schreber's early life for proud, spontaneous displays of individuality, gender, or sexuality. Instead he was forced to conform to very rigidly imposed parental expectations that covered all aspects of his existence.

In light of their coercive methods, it is tempting to speculate that Schreber's early relationship to his parents resembled the disorganized/disorienting attachments Liotti (1992) associates with the development of dissociative disorders. It is not difficult to imagine the young Schreber as torn between fear of his parents and desperate need for them, a conflict that was undoubtedly intensified as he grew older and became more aware of the approbation accorded his father's methods not only by his own family but by the outside world. Because the sadism inflicted on Schreber was disguised by high-minded medical, educational, and religious principles, his experiences of betrayal could find no corroboration. Add to this tragic situation the fact that he was actively encouraged to suppress the feelings of rage and shame one must assume were evoked by these betrayals and it becomes clear that Schreber had no other recourse but dissociation.

We have already seen that it is the crushing of trust-in-self that appears to be most decisive in the later development of his paranoid disorders. Because of the relentless discipline his parents appear to have imposed on him, Schreber would have had little opportunity to experience himself as exerting omnipotent control over them as selfobjects, an experience that, as Kohut (1971) attests, is essential for healthy self-development. Schreber's strongest hope for psychological survival appears to have lain in a massive alteration of his subjective reality such that it matched his parents' version of his childhood. In other words, he attempted to perceive himself as the perfectly obedient and loving son of infinitely wise, benevolent, and loving parents whose ministrations were instituted for his ultimate good.

To accomplish this dissociative feat in the face of daily experiences that so blatantly contradicted it, Schreber would have had to institute major changes in his self-trust organization and repudiate large portions of his self-experience. It is probable that trust-in-others and trust-in-self were greatly intensified and that he retained highly phantasmagoric and perfectionistic self-trust criteria.

Along with all awareness of the sadistic meanings of his parents' actions toward him, Schreber's rage, hatred, fear, and sadness as well as his assertive strivings for differentiated selfhood must have been sucked into the black holes of his self-experience.

Let us not forget Liotti's (1992) hypothesis that children who develop dissociative disorders are required to serve as soothing selfobjects for their fragmentation-prone parents. Unconsciously comprehending that his parents' unmet needs lay beneath their coercive methods, it is likely that young Schreber also attempted to function as an infallible provider of selfobject experiences for them. Intensifying self-as-trustworthy, Schreber undoubtedly did all he could to support his parents' perceptions of themselves as ideal parents by transforming himself into the docile, neutered little boy, who appeared to the world a shining validation of their methods. In a letter, his youngest sister described her brother's "goodhearted, friendly personality," although she also mentions his having shown "a hasty, restless, nervous nature . . . from childhood on" (Niederland, 1959b, p. 69).

Without the support of alter ego selfobjects who embodied the repudiated aspects of his self-experience, it seems unlikely that Schreber could have experienced even a semblance of self-cohesion. As long as his parents continued to impose their controlling and coercive methods, we must assume they served him, on an unconscious level, as alter ego selfobjects. We have seen that abusive parents often engage in sadomasochistic enactments with their children. As the betrayed in relation to his parents as betrayers, Schreber was enabled to keep alive hope that his martyrdom would one day be rewarded.

This relatively stable situation appears to have been dramatically disrupted by the changes that occurred in the family following his father's head injury. Severely depressed, suffering from headaches, and prone to periodic rages, Schreber's father withdrew from all but brief and superficial contacts with his children. Indeed, "the only person whose presence he could stand was his wife" (Niederland, 1968, p 102). As her husband's nurse and colleague, Pauline Schreber must have had far less time for her children. Judging from his later reactions to being excluded from contact with those he needed as selfobjects, it seems that Schreber experienced the sudden cessation of his parents' vigilant scrutiny and control in itself as traumatic. Even if the discipline he received was harsh and unyielding, it was, at least until this point, predictable and reliable. Ten years later, when Schreber was 19, his father died of an intestinal blockage.

Not only did his father's illness and death deprive Schreber of his alter ego selfobjects, these events also appear to have crushed his heightened self-as-trustworthy. Here was irrefutable evidence that he had failed dismally as the provider of his father's needs.[3] It is probably significant in this regard that the height of Schreber's paranoid symptomatology developed when he was 53, the age at which his father died.

It seems likely that Schreber responded to these retraumatizing betrayals by deepening his dissociative reaction and strengthening his adherence to his myth of an Edenic childhood. His precarious stability apparently depended on his maintaining a very safe, orderly, and placid existence close to home. Schreber's life appears to have contained no adolescent rebellion, no "Sturm and Drang" period, no torrid love affairs, and no adventurous episodes (Lothane, 1992). At age 35, he went directly from the familiar confines of his parental home to married life with Sabine Behr.[4]

One year before Schreber married, his carefully engineered serenity was again smashed with news that his brother, Gustov, three years older than he, had shot himself to death. Considering that Gustov also attended law school and worked as a judge, and that both brothers worked on legal arrangements with publishers concerning their fathers' books, it is possible that Gustov served as a reassuring presence in Schreber's life, perhaps providing twin selfobject experiences. That his brother's death had traumatic meaning in Schreber's life is suggested by a delusion during his illness that he was dead and decomposing and that a newspaper containing his own obituary had been put into his hands. It is probable that this delusion referred to the death notices of his brother as well as his father (Niederland, 1968). We might well wonder if Gustov's suicide belied the myth that Schreber had created about his family life. To the extent that he identified with his brother, he might well have worried that he too would fail in his desperate bid for psychological survival.

Schreber's Breakdowns

There are many competing theories on the underlying causes of Schreber's breakdowns, but most contemporary experts on the case agree with Schreber that his candidacy for election to the Reichstag was instrumental in bringing

[3]What is commonly regarded as "survivor guilt" may, in many instances, be better understood as shame over failure to live up to immature criteria for self-as-trustworthy.
[4]Unfortunately, according to Lothane's (1992) investigations, Schreber's wife betrayed him cruelly when he most needed a staunch ally and advocate. She was instrumental in having him transferred from a private hospital to a state insane asylum.

about his first hospitalization and his promotion to the high office of Senats-präsident of the Superior Court of Appeals in Dresden led to his second. At the onset of both of these breakdowns he attempted suicide. Niederland (1951) noted that since the two illnesses occurred under similar circum-stances, they must have "a common denominator." He asserted that Schreber fell ill "after having been put in the unbearable situation, before each out-break, of assuming an active masculine role in real life" (p. 41).

I agree that Schreber's breakdowns were, in part, precipitated by his having adopted an active, self-assertive, "masculine" stance on both occasions. How-ever, my understanding of the significance of this behavior is considerably different from Niederland's. He asserted that Schreber's greatest dread was of castration, his punishment for taking the place of the father, a formulation consistent with Freudian theory. My understanding depends on the assump-tion that Schreber's dissociative reaction to early parental betrayals of self-trust included his repudiating experiences of himself as bold, active, independent-minded, and self-assertive in the hope that doing so would enable him to hold on to some shred of selfobject relatedness to his parents.

What was most notable about Schreber's candidacy to the Reichstag pre-ceding his first breakdown was the fact that he lost the election. To add insult to injury, a local newspaper ran the humiliating headline: "Who, After All, Knows Dr. Schreber?" (Lothane, 1992). After daring to display his masculine ambitions in this highly exposed public way, an attempt, perhaps, to rescript his trauma scenarios through a behavioral enactment (see Chapter 4), his defeat may well have recapitulated an often-repeated scenario in his child-hood. Once again a display of "masculine" self-assertiveness was brutally and shamefully crushed. As Lothane (1992) pointed out, Schreber failed to men-tion his defeat in the *Memoirs*, further evidence of the unbearable pain he felt over this public humiliation. Thus it appears that Schreber's first breakdown was precipitated by a retraumatizing betrayal. His attempt to reintegrate his disavowed masculinity in the hope of finally receiving praise and acceptance from the outside world only resulted in another trauma.

Because his second breakdown occurred shortly after having been pro-moted to the position of Senatspräsident, he may well have experienced this promotion as an invitation to a similar disaster. Perhaps he anticipated an-other humiliating defeat if he failed to function flawlessly in accordance with his highly unrealistic and perfectionistic criteria for self-trust. Just as he had at the time of his first breakdown, Schreber tells us, he again suffered from "mental overstrain," caused by "a very heavy burden of work." Although as

Senatspräsident he was undoubtedly confronted by an increase in responsibility, it is probably more to the point that he could not bear the strain of warding off what he feared was inevitable psychic catastrophe.

It is also possible that his unsuccessful efforts to have children contributed to his breakdowns. Suffering from diabetes, his wife had six miscarriages, two of which were stillborns. Here again his hopes of demonstrating his masculine power resulted in shameful disappointment. Indeed, a contributing factor in his second breakdown may have been Sabine's suggestion that they adopt a child, which for Schreber may well have represented an intolerable admission of his failure as a man. Lothane (1992) provided some evidence to support a speculation that the baby girl she proposed they adopt at that time, Fridoline, and whom they did adopt when she was 13 years old, after Schreber's discharge, was the product of an affair Sabine had during Schreber's first hospitalization.

If Schreber's breakdowns were precipitated by shattering retraumatizations they must also be understood as desperate appeals for the therapeutic selfobject connections he would have needed to restore his crumbling self-experience. Tragically, these appeals went largely unheeded. The psychiatric establishment on whose doorstep Schreber laid his hope for recovery not only failed to provide a healing environment for him, it assailed him with further self-trust betrayals. Lothane's (1992) account of Schreber's mistreatment by all those to whom he entrusted himself, including his psychiatrists, hospital attendants, and his wife, lends poignant meaning to Schreber's charge of "soul murder."

Paul Flechsig, a highly respected German psychiatrist, was the man to whom Schreber turned for help at the outset of his first breakdown. One imagines that Schreber longed to represent him in selfobject fantasies as an idealizable paternal selfobject who might have alleviated the pain and anxiety of Schreber's traumatizing election defeat. That Flechsig dismally failed to demonstrate his trustworthiness as a provider of selfobject experiences is evidenced by Schreber's contention that, during his first admission to his hospital, Flechsig told him "white lies." These, according to Lothane (1992), consisted in attributing Schreber's illness to poisoning from the potassium bromide prescribed for him by another doctor, and diagnosing him as suffering from syphilis, which he did not have. By reducing Schreber's difficulty to a matter of drugs and brain response, a diagnosis consistent with his attempt to find somatic bases for all mental disorders, Flechsig deprived Schreber of the empathic understanding he undoubtedly needed.

Yet, Schreber's very use of the euphemistic expression "white lies" indicates his unwillingness to relinquish his trust in Flechsig. Despite feeling misunderstood and wrongly treated by Flechsig the first time, he still returned to him for treatment following his second breakdown. How else can this seemingly inexplicable behavior be understood than as an intensification of trust in another potential betrayer? Just as he had once intensified trust in his father as part of his efforts to reorder his subjective reality in childhood, Schreber's *Memoirs* make it clear he did the same in relation to Flechsig. For example, he writes, "Dr. O, whom I had consulted, made me take a week's sick leave, which we were going to use to consult Dr. Flechsig, *in whom we placed all our faith since his successful treatment of my first illness* [italics added]" (p. 38). In his use of "we," Schreber was clearly referring to his wife, whom he noted "worshipped" Flechsig for restoring her husband to health following his first breakdown (she kept Flechsig's photograph on her night table). Further evidence of his intensified trust in Flechsig is to be found in his description of his meeting with Flechsig: "Flechsig developed a remarkable eloquence which affected me deeply. He spoke of newly discovered sleeping drugs, etc., and gave me hope of delivering me of the whole illness through one prolific sleep" (quoted in Lothane, 1992, p. 46).

In his need to experience Flechsig as a benevolent, omnipotently idealizable selfobject, he hailed as eloquent the same sentiments he once decried as "white lies," i.e., that his illness was of an organic nature and that drugs would cure him. In fact, the sleep medication Flechsig prescribed, which he took in his mother's house the next night, failed, and in an agitated state he attempted suicide. The following morning he returned to Flechsig's hospital.

Ironically, the treatment offered him by Flechsig is strongly reminiscent of the coercive measures advocated by his father. Flechsig defended the "moderate" use of physical restraints, and he was an ardent advocate of what would now be called "chemical straitjackets" (Lothane, 1992). Despite his finding that Schreber had been overmedicated with bromides he continued to prescribe them for him. Indeed, Schreber appears to have found enough similarity between his father and Flechsig to warrant an attempt to rescript the trauma scenarios of his childhood within the context of this purportedly therapeutic relationship (see Chapter 6). Like the powerful and celebrated father of his childhood, Flechsig as the Rector Magnificus of Leipsig University must have appeared God-like to him in his power over others. Proud, authoritarian, overbearing, and eccentric in his dress, Flechsig was also a reformer at heart: He proselytized the organic etiology of psychopathology. Like the reclusive father of his adolescence, Flechsig also kept himself tantalizingly inaccessible to his patient. Schreber complained that Flechsig "experimented" on him "from a distance" and it is easy to see how he might have felt that way about receiving drug therapy instead of being engaged by him in a therapeutic dialogue. His ailing father had drawn closer to his mother as he distanced himself from Schreber. Flechsig also favored a woman on whom Schreber was dependent while keeping aloof from him: He treated Schreber's wife as a private outpatient, while he treated Schreber as an ordinary inmate of his hospital.

Instead of encouraging the close albeit stormy therapeutic relationship that would have enabled Schreber to work through the traumas he experienced at the hands of his parents, Flechsig subjected Schreber to experiences that matched or exceeded in sheer brutality and deceit those to which he appears to have been subjected as a child. For example, while at Flechsig's hospital Schreber reports having been dragged from his bed by two attendants and on resisting being beaten in a billiards room. Flechsig, he reports, denied the whole occurrence.

There is little doubt that the worst of Schreber's adult betrayals involved his being sent to a state hospital.[5] The *Memoirs* are as much a record of his efforts to come to terms with betrayals of his trust by the mental health professionals purporting to help him as it is an indictment of his early life.

A Self-Trust Understanding of Schreber's Delusions

One of Freud's (1911) major contributions to the understanding of psychosis was his discovery that paranoid delusions are restorative. "The delusional formation, which we take to be the pathological product," he observed, "is in reality an attempt at recovery, a process of reconstruction" (p. 71). Kohut (1971) suggested one means by which delusions represent an attempt at recovery: They replace cohesive narcissistic configurations (selfobject fantasies) and provide relief from intolerable states of fragmentation. Freud's (1937) idea that delusions contain "kernels of historical truth," another invaluable contribution, has been borne out by many subsequent investigators such as Josephs and Josephs (1986) and Stolorow et al. (1987).

Incorporating these insights into a self-trust perspective, I understand delusions to crystalize the dissociatively altered subjective reality of the paranoid person into a coherent construction of beliefs and expectations, thus stabilizing a disintegrating self-experience. This delusional construction promotes

[5]See Lothane's (1992) account of the events leading to the worsening of Schreber's condition and the circumstances of his institutionalization.

self-restitution in the following ways: (1) It concretizes or gives symbolic expression to traumatizing betrayals, thereby giving form, albeit disguised, to memories, affects, and meanings that may be unconscious; (2) it attempts to rescript trauma scenarios and to confirm drastically diminished and/or intensified self-trust dimensions; and (3) it substitutes for unconscious selfobject fantasies shattered by trauma. Viewed in terms of this understanding, Schreber's delusional construction is a masterwork!

Niederland (1984) summarized Schreber's delusional system as it is revealed in the *Memoirs* as follows:

> He felt he had a mission to redeem the world and to restore it to its lost state of bliss.
> This mission must be preceded by the destruction of the world and by his personal transformations into a woman.
> Transformed into a female, he—Schreber, now a woman—would become God's mate, and out of such union a better and healthier race of men would emerge. (p. 10)

Schreber's perception of the world as needing redemption appears to symbolically concretize his experience of growing up and living as an adult in an environment in which his trust was repeatedly betrayed, his psychological and bodily integrity was frequently violated, and his experience of cohesive selfhood was constantly endangered. The role of redeemer delusionally extended his childhood position as the trustworthy provider for the selfobject needs of others. At the same time, because the redeemer is himself God-like, his trauma scenarios of victimization were rescripted. No longer the helpless victim, the betrayed, he claimed for himself the power of those who betrayed him.

The idea that his conscious delusional constructions were attempts to replace his shattered unconscious selfobject fantasies is well-illustrated by his descriptions of the hereafter in the opening chapter of the *Memoirs*. After death, according to Schreber (1988), souls experience a state of continual bliss derived from their beholding of God. This ecstatic prospect seems to provide an ingenious substitution for the selfobject fantasies of mergers with omnipotent idealized paternal figures which were repeatedly shattered by the betrayals he sustained at the hands of his parents and Flechsig—betrayals that were due not only to their abusive treatment but also to their neglect, rejection, and abandonment of him. It seems likely that the lost state of bliss to which Schreber believed he would return the world refers to his illusion of having lived in perfect happiness as a child, another fantastical rescripting of trauma.

Schreber (1988) developed the notion that the earth had been destroyed and that he was "the only real man still surviving" immediately after his wife failed to visit him in Flechsig's hospital following his second breakdown.

> A further decline in my nervous state and an important chapter in my life commenced about the 15th of February 1894 when my wife, who until then had spent a few hours every day with me and had also taken lunch with me in the Asylum, undertook a four-day journey to her father in Berlin, in order to have a holiday for herself, for which she was in urgent need. My condition deteriorated so much in these four days that after her return I saw her only once more, and then declared that I could not wish my wife to see me again in the low state into which I have fallen. (p. 44)

In choosing to visit her ailing father instead of her tormented husband, Sabine all but rubbed in Schreber's face his incapacity to exercise omnipotent control over those he needed to provide him with selfobject experiences. Proclaiming himself the only surviving human, Schreber attempted to demonstrate his transcendence over his need for selfobjects. When Schreber did see Sabine again he reported, "I no longer considered her a living being, but only thought I saw in her a human form produced by miracle in the manner of the 'fleetingly-improvised-men'" (p. 44). In describing her as less-than-human and phantom-like, Schreber appears to concretize his experience of his wife as a betrayer, no better than the many people in his life whose availability as selfobjects was unpredictable, unreliable, and sporadic. As Niederland (1963) and Orange (1993) point out, the fleetingly improvised men may also allude to the little figures used as illustrations in his father's books. Thus, Schreber linked Sabine with those figures in his past whom he had experienced as cruel and depriving. I must agree with Lothane's (1992) assessment of Sabine's absence as a "trauma within a trauma."

As Freud (1911) first observed, God, a central figure in Schreber's delusions, combines elements of his father and his psychiatrist. However, since Freud was convinced that these men were objects of homosexual desire, he failed to recognize that Schreber's delusions revealed them as his chief betrayers. Schreber appears to have assigned to God many of the negative qualities shared by his father and Flechsig that relate to disavowed perceptions of them as betrayers of his self-trust. Far from omnipotent or benevolent, Schreber's God is a profoundly vulnerable deity who keeps potentially destructive humans at a safe distance. Like the two men whose needs for sadistic domination over Schreber were born of weakness and fear, his God experienced human need for selfobject connectedness as threatening and dangerous.

Much as Schreber's father and his psychiatrist hid their betrayals behind the espousal of high-minded principles, so God's language cannot be taken on face value. He is a hypocrite! As Katan (1959) pointed out, the so-called "ground language" of Schreber's God reverses meanings and relies on euphemisms. As an example, Schreber mentions a number of words whose meanings have been changed into the reverse: "Reward" means "punishment," "poison" means "food," "unsacred" means "sacred." Such reversals and euphemisms appear to represent his father's disguised sadism. Katan observed that

> this is the language spoken by a father who does not punish his son for the sake of punishment but for the child's own good—a father who wants to drive the devil out of his son, who wants to make him pure so that he will not masturbate again and will not spread "repugnant odors" or even worse soil himself. . . . Under cover of having his son's interests at heart, he submits him to a treatment of relentless testing and tongue-lashing. (p. 146)

Schreber's God is incapable of empathy. Schreber (1988) explained, "*[W]ithin the order of the World, God did not really understand the living human being* and had no need to understand him because according to the Order of the World, He dealt only with corpses" (p. 75). Here again Schreber apparently condensed representations of Flechsig who was famous for his discoveries made on the brains of cadavers and his father whose experiments were better suited to corpses than living, feeling children, and assigned them to God. Schreber's assessment of God as "completely unable to learn from experience," appears to reflect the fact that the betrayals he suffered at the hands of both men were repetitious in nature.

Nowhere is the self-restorative meaning of Schreber's delusions more clearly evident than in his descriptions of "miracles" scattered throughout the *Memoirs*. In the opening paragraph of Chapter XI, "Bodily Integrity Damaged by Miracles," Schreber wrote:

> From the first beginnings of my contact with God up to the present day my body has continuously been the object of divine miracles. If I wanted to describe all these miracles in detail I could fill a whole book with them alone. I may say that hardly a single limb or organ in my body escaped being temporar-

ily damaged by miracles, nor a single muscle being pulled by miracles. (quoted in Niederland, 1959b, p. 75)

Niederland's (1959b) discovery that these miracles derived directly from the physical manipulations and contraptions described and illustrated in Moritz Schreber's books "broke the code" of Schreber's delusional system. He observed, "The father's apparatus of belts and body straps give new sense and meaning to such divine miracles as 'being tied-to-earth,' 'being tied-to-celestial-bodies,' or 'fastened-to-rays' (p. 77). For example, the "compression-of-the-chest miracle" appears to originate in the "geradehalter," a bizarre contraption consisting of a system of iron bars fastened to the chest of the child and a table near which the child sat. By delusionally transforming these abusive experiences into "miracles," Schreber rescripted some of his most horrifying traumas. As the object of miracles, he proclaimed his specialness; his selfobject fantasies of mirrored grandiosity found delusional replacement.

Schreber's *Memoirs* also contains indications that Schreber may have experienced many of his father's sadistic experimentations as sexually abusive. He repeatedly linked his expectation of being "unmanned" or transformed into a woman with his fear of being sexually abused. For example, describing the persecution he experienced at Flechsig's hospital as attempts to "forsake" or "abandon" him, he wrote, "[I]t was thought that this could be achieved by unmanning me and allowing my body to be prostituted like that of a female harlot" (p. 99). A few pages later he observed, "[M]ost disgusting was the idea that my body, after the intended transformation into a female being, was to suffer some sexual abuse, particularly as there had even been talk for some time of my being thrown to the asylum attendants for this purpose" (p. 101).

It is easy to understand how a child subjected to the contraptions recommended by Schreber's father to prevent masturbation might have experienced himself as sexually abused. One particularly cruel device described by Niederland (1984) was attached to the genital area at bedtime. It contained sharp spikes which stabbed the penis as soon as an erection occurred and simultaneously set off an alarm clock that awakened the child and his parents. Whether or not this device was ever used on Schreber, it seems probable that he learned that any pleasurable activity involving his genitals was not only forbidden, it was likely to result in pain and humiliation. Little wonder that he feared retraumatization if he demonstrated behavior typically associated with masculine assertiveness.

Schreber's father also prescribed enemas as the "most subtle form of laxative" (Niederland, 1959b, p. 73). In one book, *Die Kaltwasser-Heilmethode in thren Grenzen und ihrem wahren Werthe [The Cold-Water Therapeutic Method: Its Limits and True Value]* (Schreber, 1842), the repeated administration of cold water enemas is justified for a variety of reasons. In another book (Schreber, 1852) he advocated that these be administered to a child starting at the age of three months. If, as Niederland (1984) contended, Schreber's references to such things as the "coccyx miracle" and "the urge to shit . . . miracled up" relate to his having received cold water enemas, it is probable that he experienced them as a form of anal rape.

It is quite possible that Schreber's fears of being "unmanned" and transformed into a woman also relate to his having discovered that Flechsig advocated and actually performed castrations as a means of treating neuroses and psychoses (Niederland, 1968, p. 104). Orange's (1993) understanding of the relationship between Schreber's delusion of becoming a woman and his expectation of being sexually abused is compatible with a self-trust perspective:

> Schreber's own sense of vulnerability and of being used was clearly tied to the experience of sexual abuse. He may have identified this vulnerability and the accompanying shame as equivalent to becoming female. If Schreber had been sexually abused as a child—not impossible in a family where children were experimental subjects—he would understandably experience any threat of sexual abuse as "unmanning," depriving of all autonomy, and as central to the stealing of his soul. (p. 150)

For Schreber, the notion of being transformed into a woman also appears to have had very positive meanings. At the outset of his second breakdown he reported having the thought that "it must be very nice to be a woman submitting to the act of copulation." To understand this aspect of Schreber's delusion, we must bear in mind that the men Schreber longed to represent in selfobject fantasies of idealized merger—his father and Flechsig—chose the company of woman over closeness with him. As a woman mated with God, Schreber could achieve, by means of a delusional replacement, the experience of idealized merger with an idealized paternal figure. By experiencing himself as a woman in the masochistic position of submitting to intercourse, Schreber also installed God as an alter ego selfobject.

Assigning his disavowed masculinity to God, Schreber attempted to place God in the role once occupied by his father. Meissner (1978) viewed this aspect of Schreber's delusion in similar terms: "The persecutor relation . . . was the only one that Schreber could attain with his father. The price of the relation with the father, therefore, was subjugation and submission, just as the price of becoming the special agent and instrument of God's divine purposes for redemption of the world was his transformation into a woman" (p. 110). It is also probably that Schreber's delusion of mating with God and bearing a new breed of healthy humans rescripted the traumas of Sabine's miscarriages; his hope of experiencing the pride of parenthood was delusionally restored.

A number of recent Schreber scholars have questioned the assumption that Schreber was actually abused by his father. For example, Israëls (1989) criticized the "domestic tyrant genre" of psychoanalytic literature, most notably the writings of Katan (1959) and Niederland (1984) as hodiecentric, that is, distorting the past by viewing it in terms of the present. Lothane (1992) blamed the "horrific imagery" created by Niederland's "exaggerated descriptions" of Moritz Schreber's posture-improving appliances for establishing his reputation as a malevolent sadist. We have no proof that Schreber was physically or sexually abused by his father or even made to wear his orthopedic restraints. In fact, there are some reasons to believe he was not. For example, Richard Ulman (1994, personal communication) suggested that Schreber would have shown more violent, sadistic behavior if he had been systematically brutalized. To my mind, the repeated betrayals of self-trust that give rise to paranoid experience do not necessarily depend on abusive physical acts. As I see it, even if Moritz Schreber and his wife followed a small portion of the child-rearing advice contained in *Kallipädie* (Schreber, 1858) in their upbringing of Schreber, he might still have experienced failures in empathic responsiveness severe enough to constitute devastating betrayals of self-trust; the alteration of his experience of subjective reality might still have involved a paranoid process, and the content of his delusions might still have embroidered on images found in his father's books—evidence of his heroic efforts to rescript his trauma scenarios.

Freud and Schreber

In the previous chapter we saw that many of Freud's theoretical constructs (such as the death instinct and the repetition compulsion, his understanding of sadomasochism and the psychological development of women) reflect his dissociative alteration of subjective reality following his traumatic betrayals. Freud's interpretations of the Schreber case may also be seen as part of his effort to rescript his own trauma scenarios. Once again he seems to have preferred to find guilt and fear over the expression of sexual, in this case homosexual, urges, rather than to give credence to the possibility that his patient was a survivor of traumatizing betrayals inflicted by those on whom he utterly depended for his psychological survival.

Bloch's (1989) insights into the relationship between Freud's retraction of the seduction theory and his interpretation of the Schreber case add considerable weight to my contention that Freud's own self-trust betrayals influenced his theories. She suggested that Freud's "phenomenal misreading" of the *Memoirs* cannot merely be ascribed to his ignorance of Schreber's background. Although specific information about Schreber's life was meager at the time of Freud's (1911) paper, Bloch points out that Freud certainly had access to the widely popular textbooks written by Schreber's father. Yet, Freud stated in a footnote to his paper that apart from learning Schreber's age, "I have made use of no material that is not derived from the actual text of the *Denkwurdigkeiten*" (p. 46). Bloch questioned whether Freud chose to remain ignorant of the father's writings for fear that he might have come upon information he preferred not to know.

Despite Freud's recognition that Schreber's descriptions of God thinly disguised his experience of his father, Freud failed to consider that Schreber's indictments of God as his persecutor might have been based on actual experience. Instead, he explained Schreber's complaints about God's cruelty and sadism in terms of the paranoid transformation of love into hate. And he repeatedly paid high tribute to the father's excellent reputation, writing, for example, "Such a father as this was by no means unsuitable for transfiguration into a God in the affectionate memory of the son from whom he had been so early separated by death" (Freud, 1911, p. 51).

Bloch (1989) suggested that Freud's relationship with his own father was responsible both for his retraction of the seduction theory and his exoneration of Schreber's father. She observed that before his father's death, Freud had not excluded him from charges of responsibility for the perverse sexual traumas that he posited as the cause of hysteria. In a letter to Fliess (February 11, 1907), he stated, "Unfortunately my own father was one of these perverts and is responsible for the hysteria of my brother and those of several younger sisters" (Masson, 1985, p. 281). Referring to a dream Freud had the day after his father's funeral which included a sign that read either, "You are requested to close the eyes," or "You are requested to close an eye," Bloch wrote:

> Freud thus leaves no doubt that it was *his* eyes he was directed to close. . . . At the time of his father's death, he was "in all cases" still accusing "the father, not excluding my own" of perverse acts. . . . The admonition "to close the eye"

could therefore only be an injunction to cease his analysis of his father's character and behavior and their role in his children's neurosis. (pp. 189–190)

Thus, there appear to be stronger connections between Freud and Schreber than those joining them in psychoanalytic history. Both employed enormous creativity in the service of rescripting their trauma scenarios, exonerating their parents from blame for self-trust betrayal, and paying the heavy price of repeated retraumatization.

Part II

TOWARD A PSYCHOTHERAPY

OF TRUST

SELF-TRUST AND THE

THERAPEUTIC RELATIONSHIP

[The patient's] trust or distrust is almost negligible compared with the internal resistances which hold the neurosis firmly in place. . . . his distrust is only a symptom like his other symptoms and it would not be an interference, provided he conscientiously carries out what the rule of the treatment requires of him.

Sigmund Freud (1913)

Trust must be acquired analytically, by the passing of all sorts of tests by the patient. One must have stood all the tests. Then he brings his confidence spontaneously. Neurotics have been disappointed heavily in their trust.

Sandor Ferenczi (1932)

I have yet to begin a therapeutic relationship with a person whose self-trust was not scarred by past betrayals. Some of my new patients try to prevent their recurrence by keeping me at a safe distance. Formal, remote, and suspicious, they guard themselves against the dangers they associate with closeness. Even while presenting factually accurate histories and minutely detailed accounts of their present lives, they are careful to keep their feelings to themselves, especially those pertaining to me. Other patients are just the opposite. With what often strikes me as reckless abandon, they indiscriminately reveal their most intimate thoughts, feelings, and pain-shrouded memories within minutes of our first meeting. Unfortunately these patients often come to regret their impetuosity. Having shared too much, too soon, they are likely to become overwhelmed with fear, shame, and self-loathing.

These very different styles of relating illustrate the bidirectional nature of self-trust disturbance (see Chapter 3, p. 59). My guarded patients have little trust that others will provide them with selfobject experiences while my impetuous patients trust to an inordinate degree. If patients with these two styles were compared with one another, huge differences undoubtedly would be found in the ways they experienced subjective reality and in the organization of the various dimensions of their self-trust. However, all of my patients, no matter what their self-trust organization, find themselves in the same predicament: They face what I have come to regard as *a self-trust dilemma*. Much as they long to reveal their cherished dreams, tormenting anxieties, shameful doubts, and guilty secrets, much as they crave relief from debilitating psychological symptoms, and much as they wish for a chance to realize themselves more fully, they are forced to confront the possibility that past betrayals will be repeated in our relationship.

If my hypothesis is accepted, that the betrayal of self-trust lies at the heart of trauma (see Chapter 3), the threat faced by my patients is clearly that of retraumatization. Does this mean that all psychotherapy patients are trauma victims? Is self-pathology, as Jonathan Cohen (1981) claimed, the "structural consequence" of psychic trauma? Recent conceptualizations of the treatment situation acknowledge the centrality of trauma in pathogenesis. Ornstein's (1974, 1991) view of patients as torn between a wish for "a new beginning" and "a dread to repeat" poignantly captures this self-trust dilemma.[1] Stolorow et al. (1987) elaborated these ideas into a "bipolar" conceptualization of transference. At one pole, according to these authors, is

> the patient's longing to experience the analyst as a source of requisite selfobject functions that had been missing or insufficient during the formative years. . . . the patient hopes and searches for a new selfobject experience that will enable him to resume and complete an arrested developmental process. (pp. 101– 102)

---

[1]Ornstein (1974, 1991) asserted that what patients dread in treatment is the repetition of old, self-defeating patterns of behavior in response to threats of transferential repetitions of trauma. I disagree. While patients are often dismayed and even humiliated by the need for such behaviors, they experience them as essential for psychological survival and are usually reluctant to relinquish them. What they dread are the retraumatizing betrayals of self-trust that make these behaviors necessary.

At the other pole, they see

> the patient's expectations and fears of transference repetition of the original experiences of selfobject failure. It is this second dimension of the transference that becomes the source of conflict and resistance. (p. 102)

While self-trust and its betrayal are implicit in the foregoing conceptualizations, there are two important advantages in allowing these issues to emerge from the shadows: First, the relationship between trauma and psychopathology in general is clarified, and second, previously neglected or poorly understood aspects of the therapeutic relationship can be addressed, thus facilitating treatment. In this chapter I discuss these advantages more fully. Two illustrative treatment cases are presented in Chapter 7.

DISTURBED SELF-TRUST, TRAUMA, AND DISORDERS OF SELF-EXPERIENCE

Given the mounting evidence that the abuse of children is endemic throughout the world (see deMause, 1991),[2] it is little wonder that a growing number of clinicians and researchers are finding that childhood trauma is an important predictor of psychiatric disorder among children and adults (e.g., Herman, 1992; Terr, 1991; van der Kolk, 1987). A recently conducted national survey found that posttraumatic stress is one of the leading mental health problems for women (Goleman, 1994). Moreover, trauma has been recognized as a major etiological fact in ever-increasing numbers of psychiatric syndromes. For example, extremely high rates of childhood sexual and physical abuse have been found among patients diagnosed as "borderline" (Herman & van der Kolk, 1987; Herman, Perry, & van der Kolk, 1989).

Despite these developments, relatively few patients enter treatment with full-blown PTSD. This may be partially explained by recent findings that traumatized children frequently exhibit symptoms of severe psychopathology that bear little resemblance to the classic PTSD symptom picture (Kendall-Tackett, Williams, & Finkelhor, 1993). Moreover, children with other disorders often have PTSD as an intercurrent diagnosis (March & Amaya-Jackson, 1993; Kendall-Tackett et al., 1993). Hence, adult patients, even those who suffered severe traumas as children, are more likely to complain of depression,

---

[2]Finkelhor & Dziuba-Leatherman (1994) found that children suffer more victimizations than do adults.

anxiety, obsessions, addictions, phobias, problems at work or in relationships, or merely the sense of being on the wrong track in life, than of the numbing and reexperiencing symptoms of PTSD. The question, then, is whether all of these complaints derive from trauma.

As Cohen (1980) observed, many attempts have been made to differentiate trauma from pathogenic influence in general (Cohen, 1980, 1981; Hoffer, 1952; Khan, 1963; Kris, 1956; Sandler, 1967). Much depends on one's use and understanding of the term "trauma." Ulman and I (Ulman & Brothers, 1988) reserved the term for situations in which the shattering and faulty restoration of selfobject fantasies are fully expressed in the characteristic dissociative symptomatology of PTSD. However, we also suggested that this conceptualization was relevant for a wide variety of common psychopathological conditions. And, we advocated "careful clinical exploration for possible pathological sequelae of trauma, even if not manifested in a diagnosable syndrome such as PTSD" (p. 5). Now, from the vantage point gained by employing a self-trust perspective, I am prepared to argue that trauma is an aspect of all disorders of self-experience.

Kohut did not emphasize the etiological significance of trauma per se. In his view, traumas are "clues that point to the truly pathogenic factors, the unwholesome atmosphere to which the child was exposed during the years when his self was established" (Kohut & Wolf, 1978, p. 417). In his last writings, he left no doubt as to what these pathogenic factors were. "All forms of psychopathology," Kohut (1984) observed, "are based on defects in the structure of the self, on distortions of the self, or on weakness of the self. . . . [and] all these flaws in the self are due to disturbances of self-selfobject relationships in childhood" (p. 53). As I see it, disturbances in selfobject relationships severe enough to cause "defects in the structure of the self" are likely to be experienced as traumatizing betrayals of self-trust. When serious disturbances in selfobject relations are understood in terms of self-trust betrayal, Kohut's formulations fit well within the parameters of what Cohen (1980, 1981) called "a trauma paradigm of pathogenesis."

My contention that traumatic self-trust betrayals underlie all psychological disorders goes hand in hand with my belief that dissociation and dissociative phenomena are fundamental aspects of psychological disturbance. This idea has a very long history (Crabtree, 1989; Putnam, 1989; van der Hart & Horst, 1989; van der Kolk, Brown, & van der Hart, 1989). As far back as 1784, Puysegur discovered a relationship between "magnetic sleep," or what would now be recognized as dissociated states induced by hypnotism, and mental disorders in general. Contemporary thinking about dissociation originated in the momentous discovery of Pierre Janet (1887) that the subconscious personalities of hysterics functioned as coexisting psychic centers and were constructed in response to traumatic events. As Crabtree (1993) noted, these valuable insights into dissociation and therapeutic integration, although acknowledged by Breuer, were largely ignored by Freud.

Most psychoanalysts regard repression and dissociation as quite different phenomena. For example, Davies and Frawley (1994) asserted that "repression is an active process through which the ego attains mastery over conflictual material," whereas dissociation "is the last ditch effort of an overwhelmed ego to salvage some semblance of adequate mental functioning" (p. 65). They added that repression brings about a forgetting of mental contents, whereas dissociation leads to a severing between one set of mental contents and another. They also proposed that repression and dissociation require different treatment strategies: "The working-through of repressed contents involves the process of remembering. Working through dissociative states involves an ongoing effort at integrating mental contents severed by traumatic regression and maintained in disparate ego states that alternate in accessibility" (p. 65).

Kohut's (1971) formulation of horizontal and vertical splits in the psyche also depends upon an understanding of repression and dissociation as entailing distinctly different processes. Horizontal splits, in Kohut's view, involve the repression of painful memories of parental failures to respond empathically to developmentally appropriate expressions of "archaic narcissism." Vertical splits involve the disavowal of the meaning of the experience. He observed that "the ideational and emotional manifestations of a vertical split in the psyche . . . are correlated to the side by side, concurrent existence of otherwise incompatible psychological attitudes" (pp. 176–177). He believed that horizontal splits caused by repression do not prevent the development of a cohesive nuclear self while the vertically split-off aspects of archaic narcissistic experience maintained by dissociation and disavowal do not undergo transformation and therefore remain unintegrated.

When viewed from the standpoint of intersubjectivity theory, these sharp distinctions between repression and dissociation fade dramatically. According to Stolorow and Atwood (1992), consciousness itself arises within an intersubjective context, and becomes articulated through the validating responsiveness of others. In early life, validation takes the form of sensorimotor attunement; later, it involves the validation of experience encoded in symbols. Increasingly over the course of development "unconscious becomes coextensive with unsymbolized" (p. 33).

Repression, according to these authors, may be understood as a process whereby affect states associated with emotional conflict are prevented from crystalizing in awareness: conflictual experiences are not symbolically encoded. In contrast to an intrapsychic drive theory conceptualization, the conflicts that cause repression are not thought to occur over the expression of instinctual drives, but are seen as arising in intersubjective contexts in which central affect states are not integrated because they failed to evoke attuned responsiveness from others. These unintegrated affect states remain unconscious to the extent that they pose threats to the maintenance of vitally needed (selfobject) ties. A noteworthy feature of this conceptualization is that repression is seen as interfering with the integration of experience, a function previously attributed to dissociation.

This intersubjective theory of repression is highly congruent with a self-trust perspective. From the standpoint of self-trust, repression is not viewed as involving psychological processes different from those of dissociation; rather, repression is understood as part of a dissociative process. I view repression as a means by which memories of self-trust betrayals or threatened betrayals are prevented from being articulated in consciousness or are eliminated from consciousness. In Chapter 3, I argued that dissociation results when traumatizing betrayals of self-trust create imbalances between the self-centered organizational mode and the reality-oriented organizational mode. These imbalances reflect alterations that occur in the world of selfobject fantasy and in the world of subjective reality as the betrayed person struggles to regain trust in those represented in shattered selfobject fantasies. Repression is a highly effective means by which subjective reality is altered.

In a similar vein, Gruber (1992) argued that the phenomenon Freud called repression is better explained in terms of dissociation. She observed that aspects of self-experience that undergo repression (i.e., are eliminated from conscious awareness) always have meanings that threaten to shatter selfobject fantasies. If they did not have these meanings they would remain available to consciousness. In other words, experiences are lost to conscious awareness to the extent that they threaten to disrupt trusting bonds between self and others represented in one's selfobject fantasies. They may be totally unavailable to consciousness or available to consciousness only when subjective reality is sufficiently altered by other means, depending on the self-restorative efforts undertaken (see Chapter 3).

When an experience involving or threatening self-trust betrayal is repressed—that is, totally eliminated from conscious awareness—trusting bonds with those needed in selfobject relations may more easily be maintained than when amnesia for the experience is only partial. This probably accounts for the association of repression with less severe psychological disturbance and for Kohut's assertion that repression does not interfere with the developmental transformation of self-experience.

As Ulman and I pointed out (Ulman & Brothers, 1988), the importance of determining whether repression or dissociation is primary in trauma resides mainly in the effects of such a determination on the treatment process. When repression is seen as primary, treatment tends to emphasize the need to bring repressed memories into consciousness; when dissociation is seen as primary, treatment emphasizes the need to promote the integration of self-experience.

The dissociative symptomatology of PTSD reflects a specific means of altering subjective reality in the aftermath of traumatizing self-trust betrayals. The characteristic reexperiencing and numbing symptoms both concretize the actuality of betrayals (fill in the black holes created by repression) and serve to restore self and/or others as trustworthy selfobjects (rescript trauma scenarios). However, there are virtually limitless ways in which subjective reality can be altered in the aftermath of traumatic betrayals of self-trust. It is well beyond the scope of this book, not to mention the limits of my knowledge, for me to attempt to identify the complicated mix of genetic, biochemical, and environmental factors intermingled with issues of self-trust betrayal that determine the form any given psychological disorder will assume. Yet I hope to show that an in-depth understanding of the contribution of self-trust betrayal to the overall clinical picture yields rich therapeutic benefits.

THE CLINICAL PICTURE

It is extremely rare for patients, including those with PTSD, to cite disturbances in trust as their reason for seeking psychological treatment. It is even rarer for therapists to describe their patients' problems in these terms. Nevertheless, I am convinced that from first encounter between patient and therapist to the final moment of their last meeting, self-trust and its betrayal informs the therapeutic relationship. How can this apparent contradiction be explained? As I pointed out in Chapter 1, until recently, clinicians have had no theoretical framework on which to build techniques for addressing this silent but, to my mind, everpresent aspect of the treatment process. With the clinical advances of self psychology and theories of intersubjectivity, this long-standing theoretical void has been filled.

From its inception, self psychology has recognized the "intersubjective world of the therapeutic exchange" (Lichtenberg et al., 1992, pp. 132–33). Kohut's ideas about the therapeutic relationship reflect his belief that "reality per se is unknowable" (Kohut, 1981, p. 552) and that the observer/therapist always profoundly affects the observed/patient. Recent theories of intersubjectivity have further demonstrated the impossibility of understanding the treatment situation in terms of the patient's experience alone (Atwood & Stolorow, 1984; Benjamin, 1990; Natterson, 1991; Stolorow & Atwood, 1992; Stolorow et al., 1987). For example, Benjamin observed that a "Troublesome legacy of intrapsychic theory [is] the term *object*" (p. 34). Intersubjectivity considers two participants in a relationship, not as subject and object but as subject and subject. Similarly, Stolorow and his collaborators defined intersubjectivity as the field of intersection between two subjectivities. Natterson argued that intersubjectivity should replace the notion of countertransference. In his view, the therapist's fantasies and desires, while crucial to the therapeutic process, are not mainly reactive phenomena.

Since subjectivity is itself powerfully affected by the organization of a person's self-trust, it follows that intersubjectivity is also influenced by the configurations of self-trust between two people who form a relationship. It is meaningless to view the therapeutic relationship only from the vantage point of the patient's self-trust. The therapist, as much as the patient, enters the therapeutic relationship with a unique organization of self-trust shaped by the vicissitudes of selfobject relations. No two therapists will have exactly the same reaction to the doubt, skepticism, and suspicion evinced by some patients, or the blind faith shown by others. Just as patients dread retraumatizing betrayals of self-trust in the therapeutic relationship, so do therapists. What actually transpires between patient and therapist in large part reflects the highly individual configuration created by their different self-trust organizations and their mutual vulnerability to self-trust betrayal.

Richard Ulman and I (1988) expressed the view that in treating trauma survivors "the most significant countertransference issue concerns the therapist's unconscious selfobject fantasies of the patient" (p. 24). We reconceptualized such treatment pitfalls as the "conspiracy of silence" (Krystal, 1971), "therapeutic enthusiasm" (Klein, 1968), and "therapeutic pessimism" in terms of what we called "countertransference selfobject fantasies." We noted that when empathically understood, these fantasies enhance the reconstruction and working-through of the unconscious meaning of trauma. However, when patients are represented in the therapist's selfobject fantasies, empathic understanding is often difficult to come by. Since such fantasies come to organize the therapist's self-experience, disturbances in the therapeutic relationship are likely to provoke such intense feelings that understanding is obscured. A self-trust perspective helps in this process. Therapists made aware of the organization of their own self-trust are likely to become highly sensitive to changes in trust in themselves as providers of selfobject experiences for their patients and changes in their trust in patients as providers of selfobject experiences for them. Once aware of these changes, they are better able to address therapeutic disruptions.

Thomson (1994) described an experiment using intersubjectivity theory to examine his "countertransference experiences" over a four-month period. His unusually candid, at times courageous, disclosures about himself and his interactions with two patients provide an excellent opportunity to demonstrate the effectiveness of a self-trust perspective. In one case, a male patient's silence left Thomson feeling frustrated. Referring to the fact that his classical training "induced in me a prereflective need to regard his silence as a resistance" (p. 129), Thomson either met the patient's silence with silence of his own or attempted to "push" him to speak. Enraged, the patient criticized Thomson's "nonresponsiveness." Thomson reported becoming angry because he felt he had been responsive and encouraging. When the same patient accused him of sounding "technical and unsympathetic" in his reaction to news of the death of one of the patient's friends, Thomson felt "defensive." From his perspective, he had been empathic. Intending to demonstrate his empathy for the patient's feelings, he made a number of remarks that enraged the patient further and intensified the disruption in the therapeutic relationship. Anticipating the emergence of intense affects in another patient, a woman, Thomson felt "a need to be reassuring." She complained that Thomson's silence made her feel alone and she suggested that this posed "a problem" for Thomson. She became enraged when Thomson responded with a reassuring comment.

Let us now attempt to understand the patients' reactions from a self-trust perspective. According to Thomson, the male patient's parents were "unable to respond affectively to him in early life." Quite probably, the patient's parents betrayed his trust in them as providers of his selfobject needs. The patient's references to Thomson's "nonresponsiveness" suggest that he feared a retraumatizing betrayal of his trust in Thomson as an affectively responsive provider of selfobject experiences. The female patient's parents also "failed to provide an empathic presence" and she suffered "the loss" of her elder sister during adolescence. She too appears to have perceived Thomson's reaction to her (his silence) as threatening a retraumatizing betrayal. Indeed, she said, "I feel a great distrust of you, I can't afford to let go" (p. 138).

Thomson understood his reactions to both patients as stemming from "a prereflective attitude that led [him] to believe that [he] was personally responsible for the disappointments and that [he] should therefore be able to relieve them" (p. 141). Thomson seems to suggest that this is a misconception born of his countertransferential need for "an affiliatively affirming selfobject" (Lichtenberg, 1983). From a self-trust perspective, Thomson *was* personally responsible, at least in part, for his patients' disappointments within the therapeutic relationship. It was his actual behavior that threatened them with retraumatizing betrayals, just as their actual behavior appears to have threatened him.

How would the disruptions that occurred between Thomson and his patients be understood from a self-trust perspective? Let us consider one of Thomson's self-disclosures:

> In the past I had recognized that my need to see myself as sensitive, loving, well-motivated, and so on had had an influence on my choice of profession. I had gained some degree of understanding from experiences similar to this one that my need for such a self-image arose from early experiences. I had come to believe that I had been needed then as a gentle, loving selfobject. (1994, p. 139)

It appears that intensified self-as-trustworthy is a prominent feature of Thomson's self-trust organization, that is, he has an unusually strong need to experience himself as a trustworthy provider for the selfobject needs of others. His criteria for this self-trust dimension appear to be fairly perfectionistic; he must always be regarded as sensitive, loving, well-motivated, etc. We might further speculate that the selfobject fantasies that structure his self-experience largely consist in images of himself as providing selfobject experiences for others.

It seems likely that his patients' accusations and criticisms threatened Thomson with self-trust betrayal. They were, in effect, informing him that he was not the trustworthy provider he believed himself to be. His reaction was most intense with the woman patient. As he noted, "Women patients who even hinted that I might not be kind or that I might be destructive . . . threatened to undo defense against an entirely different but repressed self-image, which contained guilt-ridden anger" (p. 139). It is probably safe to assume that Thomson's original betrayals of self-trust involved a woman. His difficulty in accepting his responsibility for frightening his patients with the prospect of retraumatizing betrayals stems from the fact that his very experience of cohesive selfhood was at stake.

Describing his successful effort to restore his therapeutic relationship with his woman patient, Thompson noted: "the most urgent task was to take my own disrupted state in hand. I did not find this at all easy" (p. 140). Citing Lichtenberg (1983), Thomson advised therapists who find themselves in similar situations to "search for insight through empathy and introspection" which includes an "inquiry into those preflective attitudes that form the underpinnings of his [the therapist's] character" (p. 141). I believe when these underpinnings include one's self-trust organization and that of one's patients, the task becomes a great deal easier.

Therapists adopting a self-trust perspective need not abandon the general treatment approach advocated by self psychologists who accept the refinements of intersubjectivity theory. They would still employ "an empathic-introspective observational stance as the basic mode of analytic listening" (Schwaber, 1981) and their understanding would still be guided by a realization that "the psychoanalytic process is inherently an intersubjective one, shaped by the continuously shifting psychological field created by the interplay between the differently organized subjective worlds of patient and therapist" (Stolorow, 1994, p. 28). (They would, however, bear in mind that one's subjective world is powerfully determined by one's unique self-trust organization.) Moreover, the analysis of what have variously been called empathic failures (Kohut, 1971, 1977, 1984), selfobject failures (Stolorow et al., 1987) or ruptures in selfobject transference ties (Stolorow, 1994) would still occupy a central position in the treatment process.

Self psychologists tend to view the entire treatment process in terms of the establishment, unfolding and working through of what Kohut (1971, 1977, 1984) identified as "selfobject transferences." These are therapeutic relationships in which the patient perceives the therapist as providing mirroring, idealizing, twinship, or alterego experiences that were absent, insufficiently available, or traumatically aborted in the selfobject relationships of childhood. Kohut appears to have conceptualized selfobjects and selfobject transferences in all or nothing terms. In other words, in Kohut's view, patients either experience their therapists as selfobjects or they do not; a selfobject transference exists or it does not. Kohut did take note of certain qualitative aspects of selfobject relatedness. For example, the establishment of selfobject transferences might be "resisted," they might change character, shifting from idealizing to mirroring or vice versa, and they might undergo transformation from "archaic" to more mature forms. However, once these transferences come into being, or "click into place" (Kohut, 1984), he envisioned them as enduring in a fairly consistent way.

Stolorow and his colleagues (1987) refined this conceptualization considerably. They regarded the treatment process in terms of the continual oscillations between "the selfobject dimension" in which the patient experiences the therapist as providing selfobject experiences that were missing or insufficient during the formative years and "the repetitive dimension," which is a source of conflict and resistance. The two dimensions repeatedly move between the experiential foreground and background of the transference according to the patient's varying perception of the therapist as attuned to his or her emotional states and needs. Thus, the patient's experience of the therapist as a selfobject is seen as conditional and impermanent.

With a self-trust perspective, the distinction between what Stolorow and his colleagues regard as the selfobject dimension and the repetitive dimension of the transference becomes difficult to maintain. Consider, for example, a patient with highly intensified trust-in-others whose unquestioning trust in the therapist as selfobject functions to ward off the terror of a retraumatizing betrayal. What does it mean to say that the selfobject dimension of this transference is in the foreground? Such a statement does not convey, for example, the degree of dissociation required to maintain the state of selfobject relatedness, nor does it convey the degree of vulnerability of the selfobject bond should the therapist fail to meet the patient's highly immature and perfectionistic criteria. Moreover, to say that the selfobject dimension is in the foreground conveys no information about selfobject relatedness resulting from the patient's experience of providing selfobject experiences for the therapist. For most self psychologists, a selfobject transference refers only to an experience of the therapist as providing selfobject experiences for the patient. From a self-trust perspective, the therapeutic relationship is just as powerfully affected by patients' experiences of themselves as selfobjects for their therapists and by therapists' experience of the patients as selfobjects (see Chapter 8).

What changes with the adoption of a self-trust perspective? When a self-trust perspective is employed, one is less inclined to ask if a specific selfobject transference exists (the Kohut question) or if the selfobject pole of the transference is presently occupying the experiential foreground or background (the Stolorow question). Rather, one would consider the quality of relatedness between patient and therapist at any given moment in an attempt to determine the extent to which each experiences self and other as trustworthy in providing selfobject experiences. They would also attempt to determine the nature of the self-trust criteria employed.

TESTING, RECONSTRUCTING, WORKING THROUGH

A self-trust perspective highlights three interrelated elements of the treatment process: testing, reconstructing, and working-through. Although these three aspects of treatment are to be found throughout the course of any therapeutic relationship, testing is likely to predominate in the first phase of treatment; reconstructing, in the second or middle phase of treatment; and working-through, in the third or final stage of treatment. Consequently, I refer to the beginning, middle, and end phases of treatment as testing, reconstructing, and working-through. [3]

Phase 1: Testing

Kohut (1984) contended that selfobject transferences arise spontaneously and require no active encouragement from the side of the therapist. Describing the familiar clinical situation in which patients vehemently blame therapists when their condition deteriorates after an initial period of marked improvement, Kohut explained, "What happens is nothing else but the transference clicking into place. . . . the analytic situation has *become* the traumatic past and the therapist has *become* the traumatizing selfobject of early life" (p. 178).

In my view, selfobject transferences appear to arise spontaneously only when issues of self-trust are ignored. Therapists are not represented in their patients' selfobject fantasies unless they meet their criteria for self-trust. Of course, certain patients do make snap judgments, and some whose trust-in-others is extremely intensified represent therapists in selfobject fantasies on the basis of hearsay, before they ever meet. There is no such thing as a traumatizing selfobject; someone experienced as betraying or likely to betray one's self-trust will not be represented in one's selfobject fantasies. Patients whose conditions deteriorate and who noisily reproach their therapists following a period of improvement do so not as a result of the selfobject transference "clicking into place." Their conditions deteriorate because the selfobject relatedness between themselves and their therapists is in danger of "clicking out of place." They are enabled to protest only in light of the fact that the treatment situation is not the traumatic past and the therapist is not the traumatizing betrayer. Because the therapeutic relationship was experienced as trustworthy, however briefly, patients expect their therapists to grasp the meaning of their protests and to respond in ways that will reestablish trusting therapeutic bonds. The clicking into place Kohut described is likely to occur after patients have tested the selfobject potential of the therapeutic relationship and have found it reasonably trustworthy.

[3]Compare this scheme to the one developed in Ulman & Brothers (1988).

Just as psychologically well-functioning parents are ideally equipped to provide experiences for their children that promote the maturation of self-trust (see Chapter 2), so the therapeutic relationship is ideally structured to provide experiences for patients that promote the restoration of damaged self-trust. It is the consistent, reliable, predictable, and dependable behavior of parents or caretakers that facilitates the maturation of self-trust in children. And it is the regularity of appointments, the consistency of session duration, the fairness of fee arrangements, etc., that help to promote the restoration and maturation of self-trust in the therapeutic relationship.

However, these features of "the holding environment" (Winnicott, 1960) of the treatment situation are not sufficient to bring about lasting changes in the organization of a patient's self-trust. We have seen that the therapeutic relationship confronts all patients with a self-trust dilemma. They must risk retraumatizing betrayals if they are to pursue selfobject connectedness with the therapist. The "dread to repeat" always haunts the search for "a new beginning" (Ornstein, 1974). As a consequence of finding themselves in this predicament, patients continually test the trustworthiness of the therapeutic relationship. Although patients may actively design and carry out tests of therapeutic trustworthiness in a deliberate, conscious way, these are fairly infrequent occurrences. Much more commonly, patients construe what tran-spires within the therapeutic relationship, either consciously or unconsciously, as tests of trustworthiness (see Ferenczi, 1932). The unique self-trust organi-zation of each patient and the criteria used to evaluate self-trust determines the meaning of these tests. Thus, for example, one patient may construe the meaning of events in the therapeutic relationship primarily as tests of the trustworthiness of the therapist in providing selfobject experiences, while another patient may construe similar interactions as tests of his or her own capacity to elicit selfobject experiences from the therapist. They are both concerned with protecting themselves against the possibility of retraumatizing betrayals. The first patient dreads betrayal by the therapist while the second dreads self-betrayal.

Weiss (1986), an ego psychologist, advanced a similar view of treatment:

> the psychoanalytic process is in essence a process by which the patient works with the therapist, both consciously and unconsciously, to disconfirm his pathogenic beliefs. He does this by unconsciously testing his beliefs in relation to the therapist and by assimilating insight into them conveyed by the thera-pist's interpretation. (p. 101)

Weiss conceptualized these tests as efforts to repeat the past rather than to remember it, an idea that resembles Freud's conceptualization of transference as arising from the repetition compulsion. Insofar as Weiss's formulations grow out of a traditional psychoanalytic framework, they stress belief and insight rather than trust and empathy. However, many of his ideas are readily translatable into the language of self-trust. For example, Weiss mentioned that certain patients test the "limits" of the therapeutic relationship. From a self-trust perspective, there are a multitude of meanings in such tests. For example, certain tests of limits may involve the patient's need to confirm some intensified dimension of self-trust. Think of patients whose main criterion for highly intensified trust-in-self is the exertion of total control over others. Their insistence upon arbitrary changes in appointment times, requests for fee reductions, or demands of contact with the therapist outside of sessions may represent an attempt to confirm this intensified self-trust dimension. Some patients who test the limits of treatment in identical ways may be seeking to confirm intensified others-as-self-trusting. They unconsciously hope their demands will be turned down as evidence that their therapists can take care of their own needs (see the treatment of Ruth, next chapter).

Events in the therapeutic relationship most likely to be construed as failed tests of therapeutic trustworthiness are those that have come to be known as empathic failures, selfobject failures, or ruptures in the selfobject transference tie. For Kohut (1984), the therapist's selfobject failures or "errors in empathy" are basic to psychoanalytic cure because they contribute to the "laying down of psychological structure" by means of transmuting internalization" (see Chapter 2). This view is incompatible with a self-trust perspective. To the extent that empathic errors are construed as failed tests of trustworthiness, they signal the imminence of retraumatizing betrayals. Under these circumstances the psychic glue of selfobject relatedness loosens, giving rise to disintegration anxiety and dissociative efforts at self-restitution. It is difficult to imagine that such experiences would contribute to the restoration of cohesive selfhood. It is primarily the working through of failed tests of therapeutic trustworthiness that is curative (see Bacal, 1985; Stolorow et al., 1987).

Patients' tests of the therapeutic relationship often powerfully affect therapists' self-trust. Because the meanings of these tests are rarely easy to grasp, and because they threaten to disrupt the treatment process, therapists often experience uncertainty and anxiety when confronted with them. Moreover, therapists also construe events in treatment as tests of the trustworthiness of the therapeutic relationship. The extent to which patients pass or fail these tests strongly affects the success of treatment.

In writing about the initial phase in the treatment of trauma survivors, Ulman and I (1988) spoke of the patient's vacillations between resistance to and establishment of selfobject transference fantasies. When "resistance" to the establishment of selfobject transference fantasies is thought of in terms of the fear of retraumatizing betrayals of self-trust within the therapeutic relationship on the part of both participants and the concomitant need to dissociatively alter experiences of subjective reality, the advisability of retaining the concept "resistance" becomes debatable. No matter how it is reinterpreted, a pejorative aura clings to the term. Even if one adopts Kohut's (1970) view of resistance as motivated by the "anxieties of an insecurely established self" and the "danger of the self's disintegration," it is still likely to be thought of as undesirable. "Don't be afraid," we seem to be saying to the patient experienced as reluctant to represent the therapist in selfobject fantasies, "your therapist will not betray you." It is hard to think about resistance without thinking about helping the patient to overcome it, a stance antithetical to empathic understanding. To my mind it is preferable to think about the complex set of behaviors, attitudes, and expectations called resistance as attempts by patients and therapists to avert retraumatizing self-trust betrayals by testing the trustworthiness of the therapeutic relationship.

Phase 2: Reconstructing

Reconstructing involves the analysis of past betrayals of self-trust in the lives of patients and the subsequent changes that occur in selfobject fantasies and in the experience of subjective reality. Everything a patient does or says in sessions contributes toward reconstruction. The histories provided by patients, their memories of past betrayals, their present-day concerns outside of the therapeutic relationship, their dreams and fantasies, as well as inferences made on the basis of tests of trustworthiness within the therapeutic relationship are all used in the service of reconstruction. When therapists, employing an introspective-empathic stance, reconstruct the meaning of past betrayals for patients and interpret to them how they have altered subjective reality in light of these betrayals, they invariably strengthen the bonds of self-trust upon which therapeutic success depends.

Reconstructive efforts begun early in treatment are continuously refined. However, it is during the middle of a treatment, after the trustworthiness of the therapeutic relationship has been established to some degree, that reconstructing reaches its height.

Phase 3: Working-Through

From a self-trust perspective, working-through refers to those elements of the treatment process involving responses to failed tests of therapeutic trustworthiness. We have seen that patients are likely to construe as failed tests of trustworthiness those disruptions of the therapeutic relationship resulting from what they experience as failures in their therapists' empathic responsiveness. It is at these moments that the threat of retraumatizing betrayal looms most menacingly. Stolorow (1994) cogently described the therapeutic task in the aftermath of failed tests of trustworthiness that have disrupted selfobject connectedness between patient and therapist:

> the analyst investigates and interprets the various elements of the rupture from the perspective of the patient's subjective frame of reference — the qualities or activities of the analyst that produced the disruption, its specific meaning, its impact on the analytic bond and on the patient's self-experience, *the early developmental traumata it replicates* [italics added], and especially important, the patient's expectations and fears of how the analyst will respond to the articulation of the painful feelings that follow in its wake. (p. 51)

Since from a self-trust perspective "the early developmental traumata" to which Stolorow refers are past betrayals of self-trust, the result of the process he describes is the alleviation of fears of retraumatizing betrayal in the therapeutic relationship. When therapists nondefensively acknowledge their "errors in empathy," and thereby take responsibility for the threatened betrayals, their trustworthiness is demonstrated directly and persuasively. With their trust in the selfobject relatedness between themselves and in their therapists confirmed, patients are likely to experience a surge of well-being. As the need for dissociative diminutions and intensifications of self-trust lessens, experiences of self and others gain clarity and sharpness. Little by little, they are enabled to integrate memory, meaning, and affect and to regain a sense of wholeness and self-worth.

THE RESCRIPTING OF TRAUMA SCENARIOS WITHIN THE THERAPEUTIC RELATIONSHIP

Tests of self-trust tend to occur within the therapeutic dialogue among patients who have experienced few significant betrayals of self-trust in the course of development and for whom criteria for self-trust are relatively realistic, abstract, complex, and differentiated. Because these patients rarely experience the terror of disintegration anxiety, they are apt to call attention to failed tests of therapeutic trustworthiness when they occur by spontaneously expressing strong negative feelings, including shame and rage. They can well afford to protest loudly and strenuously.

The situation is quite different for patients who have suffered severe and/

or frequent betrayals of self-trust and whose criteria for self-trust remain relatively unrealistic, concrete, simple, and undifferentiated. Because the danger to self-preservation posed by threatened betrayals is so great, they may not express their distress directly and verbally. Instead, when faced with retraumatizing betrayals they are likely to attempt to confirm dissociatively intensified self-trust dimensions through behaviorally enacted rescriptings of past trauma scenarios. Moreover, these rescriptings of trauma often take the form of sadomasochistic enactments (see Chapter 4). When therapists fail tests of trustworthiness and are unable to recognize and acknowledge their failures, sadomasochistic rescriptings of past trauma scenarios are likely to be enacted both outside and within the therapeutic relationship.[4]

Sadomasochistic rescriptings of trauma scenarios may occur at any point in a therapeutic relationship. A good example of an attempt at such rescripting occurred early in my treatment of Jill, a young woman whose mother died while she was away at college. Several months into the treatment her attendance became erratic. Within a few hours of failing to appear for a scheduled appointment, she would phone me to say that although she had intended to come, something had prevented her from doing so. As time went by and Jill missed more appointments than she kept, I all but gave up on my hope of keeping her as a patient. Needless to say, my trust in her to provide validating selfobject experiences for me plummeted.

With time, encouraged by my realization that Jill had no intention of abandoning treatment, I discovered the meaning of her behavior. I learned that all during Jill's childhood, her mother had resisted her efforts at self-differentiation with guilt-inducing complaints. Jill, I surmised, had grown up with the unconscious belief that her mother's survival depended on her supportive presence. The self-trust dilemma she confronted in the therapeutic relationship, therefore, seemed insoluble to her. Much as she longed to experience me as a trustworthy provider of her selfobject needs, she feared that I, like her mother, required her presence for my psychological well-being. Worse still, she dreaded a retraumatizing catastrophe if she failed to meet my presumed need for physical closeness.

In the session just prior to the onset of Jill's absences, I suggested that she increase the number of sessions from two to three a week, believing she

---

[4]Ornstein (1991) also related the emergence of sadomasochistic or "self-defeating" behaviors in treatment to childhood traumas. She viewed them as "transference symptoms" in which "archaic defense organizations" and "newly developing psychic structures" find a compromise solution.

would benefit from the greater frequency. Unfortunately I inadvertently intensified Jill's dilemma: Like her mother, I seemed to Jill to want more contact than she herself thought necessary. This violated one of her criteria for trust-in-others, namely, that the other person respect her wish for distance and privacy. She construed my suggestion of more frequent sessions as a failed test of trustworthiness. She feared that once again she would be forced to relinquish her efforts at differentiation (e.g., setting the number of sessions that suited her needs) to avoid a traumatic loss.

By skipping sessions, Jill attempted to rescript the original trauma of her mother's death through enactments that had masochistic as well as sadistic elements. Although she (masochistically) deprived herself of contact with me, she now controlled the situation: She would not be left by the woman she needed. Turning the tables, it was she who (sadistically) "died" for me by not showing up. Jill's phone calls following her absences were necessary to determine if I had survived without her, another test. It was not until I conveyed my understanding of the meaning of Jill's tests, and her efforts to rescript the trauma of her mother's death, that she was enabled to keep all of our scheduled appointments.

Both of the treatment cases presented in the next chapter provide additional illustrations of attempts to rescript trauma scenarios by means of sadomasochistic enactments within the therapeutic relationship.

Chapter 7

THE TREATMENT OF SELF-TRUST

BETRAYAL: TWO CASE STUDIES

The psychotherapy of . . . a patient usually involves a prolonged process of drawing near to and then taking flight from the therapist, over and over again, while slowly and secretly the capacity to "trust" is growing.

Harry Guntrip (1969)

I have argued that traumatizing betrayals of self-trust are elements of all disorders of self-experience. In the lives of the two patients whose treatment I now describe, self-trust betrayals occurred early and repeatedly. Their therapeutic relationships with me reflect the profound alterations that occurred in both realms of their self-experience (in their selfobject fantasies and in their experience of subjective reality) as well as their courageous efforts at self-restitution. Although it is clearly impossible to fully present the rich complexity of my ten-year treatment of Ruth and my eight-year treatment of Mark, I have attempted to give the flavor of treatment conducted in accordance with a self-trust perspective.

RUTH

Looking back, I realize it was not so much the unexpected candor of Ruth's pressured revelations about herself during our first meeting that left such an indelible impression on me; it was her remarkable appearance. Although slim and attractive at 42, she had obviously attempted to camouflage the inevitable effects of time in ways that seemed to me touchingly misdirected. Her faded jeans, fringed shirt, and sandals—tribute, I imagined, to a "hippie" youth in the 1960s—contrasted incongruously with her mature features and body. At least four strands of beads hung from her neck and many hoops of silver studded with turquoise or onyx circled her wrists, fingers, and multiply pierced earlobes. I wondered if she had worn this astonishing collection of jewelry in the hope of so bedazzling would-be admirers they would overlook her pronounced limp, the aftermath, she explained with elaborate nonchalance, of childhood polio contracted when she was three. Her dramatically made-up Cleopatra eyes remained fixed on mine in what I felt was an imploring gaze—except when the smoke of an ever-present cigarette caused her to squint.

The jangling effect of the poignant and the brash in Ruth's appearance was echoed in two rapidly alternating, at times almost simultaneous, personas. One moment she was a tough, eternally young proponent of a sex, drugs, and rock 'n roll morality, a gritty survivor; the next, she was a frail, anxiety-ridden, aging woman who barely made it through her day, a helpless victim.

In that first meeting and for many months afterward, Ruth made no attempt to connect her handicap with the distress that had prompted her to seek my help. In fact, she presented her life as if it were no more than a bewildering series of inexplicable catastrophes. Glossing her past, Ruth maintained a detached, ironic tone as she mentioned having endured a childhood marred by numerous unsuccessful operations on her polio-damaged legs, a miserable adolescence filled with heartbreaking rejections, a doomed marriage, a postpartum depression, and devastating disappointments in her relationships with men. She spent the largest part of the consultation detailing the events in her current life that had propelled her into my office.

Mostly she wanted to talk about Russ, her latest boyfriend. A "hunk" she called him, much younger than she, with muscles, curly hair, and a leather jacket. Ruth admitted that he drank and drugged to excess and that he often mistreated her. He was critical and ill-tempered much of the time and he demanded that she perform sexually in ways she found degrading. Still, sex with Russ was what she lived for. He made her feel young, glamorous, and, above all, undamaged. Her expression was soft as she reminisced about their early days together but turned abruptly stiff as she confessed her suspicion that he had been seeing another woman. I now understood why her request for an immediate appointment with me had been charged with urgency. Life without Russ would be unrelievedly bleak, not worth living she said. How could she face his rejection alone? She worried about going to pieces.

Ruth's openness in describing her sex life and her drug use that day—far too open considering we had just met—had a reckless, devil-may-care quality. I wondered how to respond, worrying, on the one hand, that I might humiliate her and discourage future openness if I questioned the wisdom of her seemingly uncensored revelations, and, on the other, concerned that she might feel unsafe with me if I remained silent. "You seem to be in a hurry to let me know you," I finally said. "You must be in a lot of pain right now." Although she said nothing, the tears that sprang to her eyes informed me of her relief at being understood.

Ruth seemed surprised when I identified as aspects of posttraumatic stress disorder the psychological symptoms she accepted as a way of life—recurring nightmares filled with images of mentally or physically defective children, rapes, and medical tortures, reliving experiences, intrusive thoughts, feelings of estrangement from others, and, worst of all, a pervasive, haunting anxiety. She spoke of waking each day to face "a black void," a feeling of unspeakable aloneness. Only marijuana, cocaine, codeine, and what she called "V and V" (vodka and valium) eased her terror.

When I let her know the session was over, she seemed to have difficulty collecting herself. She thanked me profusely and said she felt better than she had in some time. We quickly made arrangements to meet twice-weekly. She also agreed to consult a psychiatrist so that her addictive use of tranquilizers could be monitored. I was intrigued by the complexities of her self-presentation and exhilarated by her unambivalent confidence in me. Her reckless, overly trusting manner struck a responsive chord in me. Although I attempted to bear in mind my own tendency to place inordinate trust in patients (a reflection of my intensified trust-in-others), I only barely managed to tone down my excitement.

When, years later, I asked if I could describe her treatment in this book, she presented me with the small clothbound journal she sometimes brought to sessions. Among random thoughts, dreams, and reactions to other people were jotted messages to me. With Ruth's permission, I include excerpts from this journal as counterpoint to my own description of events. The following note, which appears soon after our initial meeting, captures the powerful immediacy of her writing.

I went to the bathroom and looked in the mirror and asked God to please let the psychiatry work so I wouldn't feel like shit anymore and I'd be okay alone, and on top of it. I mean happy. I only write in here when I'm freaked or crying or both.[1]

---

[1] Italics added to indicate Ruth's writing.

As Ruth's entry makes clear, she sought my help to solidify her self-experience as the survivor. She hoped I would support her efforts to eradicate the needy, vulnerable, excruciatingly painful aspects of herself in order to achieve self-sufficiency. What I discovered only after reading her journal was that it recorded the voice of her victim self.

Phase 1: Testing

When Ruth returned for her next session she seemed more relaxed. Yet a trace of sheepishness in her expression led me to ask how she felt after revealing so much about herself. Her denial of any misgivings rang with bravado: "I figure, what did I have to lose—you weren't going to report me to the vice squad!"

Over the course of the next several months, I managed to piece together a more complete picture of Ruth's trauma-filled background. The repeated hospitalizations she endured during her childhood and adolescence entailed wrenching separations from her parents and humiliating surrenders of bodily control to doctors and nurses, many of whom treated her modesty and fear with brutal insensitivity. Her physical pain during recuperation periods was amplified by crushing disappointment as the failure of each new operation became apparent. In her survivor persona she railed against those who mistreated her; in her victim persona, her contempt and loathing were clearly directed toward her own body.

Ruth made a point of informing me that her early years were not without many happy memories. She managed to compensate for her inability to participate in active play by capitalizing on her wit and imagination. The repertoire of fantasy games she invented for the neighborhood children won her a measure of popularity. "I even remember two girls fighting over the honor of being my 'best friend'," she boasted. Adolescence was quite another story. Being "different," she discovered, was no longer a social advantage. Most painful for Ruth was feeling that she was unattractive to boys. At one particularly distressing party, she was approached by "the cutest boy" there. All went well, she recalled, while they remained seated. As soon as they stood up to dance and her limp became apparent, the young man disappeared.

Despite many absences from school, Ruth was a superb student. She majored in education at college to prepare herself for a career as a teacher of disadvantaged children. While an undergraduate, she met her husband, Daniel, a graduate student in history. Given her penchant for clothing reminiscent of the era, I was hardly surprised when she spoke nostalgically of the 1960s and the joys of being cocooned in her marriage and a circle of talented, intelligent, unconventional friends. This brief interlude of drug-saturated contentment in Ruth's life was shattered by Daniel's announcement when she was seven months pregnant that he was homosexual. After the birth of a son she suffered a postpartum depression so severe she required treatment with psychotropic medication. Several years later Daniel moved to his own apartment. According to Ruth, the sense of irrecoverable loss she experienced after they could no longer keep up the pretense of married life was compounded by the defections, one after another, of members of their social group. A period of driven promiscuity followed during which Ruth lived through numerous nightmarish episodes including a brutal rape by a man she picked up in a bar.

Ruth's detached "survivor" posture dissolved completely only when she spoke about how hard her illness had been on her mother. Then tears trickled down her cheeks and she looked hunched and small in her chair. "Taking care of a sick kid was too much for the 'prima donna'," Ruth said in a feeble effort to sound sardonic. She observed that having once led the glamorous life of an actress, her mother found caring for a desperately ill child impossibly tedious. "Oh, she slaved for me," Ruth said, recalling the countless hot compresses her mother had applied to her legs, the grueling visits to doctors and physical therapists, and the anxious moments spent in hospital waiting rooms. "But she never lets me forget it. Nothing I do is ever enough to make up for her sacrifices. She'd take the prize for best guilt producer of the century."

To make matters worse, according to Ruth, her mother had not received much help from her father, a self-taught intellectual who worked long hours in a factory. He never visited Ruth in the hospital, nor spent much time at her bedside. Ruth's voice sounded hushed and reverent as she explained that he loved her so much, he couldn't bear to see her in pain. I suspected that Ruth had a great deal at stake in convincing herself of the truth of this assertion. She smiled lovingly as she described the many ways in which her father attempted to promote her recovery. He built an apparatus that helped her to walk and special supports for the pedals of her bicycle that enabled her to ride with her friends. He strongly and consistently encouraged her to feel that she could transcend the limitations of her illness and have a normal life. Moreover, he heartily applauded Ruth's intelligence and engaged her in spirited discussions about literature, history, and current events. His evident pride in her intellectual ability contrasted sharply with her mother's indifference.

Over the course of her first year in treatment I sensed a deepening of Ruth's connection to me. She reported feeling less depressed and anxious, and her wonderfully ironic sense of humor surfaced often in sessions. For example, when I mentioned her initial efforts to minimize the effects of polio on her life, she joked, "I guess you could call me a closet cripple." She seemed to enjoy the subtle changes she observed in the way she acted with Russ, changes I attributed to a strengthening of our relationship. She confided that she now resented having to spend what seemed like hours performing oral sex when his drug use interfered with his ability to reach climax. She also reported refusing, for the first time, to comply with particularly objectional demands he made during sex.

She related the following dream fragment during this period:

> My face hurts, like I have a spectacular "zit." I squeeze it. A diamond or maybe just a shiny piece of glass comes out.

Asked what she made of the dream, Ruth shrugged and said, "You tell me. I'm not very good at figuring myself out." I suggested that we understand the dream as representing both her aching need to reveal her inner beauty and her doubts about her worth. Perhaps therapy provided an opportunity for self-disclosure that would permit her to gain a firmer sense of self. She seemed pleased with my interpretation. Looking back on this dream, however, I realize that I had not fully appreciated the significance of the diamond versus glass image. Diamonds are hard and invulnerable, the stuff of survivors, whereas glass, like Ruth's victim self, is vulnerable to shattering. With this dream Ruth had entrusted to me one of the central problems in her life: her failure to integrate two widely discrepant and alternating experiences of self.

Early in the second year, I decided to mention my objection to Ruth's chain-smoking during sessions. Although, from the start, I would have preferred that she not smoke in my office, I thought it best to tolerate it for a time. Given the strength of her addiction, I was reluctant to confront her with a request she might find too difficult to meet before our relationship proved sufficiently resilient. Finally, spurred by complaints by other patients about the cigarette smell in my office, I asked if she felt she could postpone smoking until after our sessions. Without saying a word, Ruth put her cigarettes away. I thought she made a special point of mentioning how helpful therapy had already been. By the end of the session I noticed an appreciable dip in her vitality. She spoke dejectedly of her loneliness and her worries about the future. "I want to be able to feel fine by myself," she said defiantly and then added ruefully, "but I don't."

> *Repercussions of the smoking thing—very angry, anxious. I put a lid on it. I've done everything not to write this, i.e., a valium 5. At first I thought it was restrictive, but I*

*think it goes deeper. Non smokers are so self-righteous, judgmental, joggers, yuppies –
it separates me from them. Makes you further away from me. In a way its rejecting
something basic to who I am. This issue makes me feel in some way abandoned (not
supported by you). I never would have gone to a shrink who said I couldn't smoke.
Shrinks should expect neurotics to have bad habits.*

A few moments into our next session Ruth pulled out a cigarette, caught
herself, and blurted, "I don't know if this is going to work. I'm not sure I can
go without a smoke for 45 whole minutes." Ruth's tone left no doubt that
she was irritated with me although she immediately launched into an account
of a recent phone conversation with Russ. When I interrupted to comment
on what I assumed were her unverbalized feeling, she looked astonished.
After a few halfhearted denials of her anger and feeble assurances that my
request was understandable, she stopped herself. She *was* "pissed." Nicotine,
she said, was her favorite drug. Nothing could stop her from smoking. Sounding close to tears, she added, "I hate that you don't want me to smoke in your
office – like you would never have anything to do with such a disgusting
habit."

As tears spilled down her cheeks, I acknowledged having disrupted her
experience of feeling understood and appreciated by me, feelings that I assumed reflected selfobject fantasies in which I was represented as providing
mirroring and twin selfobject experiences for her. "I'm afraid I really insulted
you," I said. "It must have been a shock to hear that I can't accept your
smoking when it's so much a part of your style. And to hear it just when
you've begun to count on me as someone who appreciates and respects you
as you are, someone enough like you to understand what smoking means to
you." Ruth nodded her agreement.

By complaining about her smoking, I had unintentionally communicated
my reluctance to support what was for Ruth as essential an ingredient of her
survivor persona as the rose she had audaciously tattooed on her breast.
Chain-smoking reflected one stringent criterion for trust-in-self: that she demonstrate toughness overriding such conventional concerns as vulnerability to
lung cancer or heart disease. I promised not to try to cure her nicotine
addiction but insisted that she reduce her smoking in my office. After a few
moments Ruth looked at me warmly and laughed. Calling me "a tough lady,"
she agreed not to smoke during sessions. I vaguely realized I had passed an
important test, but its meaning eluded me.

Soon I noticed a marked change in the way Ruth addressed me. Almost
every other sentence was a question. What did I think? Was she doing the

right thing? Was this the way to manage this person or that situation? Initially, I tried to understand this development in self-psychological terms as indicating that Ruth had begun to represent me in her selfobject fantasies as an omniscient, idealized parental figure. But the urgency I detected in her plea for answers told me that something more was at stake for her. Moreover, her customary bravado had all but disappeared. She seemed to have lost her confidence in her own ability to make decisions, even to think logically.

I decided to resist the temptation to answer her questions directly until I better understood the change in her and instead encouraged her to think through her decisions in my presence. Unfortunately, I ignored the bleak look I sometimes noticed in her eyes after she had produced an answer to one of her own questions. Was it sadness, resignation, despair, or maybe, a combination of all three?

> *The initial relief at doing something about myself (being in therapy) started to wear off—probably some time yesterday. Am getting depressed again. Don't know what to do. Can't even balance check book. I'm so lonely. Feel like I can't make decisions. Who to call. What to do. Where is my will—what is it. I was looking at myself—felt fat and dumpy. I'm crying.*

> *Mixed feelings about coming. I don't feel better. I don't know if coming is helping me anymore, but I feel like it's my lifeline or hope.*

Her bid for guidance seemed particularly urgent after she received an invitation to a party planned by a friend of hers. A single man had also been invited and she wondered if I thought the pleasure she stood to gain from a "conquest" outweighed the danger of feeling "done in" if he rebuffed her. "Tell me if I should go or not," she pleaded. "I don't know what to do." I commented that her obvious desire to have an experience that would demonstrate her desirability to a man was balanced by her fear of a traumatizing rejection, but I offered no advice.

Even before Ruth took her seat for our next session it was evident to me that something was very wrong. Not having taken her usual pains to disguise her limp, she seemed to drag half her body like a dead weight. She sank heavily into her chair without speaking. For the first time, her eyes, dull and flat, avoided mine. When she finally spoke after an uneasy silence her voice was icy and reproachful. The party had been a disaster. The agonizing self-consciousness she experienced while waiting for the man to approach made her feel that she had reverted to adolescence. When he did strike up a conversation she was certain he noticed her embarrassing gratitude. Although he was attractive and polite, something about him, she could not recall exactly what, frightened her. At the end of the evening, he asked if he could drive her home. All misgivings forgotten, she agreed. Impulsively, she decided to invite him in for a drink, a prelude, as she well knew, to going to bed with him.

Ruth described feeling flattered and "turned on" by his obvious desire for her. Without warning, however, he became violent. He punched and bit her until she feared for her life. From Ruth's description of her reactions—she became paralyzed, frozen, as if she had stepped outside of her body to observe the scene—I realized that while undergoing this abuse, she had slipped into a dissociated state. When she awoke in the morning she was relieved to find him gone but dismayed by the marks and bruises that covered her body.

Ruth insisted that she was not upset about having been violently attacked. "It's not as if this was the first time," she said. It was Russ's reaction that had been devastating. When he visited the next night, she flaunted her infidelity by letting him see her bruises. She admitted thinking it "served him right" for talking about other women. But when he called her "tramp" and "slut" and said that she disgusted him, she became distraught. Despite her pleas, he stormed out of her house, threatening never to see her again. He would not return her phone messages.

Ruth's voice was dry and expressionless as she tried to convey the feelings of ugliness and emptiness that gripped her. With her arms wrapped around her chest and her head turned to one side, she seemed to shrink from contact with me. "What's the point of living?" she asked. "I'd jump off a bridge if I had the guts." Although she spoke of killing herself, I felt her words contained a message of unexpressed rage at me. Supposing that her painful experience had disrupted her selfobject fantasies, particularly those in which I was represented as a protective idealized maternal figure, I asked if she had been disappointed in my failure to protect her from this humiliating abuse and the painful blow of Russ's rejection. Ruth said nothing but shrugged as if to indicate the pointlessness of my question. "It would have been good if you had stopped me from going," she finally said, "but you didn't. I went. Now I feel like dying. I don't know what to do."

Although it was clear that I had failed her in some critical way, I felt that I was the one betrayed. My intensified trust-in-others and sense of myself as a trustworthy provider of selfobject experiences for others (self-as-trustworthy) was shaken by her dismissive rejection of my efforts to understand what had gone wrong. I fought the temptation to defend myself angrily. "Hey, lady," I wanted to protest, "I didn't do anything to hurt you. You were the one, after all, who decided to go to the party. It wasn't my poor judgment that landed you in bed with a maniac. I never told you to rub your unfaithfulness in your boyfriend's face."

He said he won't be my lover ever again. I don't know if I can live with that. I begged. The bruises on my body freaked him. I let the phone ring 50 times but he wouldn't answer. He can't stand that I let someone else abuse me. I had to go to that stupid party. For that he let me go. He has been central to every thought for the last few weeks. How can I go on without him. I can't even figure out if I want to live. Please, please help me. My mind is on a rollercoaster.

In session after session, Ruth agonized monotonously about losing Russ. Shunning makeup and jewelry as she withdrew into a sullen, depressed state, she looked old and tired. My anger at her for reversing her trusting, appreciative stance toward me disappeared as I grew increasingly concerned about her. Struggling to understand how I could repair the disruption in our relationship, I asked many questions. "I don't know, I don't know. I don't have a clue," she responded, sounding more and more despondent and disconnected.

Just when I feared the treatment had become hopelessly stalemated, Ruth reported the following dream:

I'm in bed with Russ and feel his body, but I don't hear him breathe. I wonder if he's dead. I feel myself shrivel up and I think I must look like a hag, old and disgusting. Then the scene shifts and I'm working in a home for strange, crazy kids. They're running wild and I can barely control them. A woman, maybe the mother of one of the children, shows up. She has a doorknob in her hand. Somehow I feel I must have it and I ask her for it. She says it's not hers to give. I feel angry and scared.

I suggested that we might understand the first scene in the dream as representing Ruth's fear that in losing Russ, she must abandon all hope of having her desirability as a woman affirmed. Without that affirmation, she experienced herself as repulsive to herself and others, much as she had as a lame adolescent. I suggested that the crazy kids might have represented the feelings of rage and shame threatening to overwhelm her, feelings she struggled to control.

Ruth agreed with my interpretations. The woman, she now thought, reminded her of me. I wondered silently about the possible phallic connotations of the doorknob. Was she experiencing me as a castrated and powerless mother? Suddenly Ruth said that on second thought what had seemed to be a doorknob was more like a light bulb. This made her think of comic book drawings in which a light bulb above a character's head indicates a bright idea. As Ruth spoke her eyes grew dreamy and she smiled gently. Asked what had come to mind, she said she was thinking of Dr. B, the psychiatrist who had treated her during her postpartum depression. Because she spoke with a Viennese accent, Ruth thought of her as "Madame Freud." "She was full of good ideas, and very sure of herself." Ruth then added pointedly, "She was willing to tell me what to do." Her advice had proved invaluable. In addition to prescribing the correct antidepressant medication, she had known just when Ruth was ready to pick up the pieces of her life. "When she announced, 'You must go back to vork'," Ruth said, imitating her accent, "I found a part-time job and that was the end of my depression." Unfortunately, Dr. B subsequently presented Ruth with an ultimatum—unless she gave up her use of alcohol and drugs, Dr. B would not continue treating her. Feeling terribly abandoned and misunderstood, Ruth left therapy abruptly.

"Dr. B," she noted, "was the wise mother I never had." A wistful note crept into her voice as she observed, "My mom never said anything helpful to me in my entire life." She wondered why no one else in her family regarded her mother as she did: "as a kind of sad joke." They were all taken in by her pretentious mannerisms, her haughty tone of voice, and her penchant for high-flown phrases. They had not seen how helpless her mother had looked when, as a child, Ruth turned to her for advice on how to deal with her handicap. She had thrown up her hands in bewildered resignation at Ruth's pleas for guidance.

"The prima donna thing was probably an act," Ruth said thoughtfully, "underneath she must have been awfully insecure. She didn't know how to get the things she wanted most—a glamorous career, a successful husband, a healthy child—so how could she advise me?" I noticed that for the first time Ruth seemed willing to speculate about psychological meanings as she attempted to make sense of her relationship with her mother. Was it her mother's lack of self-confidence that led her to live in a fantasy world, she wondered? She recalled her mother's willingness to believe that at any moment she might be offered a starring role in a Broadway show, and that the next operation cautiously advised by Ruth's doctors might be the miracle cure. Was that why her mother had never prepared her for painful and humiliating medical procedures? "I guess she just couldn't deal with the reality of anything ugly or difficult." Ruth said. She remembered that after these harrowing ordeals were over, he mother would attempt to minimize her distress. "Really Ruth," she would say, "It wasn't that bad."

Ruth also spoke about feeling ashamed when the results of an operation proved far from miraculous. Her mother, unwilling to give up on her hopes, would suggest that Ruth's recovery might have been more complete if only she had been conscientious about doing the recommended exercises. "I always felt the limp was my fault," she sighed, "proof that I didn't try hard enough for my mother." I realized that Ruth's mother's responses interfered with Ruth's experience of herself as a trustworthy provider for the selfobject needs of others.

Ruth also wondered if it was her mother's insecurity that led her to fawn over people she considered successful. When, for example, a famous European pianist and his wife lived as boarders in their home, Ruth remembered that her mother treated them "like royalty." "She really fell all over herself to serve them. It made me sick," Ruth said. Then she closed her eyes as if to shut out an unwelcome sight. She remembered an event that she placed around the age of 11 because "I was just developing breasts and felt so proud of the way they poked out my undershirt." One summer afternoon, Ruth, dressed only in an undershirt and shorts, had been left alone with the pianist while her mother and his wife were out shopping. Ruth had obediently complied with his request that she sit on his lap. She explained, "I was used to doing anything he asked because that's what my mother did." When he fondled her breasts, Ruth felt confused and upset. She pushed away from him and locked herself in her room where she remained in tears until her mother came home. Recalling the anger she saw in her mother's eyes when she told her about the molestation, Ruth said, "She looked as if I had deliberately decided to wreck her wonderful relationship with 'the celebrities'." Instead of informing Ruth's father and insisting that the boarders leave, she urged Ruth to keep quiet about the episode until she decided on "the best thing to do." After months of waiting in vain for her mother to act, Ruth managed to "forget" it ever happened.

Ruth noted that despite irrefutable evidence that her mother could not or would not provide useful guidance, she continually prevailed upon her to do so. At times she presented herself as more confused and helpless than she actually felt in the hope of coaxing her mother to come through for her. She had, after all, known what to do when Ruth was at her neediest as a sick child. Early in her relationship with Daniel, Ruth asked her mother about signs indicating to her that he might be homosexual. She mentioned his limitations as a lover and his somewhat effeminate mannerisms. Her mother simply shrugged and repeated that he was a wonderful "catch." "I guess she worried that she'd never get her gimpy daughter off her hands," Ruth said.

I suggested that her mother's failure to provide confident guidance had understandably led Ruth to long for this missed experience. Without a connection to a self-trusting maternal figure she felt terribly alone and endangered, compelled to intensify her neediness in the hope of extracting the response she needed. Finally understanding what had disrupted Ruth's trusting connection to me, I added, "You wanted to believe that I, like your old psychiatrist, am a wise, secure woman who knows how to take care of herself—and you. When I refused to give you advice, I must have seemed no more self-trusting than your mother."

Phase 2: Reconstructing

It was now possible for me to begin to reconstruct the meaning of Ruth's traumatizing childhood betrayals and the ways in which she had dissociatively altered reality in their aftermath. Her mother's failure to offer guidance born of confident wisdom, a betrayal of others-as-self-trusting, had led to the most devastating experiences in Ruth's life. Her mother had not prepared Ruth for painful medical procedures, nor advocated on her behalf with hospital staff; she had not helped her withstand her disappointment over failed operations; she had not warned her about the pianist's lechery, let alone validate her reality of having been sexually abused; and she had not confirmed Ruth's intuition that her future husband was homosexual. Unable to experience her mother as self-trusting, Ruth repudiated her own competence in the hope that others would be forced by her neediness to assume a protective, guiding role.

By prohibiting her from smoking in my office, I apparently stirred Ruth's hope that she had found in me the confident, self-trusting maternal figure she longed for. Hoping to confirm this perception, she fully embraced her victim persona. Experiencing herself as indecisive and incompetent, she sought contact with me as an alter ego selfobject, the embodiment of the confident, diamond-tough aspects of her survivor self she now disavowed. Undeterred by my refusals to give her advice, she intensified her efforts by experiencing herself as less and less able to manage her life without my help.

Ruth experienced her abuse by the man she met at the party and Russ's subsequent rejection as a dreaded repetition of earlier traumas. Once again she had been hurt as a result of a woman's failure to offer self-confident advice. Disappointed in me as an alter ego selfobject, Ruth attempted to reestablish her connection to Russ through a sadomasochistic enactment whose meanings reflected her dual self-experience. On the one hand, assuming the posture of the sadistic betrayer, she hoped to turn the tables on Russ by flaunting the fact that it was she who had been unfaithful. On the other hand, by masochistically showing herself as the betrayed (hurt by the man's violence), she had hoped to elicit Russ's compassion and caring. Ruth acknowledged that "deep down" she had known Russ would "freak" when he saw evidence that she had replaced him with another man. "I just couldn't think straight," Ruth said. "All I knew was that I desperately needed him to say he loved me and wanted me and that he still found me beautiful."

Heartened by phone calls from Russ, Ruth's mood brightened over the next several weeks. Despite his admission that he had begun to see another woman, Ruth imagined she would soon win him back. The change in her mood was accompanied by another dramatic change in the way she related to me; now she maintained a pose of wary toughness which intensified with every setback in her efforts to regain her exclusive position in Russ's life. Although she again seemed to experience me as an alter ego selfobject, I no longer embodied the strength and wisdom of her repudiated survivor self. Rather I seemed to personify the weakness and uncertainty associated with her victim self. She complained that I lacked the "know-how" to help her overcome her longings for Russ; if anything they were more intense than ever. She said she needed me less as a therapist than as a friend who might join her for afternoons of movies and shopping. I was somewhat taken aback by this dramatic shift in her stance toward me, but my newfound understanding of the disruption between us helped me to appreciate the depth of her need for selfobject connectedness with me. Since I had failed to measure up as a protective guide for her victim self, she hoped to connect with me by assuming the posture of tough survivor. Her journal entries during this period convey the doubts, fears, and yearnings she now kept out of our sessions.

> *Can't wait to see you. Feel like there are too many things to talk about. Anxiety. Russ. I know I'm putting the rest of my life on hold. An incredible night of lovemaking. I still am a turn on. It worries me that my mood is so dependent on this. I'm too vulnerable. Is this a set back or can I get on with my life. Am I out of depression or is this more masking? Keep thinking about asking him to move in. I think I really love him. I want him to love me over all else. It is too crazy. Am I doing something really bad to myself?*

Responding to fears she expressed, albeit in a rather offhand way, that she would once more cave in to Russ's demeaning sexual demands in a desperate bid for his love, I suggested that her intensified need for Russ reflected my

having failed her as a wise, protective maternal figure. In her next session she
reported the following dream:

> We come to the end of a session. You put on your coat to leave. We go out
> together. There's a tiny white sandal on the steps. You pick it up. It belongs to
> someone in your family.

Ruth wept when I interpreted the dream as reflecting her wish that she might
be able to rely on me once again as the strong, guiding mother she needed. If
only I would tenderly enfold her child-like vulnerability (the tiny sandal) in
my protective embrace, she might feel like the precious, beautiful little girl
she had been before her illness.

For brief moments after this, Ruth revealed herself to me as needy and
frightened. However, she reported Russ's escalating abusiveness with cool
detachment. Then in one session she calmly reported that he had kept a
loaded gun on the pillow beside them as they had sex and had even pointed
it at her several times. I expressed concern over her indifference to this terribly
dangerous situation. "I think you need me to tell you that you must protect
yourself even if it costs you the relationship," I said. Ruth admitted that
although she never felt he would pull the trigger, she had been terrified. She
said she was grateful that I was forceful in confronting her with Russ's sadism.

> *I feel like you are helping me get it over with by the judgement you made re R. A
> small chain of no's (I said no last night). I am so sad and angry. Seeing the end for
> me and Russ and seeing nothing and no one. I feel suicidal. I feel so unloved and
> unprotected.*

Despite Ruth's fears that without Russ she would be unloved and unpro-
tected, my intervention clearly helped to restore her trust in me as a self-
confident maternal figure. Within a week, Ruth tearfully informed me that
she had ended her relationship with Russ. Although she seemed to find
comfort in our sessions, she complained that when she was away from me
she felt frightened, inconsolable. She reluctantly refused my suggestion that
she come to therapy three times a week, explaining that the extra session
would overtax her already strained finances. I suggested that we might speak
on the telephone between sessions. Noting that she had tried to call me the
previous weekend but had hung up on hearing the message on my answering
machine, she said, "When I feel desperate it seems worse when I get your
machine. Then I know I can't speak to you right away. I get more anxious

knowing that I'll have to sit and wait until you call me back." I suggested the possibility of my calling her. "You means you're allowed to do that?" Ruth responded. "Doesn't that violate some kind of shrink code?"

We arranged that I would call on Saturday mornings. These telephone chats were very brief but seemed to make a big difference. Looking back, I realize that they demonstrated my willingness to make myself available to Ruth without making her feel either reduced to shameful neediness or forced to adopt a posture of tough invulnerability. The months that followed brought many positive changes for Ruth. She decided to enter a demanding graduate program to earn the credential that would allow her to apply for a more prestigious and better paying job. And she started dating a man she met at work. Although she compared him unfavorably to Russ, she was delighted by his interest in her.

Unfortunately, this period of relative serenity in Ruth's life ended abruptly. A beloved cat was killed by vicious dogs, her brief affair petered out, her apartment was burglarized, and worst of all, after getting a "dream job" and making new friends among the other employees, she was told that she would have to be transferred to a far less desirable location. At a time when the cumulative effect of all these events seemed the most devastating to Ruth, I planned to get married.

It seemed tactless to mention something wonderful in my life when things were so difficult in hers. My intensified need to experience myself as a trustworthy provider for the selfobject needs of others interfered with my clinical effectiveness. Ruth accepted my announcement of a two-week break in sessions with apparent equanimity. However, she snapped at me when I reminded her that she could see a colleague who covered my practice while I was away. "Sure, I'm just about to see a perfect stranger," she said sarcastically. "It would take me a month just to give him the background of my crazy life." On returning I found Ruth depressed, anxious, and very withdrawn. When I suggested that I had been away during a particularly bad time, she said that it probably would not have been any different if I had been around. "I don't know what I'm doing here anyway," she moaned. "I'm not getting any better. Besides, I hate your new look." She spent some time explaining why I looked unattractive with the changes in the style and color of my hair.

I am physically (emotionally??) exhausted. Had to lie down. Obsessed with thoughts of R (negative but obsessive). I hate being awake. Very frightened about everything. Everything takes incredible energy. I feel lonely and alone. I can't believe its going to get better. I am depressed, I think. This must be related to your hair.

Although I suspected that it was not my hairstyle but my shiny new wedding ring that Ruth objected to, I hesitated about calling it to her attention. Finally, near the end of a session in the second week after my return, I noticed that her gaze had fallen on my ring. "Congratulations," she said in a harsh, mocking way, "I'm very happy for you." Then dissolving in tears she said, "I think I knew you had gotten married, but I didn't want it to be true. I guess that made your ring invisible." Then she asked bitterly, "What does your getting married have to do with me anyway?"

When I reflected how hurt and angry she sounded, Ruth sat quietly for a long time before launching into a rageful tirade. "How could you do this to me?" she railed. "You weren't supposed to find a man to marry before I found one." Then, more sadly, she disclosed her fantasy that we would both get married again at the same time, after I had "cured" her. Then we would be friends. "What a laugh!" she exclaimed bitterly, "Married women don't have time for their single friends."

Ruth was not consoled by my acknowledgment that by getting married before she did I had disrupted a cherished fantasy of our alikeness. She left my office with angry tears streaming down her cheeks.

> I think the anger I feel towards you is dangerous to me, no great insight there. The degree seems unacceptable. You are becoming a non person in my life. Its not just a defense against being hurt when I terminate.

As Ruth and I explored her anger and pain in the next few sessions I discovered that even more devastating for her than the disruption I had caused in her selfobject fantasy of twinship with me was my failure to prepare her for a painful experience. By not informing her of my plans to marry, I, like her mother, proved myself incapable of helping her deal with harsh reality. At the same time, I had not shown respect for her strength and resilience as a survivor. She experienced my withholding news of my good fortune as overprotective, a humiliating vote of no confidence in her. Ruth was contemptuous and dismissive of my efforts to acknowledge that I had indeed disappointed her in all these ways. She mentioned reading several self-help books that "give better advice than you ever do" and hinted that she might quit therapy.

The dreams she reported during this period contained images of violence and rape. In one, a retarded woman is being raped. Ruth is both the woman being raped and the rapist. The rapist explains that he is raping the woman "to relieve the pressure." Ruth's associations to the dream confirmed my suspicion that the retarded woman combined both her experience of herself as a victim and her experience of me as a therapist whose strength and wisdom cannot be depended upon. Asked what she thought of the rapist's claim that he was relieving the pressure, Ruth remembered many medical procedures that were purportedly carried out to improve her condition but which merely felt like an excuse for the doctors' sadism. "It's like they have to hurt someone to feel good about themselves," she said. I responded by suggesting that she may have experienced my getting married as deliberately hurtful to her, a sadistic act that belied my supposedly therapeutic aims. Ruth acknowledged that she had been feeling compelled to remain in a hurtful therapeutic relationship with me much as she once felt compelled to remain with Russ.

Then she mentioned feeling haunted by an intrusive memory. As a teenager she often babysat for a beautiful little girl she both loved and envied. The child seemed to embody everything polio had taken from Ruth: beauty, grace, and health. On one occasion, although she knew the child was inordinately fearful of hot water, Ruth forced her into a steaming shower with her, ignoring her terrified screams. "It's like I was under some sort of compelling pressure to do it, but I hated myself," Ruth said.

I suggested that during her tormented adolescence she may have needed to experience herself as the one who inflicts pain instead of the one who was hurt and abused. Like the beautiful little girl, I seemed to have what she now lacked. Moreover, I was responsible for her pain. Ruth tearfully acknowledged a wish to hurt me as I had hurt her. She knew how important it was to me to feel effective in treating her and she was glad I was hurt by her complaints of my ineptitude. Suddenly smiling mischievously, she confessed to secretly hurtful acts at Russ's expense. "Maybe you'll think I'm hopelessly infantile," she said, "but sometimes I did things like spit on his toothbrush or throw his clothes on the floor. They're sort of dumb but they made me feel better."

It became clear that when my marriage threatened to disrupt her experience of selfobject connectedness to me, she experienced me as sadistic and hurtful, much as she had experienced others in her life who were needed as healers and protectors. By assuming the posture of the betrayer, she hoped to rescript her trauma scenarios and avert further retraumatizing betrayals at my hands.

Phase 3: Working-Through

For an extended period of time, Ruth appeared to consolidate gains in all aspects of her life. She seemed to find increased satisfaction in her work and to delight in several new friendships. However, immediately upon her father's death following a brief illness, her sense of well-being and optimism dissolved completely.

I feel like I've lost one of my best friends. I've lost someone who really loved me—he liked me too. I don't know who the hell I'm talking about.

In the session after her father's funeral, Ruth confessed that she felt no "real grief," but a great deal of confusion about her relationship with her father. She was clear only about the role he played in helping her to cultivate her mind. "It was great to share our intellectual worlds," she said. "He introduced me to Anatole France and I introduced him to Kurt Vonnegut. But I'm not sure if we meant anything else to each other."

To our mutual dismay, Ruth's depression deepened alarmingly. Concerned about her loss of appetite, her early-morning wakefulness, her drop in energy, and her inability to feel pleasure, I suggested that Ruth consult her psychopharmacologist. Unfortunately he prescribed new medication that not only deepened the symptoms of her depression but also left her highly agitated. It was several months before a different course of medication stabilized her condition. At about this time Ruth revealed that although she always used alcohol and drugs "recreationally," she had recently become so intoxicated at social gatherings friends were embarrassed and worried about her. Moreover, her drinking was becoming more habitual. I assured her that we would continue to address the meaning of her increased reliance on drugs and alcohol together. However, since her physical and psychological health appeared to be in jeopardy, I urged her to take steps to stop drinking and recommended that she join Alcoholics Anonymous (AA). Ruth rejected my suggestion contemptuously. She had accompanied a friend to some meetings of AA and found them repugnant. "I just can't get into that 'higher power' stuff and everything that goes with it," she complained, and added, "besides my chemical dependency is not really out of control."

I feel a lot better drunk and stoned. I get my pride back and my strength back. I drink Sambucca and feel like I have wisdom. Is cool what I am or should be? Can I pull off cool? Coke gives me power. I love it. I know I can't be sober and straight and happy again.

Ruth seemed detached and withdrawn in sessions over the next several months. She reestablished contact with Russ and confessed that their meetings centered almost exclusively around sharing drugs and alcohol. Our explorations of these alarming developments led us back to the disastrous effects of the antidepressant medication. Ruth admitted feeling a great loss of confidence in me and a longing to return to Dr. B. This competent psychiatrist, she felt certain, would have chosen the appropriate medication whereas I could not even write prescriptions. Ruth agreed with my interpretation that her loss of confidence in me had contributed to her intensified use of intoxicating substances and the resumption of her relationship with Russ. Since she could not rely on me in her neediness, she was thrown back to her familiar pose of self-sufficiency. She relied on alcohol, cocaine, and sex with Russ to help her feel like her old, brash survivor self.

Shortly thereafter, her mother became very ill. Ruth was surprised to discover that she felt genuine compassion for her suffering. She found herself deeply touched by her mother's gratitude for her frequent visits and the superb medical care she obtained. When her mother died, Ruth was pleased to be able to cry for her.

Following her mother's death, Ruth admitted that her alcohol dependence was no longer in her control and we explored possible treatment modalities to augment therapy. She recalled Dr. B's ultimatum that she end her substance abuse or leave treatment, and she feared that I would do the same. I suggested that perhaps she needed me to demonstrate my confidence and wisdom by giving her a similar ultimatum. Ignoring my comment, Ruth launched into a reminiscence of her relationship with her father. She decided it was not only her mind that he appreciated—he thought she was good looking, too. "Oh, he made it clear that my mother was even better looking, but I didn't mind that," she said. Then with an embarrassed smile, Ruth recalled an incident from her adolescence. Asked his opinion about a dress she planned to wear to a party, her father joked that Ruth resembled "a French whore." Ruth admitted that he made her feel "uncomfortable—like maybe that was how he wanted me to look."

At the outset of the next session, Ruth handed me slips of paper on which she had jotted down a dream. She mentioned having the dream, which she suspected "was important for our work," the night after attending a performance of the Broadway show *Tommy*.

I call it my incest dream because it starts with a man in an army uniform and red scarf who I know is my father (my father served in the army). He comes through a big movie set along a metal pipe or tunnel to me (I'm partly a little girl and partly Tommy). Then this really creative robot machine takes over and "machines" me to orgasm. Alfred Hitchcock appears. He and I (now grown up) walk down some stairs and knock on a friend's door. She's naked and tattooed. These horrible kids run up the stairs and I keep yelling at them because I feel out of control and helpless. A militant black woman screams that people like me shouldn't be allowed to work with kids. I yell back but I think she's right.

Ruth connected Tommy, "the deaf, dumb, and blind kid who turns out to be special," with her damaged, victim self and her longing to transcend her handicap. Her father, like Tommy's, had served in the army and had been curiously absent much of her childhood. Tommy had been profoundly altered by trauma and so had she. She felt that she too had been abused as a child, not only by the pianist but by the insensitive treatment to which she was subjected by doctors and nurses. "I think being 'machined' relates to medical devices, like iron lungs and such," she added. "I never had to be in an iron lung but it always scared me to think that I might need one. I guess there was something sexual for me in all those doctors pushing and poking their instruments into me. The touching and the pain were exciting and confusing to me at times. Maybe the constant mix of pain and pleasure is the reason Russ turns me on so much."

Asked about the image of Alfred Hitchcock, Ruth said she was a great fan of his. Her secret fantasy was to be a movie star, admired by all. She wanted to be Grace Kelly in a Hitchcock film—perfect, flawless, a classic beauty— just the opposite of the ugly, naked, tattooed girl who opens the door in the dream. I commented on the contrast between the flawless survivor and the defective victim. Ruth responded by wondering if Hitchcock was also a representation of her father: He would direct her to success in life only if she acted like the flawless survivor.

Ruth remarked that a friend of hers, a therapist, had mentioned that I treated many incest survivors. She was worried that the dream would convince me that her father had actually abused her sexually. She had no memories of any physical contact with her father that had been remotely sexual. I reminded her of her discomfort when he likened her to a French whore. "Yeah, but he wasn't turned on by me," she insisted, "it was more like he wanted me to turn other men on." Then she burst into tears. "I think he couldn't stand my being handicapped; he couldn't be successful in his life, so he needed a perfect daughter to make him feel good about himself. Maybe if I could turn men on, he didn't have to think of himself as the father of a cripple." She connected her driven promiscuity after the break-up of her marriage with her wish to be the "French whore" her father seemed to admire.

Ruth sadly wondered if her father's unwillingness to spend time at her bedside when she was a desperately ill child was due less to his inability to bear her pain than the pain of his own inadequacy which her suffering forced him to confront. He could tolerate contact with her only when she assumed the pose of survivor, who, with his help, would overcome her handicap. When she required his reassurance that he loved and accepted her with her disability, he distanced himself from her.

She then recalled having spent the summer she was 10 recuperating from a particularly complicated operation. Since her mother had accepted a part in a summer stock production, she looked forward to spending time alone with her father. She felt bitterly disappointed when he announced his intention to send her to the country home of a distant relative until her mother returned. He coldly ignored her pleas that she be allowed to stay with him. She would gladly have spent days alone in her familiar room if she could be with him in the evenings when he came home from work. "It turned out to be the worst summer of my life," she said. Her relative was an angry, withdrawn woman who left her alone in a bedroom most of the time. Her father did not respond to her letters imploring him to take her home.

I suggested that the robot in her dream may have represented the father who coldly abandoned her and the sexualization of her need for his affirmation and affection. As a child she could feel lovable, beautiful, and optimistic about finding future happiness only in his encouraging, hope-instilling presence. When he abandoned her to her mother's care, as he so often did, she could no longer feel like the brave survivor. Instead, she was forced to adopt the pose of a weak, helpless victim in the hope of extracting her mother's ministrations.

Ruth agreed that she must have experienced her father's death as a retraumatizing betrayal, the final abandonment by him. She associated the militant black woman in her dream with me, mentioning a suspicion that I wanted to conclude the treatment. She was certain that I felt tired of her neediness and her continued reliance on drugs and alcohol. Perhaps I believed that her alcoholism made her unfit to work with children. I realized that I had terrified Ruth by mentioning the possibility of terminating treatment unless she gave up alcohol. After the medication fiasco had disappointed her trust in me as a confident maternal figure, I now threatened to become a cold, sadistic, robot-like paternal one. The possibility of my issuing an ultimatum like Dr. B's threatened her with another retraumatizing betrayal. I, too, might abandon her when she most needed comforting and care.

The remainder of the working-through phase dealt mainly with traumatizing betrayals by her father and the ways in which I threatened to recreate them with the therapeutic relationship. Eventually, despite her fears of feeling "reduced to ordinariness," she relinquished her dependence on drugs and alcohol considerably. Moreover, she announced her intention of joining AA as soon as she returned from a much-anticipated trip abroad. She decided she would need continued support when therapy ended which we both anticipated was soon to follow. Unfortunately, she was stricken with a severe illness on the eve of her departure. Despite being forced to cancel her travel plans and spending many dreary weeks in bed, Ruth's spirits remained high. That she continued to rely on me (by means of frequent phone conversations) and availed herself of the substantial assistance provided by friends and relatives during her illness without losing sight of her own courage and strength indicates that her treatment is nearing a successful completion.

MARK

I seem to have anticipated Mark's wariness and discomfort even before he entered my office for his first appointment. Perhaps the sounds I heard in my waiting room—a muted cough, quick little scrapes as he hung up his coat, and a faint click as he ever so gently closed the closet door—the sounds of someone trying hard to be quiet, conveyed his mistrustfulness to me. Other patients seem to do little to mask the clatter of their arrival, and I am certain that some actually mean to announce their presence through the slamming of doors and the clearing of throats. I quickly learned that such behavior would have been unthinkable for Mark.

As I greeted him, I noticed that his regular, almost classically chiseled features seemed frozen, mask-like, and that he avoided eye contact. Short and somewhat overweight, he looked mature for 26. In my office, he chose the seat farthest from mine, Then, methodically, he laid his bookbag, newspaper, and umbrella one upon the other on the floor at his feet creating a small but unmistakable wall between us. I felt an urge to tell him not to be afraid of me, that I would keep my distance, but I said nothing. Mark explained that he had been referred by Dr. C, who, after treating him for six months, had agreed the therapy was "going nowhere." Then, without any prompting, he produced the best organized history any patient has ever offered me.

Speaking slowly and carefully, as if he feared punishment for each inaccuracy, Mark described a happy early childhood as the third born in a family of four children; he has two older brothers and a younger sister. When he was six, the storybook perfection of his world was shattered by the death of his beloved father. Mark thought of himself as his father's favorite, the child who resembled him most closely in looks and temperament. He had even shared his father's taste for special ethnic foods that other members of the family found unappealing. It had seemed natural for him to study medicine, his father's profession.

Matter of factly, without any inflection in his curiously flat, dry voice, Mark described how an uncle, who visited frequently during his father's year-long battle with cancer, sexually abused him. He recalled that the first time his uncle forced him to perform fellatio was the day of his father's funeral. I shuddered involuntarily when he described his repugnant association of the chalky taste of his father's forehead as he kissed him in his coffin with the taste of his uncle's penis. At the end of a year of frequent sexual contact his uncle suddenly vanished. It was not until many years later that, at the urging of a college counselor, he questioned his mother about his uncle's disappearance. She explained that she had banished him immediately upon discovering that he had molested one of Mark's older brothers.

Next, Mark cooly described his astonishing transformation after his uncle's disappearance, a transformation that no one in his family ever acknowledged. Once skinny, active, and fun-loving, he became an obese, lonely "Momma's boy" virtually overnight. Instead of playing with his siblings and their friends after school, Mark would rush home to help his mother with the shopping and other household chores. He lavished praise on his mother for carrying on bravely after his father died, using words like loving, hardworking, and "selfless." I asked why he hadn't told her about his uncle's abusiveness at the time it occurred. "She had her hands full enough," he replied, "I just couldn't add to her worries." Then, after a pause, he said quietly, "Maybe I worried that she would be angry and disgusted with me for going along with it."

"Disgusted?" I remember repeating. Mark said no one ever spoke about sex around his mother. She had not dated after his father died. Maybe sex was offensive to her. I was curious about his mother. Why hadn't she explained her brother's disappearance? Why hadn't she tried to find out if he had molested Mark? How could she have ignored Mark's sudden and drastic transformation? I would have liked to learn more about her but I could see that Mark had something urgent to say. Leaning forward in his chair and speaking in a voice so low and tense it was almost a whisper, Mark revealed his main reason for seeking psychotherapy. Since puberty he had been plagued by fantasies of having oral sex with men that were usually triggered by intrusive memories of fellatio with his uncle. "I hate having these thoughts, but I can't help myself," he confessed. He had not had sex with a man since his uncle left, and he had never had sexual contact with a woman. Although his fondest dream was getting married and having a family of his own, he feared he was homosexual.

Mark seemed no more enthusiastic in settling the details of twice-weekly treatment with me than if he were arranging to have his car serviced or his hair cut. Noting that he took pains to find hours that suited my schedule rather than choosing ones more convenient for him, and that he quickly indicated his willingness to pay my full fee, I wondered if he feared I would retaliate for any inconvenience or burden I incurred, or if he hoped to impress me with his considerateness. Despite his apathy at the prospect of beginning therapy, I felt enormously optimistic about my ability to help him. All the signs seemed positive: I found his predicament compelling, and I must admit to feeling challenged by his evident mistrust. He would soon "warm up," I thought, as my empathy melted his reserve.

I have come to recognize that intensified trust-in-others, the result of self-trust betrayals early in my life, predisposes me to regard new patients as highly likely to provide selfobject experiences confirming my therapeutic competence. Filled with enthusiasm and eager to take the plunge into what invariably strikes me as a grand adventure, I sometimes ignore initial signs that my trust is premature or ill-advised.

Phase 1: Testing

I could hardly have asked for a more cooperative patient. Scrupulously polite, Mark arrived punctually for each scheduled session. He filled the hours with rich recollections of his childhood, finely detailed accounts of his life as a medical student, vivid fantasies, and striking dreams. The following is the first dream he presented to me:

> I was with my sister, Lisa, at school. Together we went into the boys' bath-room and walked into different stalls. Then we both urinated standing up. Suddenly a man burst in. I knew he had an office upstairs and that he shouldn't be in the boys' room. He looked odd and scary—like he was dead. He asked me to accompany him to his office. I told him to get lost, but I think he persisted.

Mark immediately remarked that the man in the bathroom must represent his uncle. "He barged into a place where he didn't belong and he took advantage of me," he said. Responding to my inquiries about the man's appearance, Mark thought of the way his father looked in his coffin. He remembered a waking fantasy from his grade-school years of his father's suddenly appearing "like a religious apparition." He mentioned his chagrin at not being able to imagine what he would say to him. Interrupting himself, Mark said he hated talking about his father and his uncle "in the same breath." He spoke at length about the differences between the two men—how kind, caring, and fun-loving his father had been and what a despicable pervert his uncle was. "If my uncle hadn't abused me," he said mildly, although his voice quivered slightly, "my whole life would be different."

Mark wondered why, in his dream, he resisted the threatening man since in real life he had passively accepted his uncle's advances. "Its hard to admit, but I enjoyed being fondled and admired," he said. "I know my uncle made me feel special. He often complimented me on my body, especially for my beautiful 'can'." I commented on the confusing mix of feelings his uncle seemed to have engendered in him: Although he had obviously enjoyed feeling special to a man who served as a surrogate father, and had even welcomed the physical contact, he had also felt exploited and demeaned by him.

Speculating on his sister's significance in the dream, Mark mentioned that even as a child he had known it was up to him to protect her. He recalled babysitting for her when they were young, defending her against bullies, and taking her side in arguments. He had continually worried about her safety. Of all his siblings she was the one with whom he felt the closest. Now, instead of Lisa, he worried about the safety of his young nieces and nephews. At this point I only vaguely appreciated the significance of the dream in illuminating Mark's self-experience. As we shall see, its meaning gradually became clearer as we returned to it during the course of treatment.

Taking stock of our progress after the first six months of therapy, I was dismayed to find that while I could have filled volumes with the material Mark provided, the therapeutic relationship seemed completely devoid of vitality. As far as I could tell, Mark had not changed in the least; he was as remote and guarded with me as on the day we met. I, on the other hand, had lost my initial enthusiasm and sense of confidence. I felt increasingly dull, if not stupid, in his presence. Uncharacteristically, I found it difficult to recall the content of sessions from one visit to the next and had constructed only a few vague hypotheses about the ways his present experience reflected his traumatic past. I rarely remembered the hours of his session without checking my appointment book. I was also disconcerted by a nagging feeling that he was doing all the work. My few interventions seemed to land further and further from the mark and to lack any sense of emotional conviction. To make matters worse, Mark told me he had been distressed to find that his longing to have oral sex with men had increased and that memories of being with his uncle had never been so vivid or disturbing.

Looking back, I realize that when I was with Mark, I would slip into a mildly dissociated state as a result of changes in my self-experience. My inability to make a dent in Mark's mistrustful armor had been a blow to my sense of myself as a trustworthy provider for his selfobject needs. His failure to give even the smallest indication that therapy was of use to him diminished my trust in him, as well as my expectation of eliciting selfobject experiences from him. That is to say, I experienced diminutions in three self-trust dimensions: self-as-trustworthy, which for me is also highly intensified, trust-in-others, and trust-in self.

I suspected that Mark was at least as uncomfortable with me as I had become with him, but in my foggy state, I found it difficult to address the situation. Not surprisingly, he was the one to bring it up. It happened near the end of a session that had begun with his recounting events on the day of his father's death. He remembered that when his mother returned from the hospital, she had called Mark and his siblings into the house. The others had stopped their games and run to her but Mark refused to stop playing. She had needed to come after him and fairly pull him into the house. He recalled that at the funeral he was noisy and "rambunctious." "I acted as though all the relatives were gathered for a happy celebration," he remarked. I noticed that while he spoke of his lingering sense of guilt at adding to his mother's distress at such a difficult time, his voice retained its customary blandness.

Suddenly he interrupted his monologue by saying, "I'm so tense. I'm always tense here—not relaxed the way I used to feel with Doug, my college counselor." This, it seemed to me, was the first time Mark addressed me with anything resembling spontaneous emotion. While I suspected that his guilty recollection of his behavior around the time of his father's death might have led him to mention his discomfort with me, I could not grasp the connection.

Responding to my request that he tell me what it had been like to be with Doug, Mark mentioned that he was tall, strong-looking, and very calm. He felt "more together" in his presence. Doug had been the first person he told of his uncle's abusiveness. With much more animation than I had yet heard in his voice, Mark described the relief he experienced after recounting the details of his incestuous experiences. "I felt lighter, unburdened," he said. "Just the thought of seeing Doug would lift my spirits."

I could not help contrasting Mark's elation on seeing Doug with the dejection and heaviness he seemed to feel with me. Mark must have had the same thought as he mumbled his goodbye without even glancing in my direction. Afterward, I sat still for several minutes struggling to hold on to feelings I would rather have pushed aside. Like Dr. C, I was not helping him. Perhaps he needed to be in treatment with a man like Doug. Convinced that I had made some grievous errors in empathy, I searched my recollection of our sessions for clues to when and how they might have occurred, but found nothing.

Waiting for Mark to arrive for his next session, I braced myself for his announcement that he was leaving therapy. I hardly expected the excitement I heard in his voice as he reported the following dream:

> I came for a session, but you weren't here. A handsome Indian man dressed like a priest or minister led me into the office. On a table between us was a basket filled with small pieces of meat. I realized that we were going to take part in some sort of ceremony. The man placed a piece of meat into his mouth and indicated that I should take the other end into my mouth. We both started to eat. I got a strong sense of communion with him — very sensual and very intense.

Without being asked, Mark described the events of the day before the dream. He had left the session thinking about Doug, the college counselor. An Indian man on the bus, not handsome in the least, caught his eye. Although he looked dirty and a sickening smell of mingled sweat and spice had turned Mark's stomach, he felt quite aroused and thought of having oral sex with the man. Abruptly, he stopped talking and looked very distressed. "I know this is an important dream" he said, "but I don't know what to make of it."

"You seem to think it's your responsibility to interpret your own dreams." I said, "You work so hard, you don't give me a chance to help you." To my astonishment, Mark's eyes filled with tears. After a long pause, he said that he knew this was supposed to be my job, but he was used to taking care of himself. After providing several examples of his self-sufficiency, Mark, without seeming to notice, slipped into describing the many ways he took care of his mother. He revealed an exquisite sensitivity to changes in her mood and health. "I usually know when she's coming down with a cold before her first sneeze," he said.

I responded by suggesting that despite the pride he obviously felt in his self-reliance and in taking such good care of his mother he might also have hoped that someone might take care of him for once. Recalling that he had complained about feeling tense in our previous session after describing his guilt at distressing his mother, I wondered if his complaint had represented a test of our relationship. After reminding him that he had risked complaining to me, I said, "Maybe you've begun to feel, just a little, that it's all right to let me know about your needs, and that you don't have to take care of me by hiding your discomfort." In response, Mark smiled at me for the first time. I could see that he was pleased by our initial efforts to address his experience of our relationship.

Returning to his dream, Mark mentioned that the Indian man in his dream reminded him of Doug, his college counselor, and of the spiritual connection he felt to him. I told him I could see that he still missed Doug. Thinking of his grief over his father's death and the paucity of male companionship in his life, I added, "It must be disappointing to be with me, a woman, when you want so much to be close to a man." Mark agreed, adding that he had wanted to mention his longings for Doug, but had kept silent for fear "I would make you feel bad." I commented on his sensitivity in wishing to spare me this injury.

After another warm smile and some moments of companionable silence, Mark revealed his fantasies as a preadolescent of having a special relationship with Jesus. With Jesus beside him but invisible to others, he imagined visiting people suffering from terminal illnesses. With just a touch of his hand he would instantly restore them to health. The grieving relatives would fall at his feet with gratitude and joy.

I suggested that when a strong, caring father dies, a little boy feels that he's lost a connection to someone who seemed God-like in his power. "How comforting it must have been to imagine Jesus beside you in your loneliness," I said. Mark nodded his agreement. Than I added, "That little boy would also have felt worried about his failure to keep those he loved and needed available to him, worried about his own strength and power."

"So I found a way to feel powerful again," Mark said with unmistakable self-appreciation. He speculated that his decision to become a doctor might have been another way to make sure he would never again feel helpless in the face of illness and death.

I wondered if the Indian priest in the dream represented more than Mark's effort to sexualize and hence restore shattered selfobject fantasies of merger with idealized paternal figures. Did the image of blissful connection to the man in the dream indicate his healthy longings for a homosexual relationship? Perhaps it was also self-representation. Mark had told me repeatedly of being called "the priest" in his family since he had been such a well-behaved, responsible, loving child. Many assumed he would actually join the priesthood. Did his dream also contain hints of his longing for a twin, someone so much like himself he would never again feel lonely and estranged from others?

Before I could pursue these thoughts, I became aware that Mark's smile had faded. After a somber silence, he blurted, "Things didn't stay so great between Doug and me. I used to complain to him that I was lonely and that I found it difficult to socialize. Doug said that I always complained about not having friends but maybe the problem was that I didn't really care about other people. I was stunned that he could think about me that way."

"You must have felt terribly misunderstood," I responded. Mark's silent tears informed me of the depth of his pain. He noted that although he saw Doug a few more times, the special feeling never returned. He confided shamefully that from then on Doug became the focus of his homosexual fantasies. Mark also described his disappointment at not being able to recapture with Dr. C the sense of blissful communion he had lost with Doug. Dr. C had refused to allow him to do any of the work in their sessions. Interrupting Mark frequently, he would weave all of the material Mark provided into what he apparently thought were brilliant interpretations, many of which concerned Mark's homosexual longings as protection against oedipal lust for his mother. Dr. C attributed Mark's refusal to accept their accuracy to his "resistance." Eventually, in the face of the intensification of Mark's symptoms, he'd given up on the treatment. "He needed to be right about everything," Mark said. "I felt bad about not letting him feel that he was right about me."

In the following session, Mark revealed another reason for the distance he had maintained between us. He interrupted a recollection of a particularly harrowing experience with his uncle by suddenly exclaiming, "I keep feeling you don't want to hear all this sordid stuff. It must turn your stomach. You can't really want to help someone who's so disgusting to you." Mark accepted my interpretation that he feared that I would react with the same repugnance to his sexuality that he had come to expect from his mother.

Phase 2: Reconstructing

This marked a dramatic turning point in the therapeutic relationship. For a while our sessions seemed to crackle with energy. Everything about Mark seemed freer, more spontaneous. His eyes, once as lifeless as a statue's, now seemed to glow. Even his voice became more animated. The formal, clinical language he initially used was replaced by a more natural "street" vocabulary.

As my dissociative fog lifted, I seemed able to hear Mark more clearly. Thoughts about his past and present life, memories of related experiences in mine, and insights into our relationship all seemed to flow.

The rhythm of our sessions also changed. In striking contrast to the dense, effortful feeling of earlier sessions, Mark now allowed comfortable silences to develop between us. At times, he seemed to test my willingness to wait for him to speak. I imagined it was gratifying for him to feel I could tend to him in this simple way. Less burdened by the need to do all the work, he seemed to enjoy much of his time with me and even engaged me in lighthearted chatter. In other sessions he wept in grief over his father's death and other painful experiences in his life. I realized however, that he rarely expressed anger at anyone except his uncle. Despite his growing awareness that his mother had disappointed him repeatedly — by failing to protect him from his uncle, by ignoring his weight gain, by neglecting his need for contact with a father figure, and by allowing him to become her helper and companion at the expense of his involvement with peers — Mark continued to maintain his reverential stance toward her. And despite his growing freedom to criticize my errors in empathy, he refused to acknowledge any feelings of anger at me.

Once, for example, he complained that I had allowed him to chat about a topic he felt was related more to my interests than to his problems, a lapse on my part that raised the frightening possibility, that I, like his uncle, would exploit him out of callous self-interest. When, after observing his tight expression and tense posture, I suggested that he might be angry at me, Mark expressed amazement that I could even imagine him feeling anger over such an inconsequential matter.

Around this time I began to notice that the boundaries of Mark's social world had expanded. His personal contacts were no longer limited to members of his immediate family and old friends from high school. New names increasingly peppered our sessions. Then the only name I heard was Maya's. Her exotic looks, her unconventional way of dressing, and her undisguised sexual interest in Mark filled him with delight. At one point Mark sighed, "I just can't imagine having sex with her, even though I know she wants it."

When I jokingly expressed surprise that he could not even imagine having sex with Maya, Mark blushed and laughed. He admitted having sexual fantasies about her, but said they made him feel guilty and ashamed. He recalled having asked his uncle if men do with women the things they were doing. "The way he said 'yes' gave me the idea he thought it was even better with women," he said. He then remembered a childhood fantasy about a beautiful naked woman hidden in a secret room of the basement where his uncle often took him. "I felt more sinful for having this fantasy than for what was going on between me and my uncle," he said.

In response to my encouragement that he elaborate on this memory, Mark thought of his childhood concern that having sex with women was something that would hurt them. He mentioned having cried out in pain when his uncle tried anal intercourse. His uncle told him it would not hurt when he got older and bigger. Nevertheless, Mark believed he had related his painful experience to his uncle's account of heterosexual intercourse and assumed women also experienced pain.

Mark then spoke about his mother's apparent repugnance toward sex. "As a school teacher she was great at explaining 'the facts of life,'" he noted, "but what she described never seemed to have anything to do with her or us." He noted that although his mother's beauty had won her many suitors she rejected them all for being "interested in just one thing," a statement that reinforced his idea that she found sexual desire offensive. I suggested that the combination of his mother's attitude and his experiences with his uncle had convinced him that he would be bad and hurtful if he had sex with a woman.

Mark sadly observed that there had been a time when his "sexiness" was associated with pleasure. On one occasion, before his father had fallen ill, the family had gone to the movies together. When a scantily clad woman appeared on the screen, Mark had called out, "Hubba, hubba!" "I remember people in the theater laughing," he said, "and my father squeezing my arm and giving me a big smile. Even my mother joked, 'Mark is going to be a ladies' man like his daddy.'" As we both laughed, I felt that Mark had never been so relaxed and spontaneous with me.

Mark's pride in himself was obvious in our next session as he excitedly revealed that he had initiated a sexual relationship with Maya. He was careful to let me know that more enabling than our explorations of the sources of his fear that sexuality was hurtful to women, or his recollection of his father's approval of him as a sexual male, was my acceptance. "Somehow I had the feeling you were cheering me on," he said.

In terms that reminded me of his adulation of his mother, Mark sang Maya's praises. He celebrated her strength of character, her caring and warmth, and her devotion to him. After a few weeks, however, his excitement and joy were replaced by gloom. Early in their relationship Mark had seen Maya almost daily. Later on, needing to catch up on his studies, he wanted less frequent contact with her. To his great dismay, Maya complained about his unavailability. She called him at odd hours, disrupting his concentration, and often insisted on having sex when he felt disinclined to be physically close to her. For a while he tried to mollify her by spending time with her at the expense of his studies and by having sex at her whim. Although Mark clearly felt repelled by her clinging, dependent, controlling stance, his reluctance to "hurt her feelings" stopped him from confronting her. I suspected that Mark's relationship with Maya recapitulated, in many respects, his childhood relationship with his mother; selfobject relatedness once again seemed to depend on his attending to the woman without regard for his own needs.

A dream he reported greatly furthered our reconstructive efforts:

> I'm in the kitchen of my mother's house. My mother and a stranger, a man I know to be an ex-convict, are sitting at the table. The man asks my mother for money. She gives him some and asks him to leave. As he prepares to go he asks my mother for more money in a seductive way that makes me see he is attracted to her. I get very angry and say in a forceful voice, "You'd better get out of here right now." The man unzips his pants and pulls them down. He has a razor strapped to his thigh. He takes it out and threatens to slash me. My mother just sits there without reacting. I think, "Doesn't she realize I'm in great danger?"

Rattling off associations to the dream in the detached manner I remembered from our early sessions, Mark suggested that the convict stood for his uncle. He wondered if the convict's attraction to his mother meant that she also had been sexually abused and if that explained her failure to notice and stop his abuse. "Maybe that's why she's so prudish about sex," he said.

Pausing suddenly, his face flushed with emotion, Mark said he realized that the convict in the dream resembled his father. He remembered his earlier dream in which a threatening man also seemed to represent both his uncle and father. Asked why this was so upsetting, Mark confided that recently he had been troubled by memories of his father as an invalid that bore little relation to the "gentle, caring guy" he had been before his illness. These memories also contradicted the myth his mother had created about his father's "saintliness" while he was dying. "I remember not being able to understand why he stopped playing and joking with me, why he just sat on the porch in his pajamas," he said, "and why he seemed gruff and angry all the time." Then he remembered even more disturbing aspects of his father's illness: He drank heavily and sometimes erupted in rageful outbursts. Instead of protecting Mark against his mother's demands for obedience as he had when he was well, his father now took his mother's side when she chastised him. Once, indignant at his father's treachery, Mark yelled at him in anger. "My mother said she couldn't believe I could be so bad, that I was going to make my father sicker. I got very upset."

I reminded Mark that in the dream he expressed anger and his life was threatened. I suggested that his psychological survival once depended on his tie to his mother. When she scolded him for expressing angry feelings, he learned a powerful lesson: His anger would cost him his mother's approval. Mark then recalled feeling angry at Maya the night before the dream for insisting that he sleep with her when he expressed a wish to return home. Lying in bed with her, after failing to protest or express his anger, he felt "mean, nasty, and hurtful." I noted that revealing his anger was similar to revealing his sexuality. "You imagine this strong part of you is destructive, that it will hurt the woman and spoil your hopes of gaining her love and affection."

"I hardly ever get angry, but when I do it always makes me feel like I've committed a punishable offense," Mark said. "Maybe I'm the convict in the dream. He demanded more than my mother gave him. In real life I would never dream of doing that." Asked what more he wanted from his mother, Mark said angrily, "Acceptance of me as I really am. I'm definitely not a priest but I don't want to feel like a criminal for being sexual or getting mad!"

Mark then provided more examples of his mother's taboo against expressing anger. For a year after Mark, then a young teenager, did something to anger his oldest brother, they did not speak to one another. When Mark complained to his mother she advised him to give his brother time to "come around." "I guess what I really needed was for her to referee an argument so that we could clear the air," he said, "but she always says anger does no good, just forgive and forget."

Reflecting on his fantasy of his father's magical appearance at school, Mark said, "Now I know what I would have said if my father showed up at school. I would have yelled at him for being so mean to me and then abandoning me. I never admitted it before but my uncle wasn't the only man who hurt me—my father's death hurt me more. He deprived me of the one thing I wanted more than anything—a father."

The dream deepened my understanding of Mark's traumatizing betrayals and the ways in which he had attempted to restore his shattered selfobject fantasies. A six-year-old's criteria for trust-in-others include invulnerability to illness, immortality, and unfailing protectiveness. By falling ill, then dying and abandoning him to his needy, controlling mother and his deceitful, sexually abusive uncle, his father had betrayed his trust in him as the most important provider of his selfobject experiences. By sexually abusing him, his uncle, as surrogate father, did the same. With his loss of trust in these male figures and the shattering of his selfobject fantasies in which they were represented, his mother represented his only hope of selfobject fulfillment. In order to maintain a trusting bond with her despite her betrayals, a massive dissociative alteration of his subjective reality was necessary. This apparently involved his transforming himself into the helpful, obedient, asexual child she required him to be. Drastically intensifying his trust in her and himself as trustworthy, Mark reorganized his self-experience around images of himself as the provider of his mother's selfobject needs. One of his highly immature criteria for self-as-trustworthy was perfect devotion to the needs of others without regard for his own. In order to maintain his dissociatively altered reality, his awareness of his parents' betrayals as well as his strong emotions, most notably his anger and his sexual feelings, were swept into a black hole in his self-experience. He apparently found some semblance of cohesive selfhood by experiencing his uncle as evil incarnate, the alter ego selfobject who embodied all of the negative and repudiated aspects of himself and his parents.

Struck by Maya's similarity to his mother—her demanding, controlling behavior belied her initial impression of being a strong, independent, and giving woman—Mark attempted to rescript his trauma scenarios by adopting the masochistic posture of the betrayed. Instead of setting limits on Maya's demands, he attempted to satisfy them as he had his mother's, apparently hoping his self-sacrifice would move her to become the woman he needed. Unfortunately, this strategy only resulted in his feeling increasingly trapped in a retraumatizing relationship.

I suspected that the dream and Mark's associations to it also reflected aspects of our relationship, that he feared I would regard him as destructive and greedy if he expressed needs directly to me or when he felt anger or sexual feelings for me. He had not yet directly expressed intense feelings that concerned me. However, having come to terms with earlier blows to my intensified trust in Mark, I felt content with the progress we were making. I was confident that each time he experienced me as helping him to understand the meaning of his dreams and memories, the feelings he had toward others, as well as the disruptions between us, he took another step closer to trusting me with strong emotions.

Phase 3: Working-Through

Soon after this session, Mark ended his relationship with Maya. Relief appeared to be his predominant feeling, although he expressed considerable anguish over hurting her. A series of similar relationships followed. Mark would become intensely attracted to a woman he experienced as strong and independent. When she showed signs of weakness or dependency, he would lose interest in her and end the relationship abruptly. Not surprisingly, he worried that he would never find a woman with whom he could be happy.

It seemed for a while that Sheila was such a woman. Mark expressed as much pleasure in being with her as he did in helping her care for her six-year-old son. She combined a successful career in business with motherhood and still made time for Mark. Mark believed she was content with her life as a single mother. After some months however, he once again looked depressed and his dreams contained many images of exploitation and betrayal. In one he exposed a scam involving prostitution, and in another a supposed friend turns out to be an imposter.

Over the next few weeks, Mark was unusually quiet in sessions and I noticed that he had gained a considerable amount of weight. His complaints about being fat seemed to contain an unspoken accusation, as if I were to blame. I reminded Mark that his weight gain in childhood had been, in part, an effort to inform his mother that something was terribly wrong in his life. "Could your gain in weight be a way of letting me know that something is wrong now?" I asked.

Cooly, Mark said that what was wrong was the treatment. "I feel fat and miserable," he said. "I think I'm getting worse. I don't think you can help me any more. Maybe I really need to see a male therapist." Collecting myself after a stunned silence, I encouraged Mark to say more about his wish to leave therapy. He repeated that he hated how he felt and that therapy was not helping him. Finally as the session ended, I murmured something about the inadvisability of his leaving treatment without our understanding what had gone wrong and Mark agreed to return.

In the days until our next session, I worried continually about Mark's threat to end therapy. I felt depressed, anxious, and very angry at him. My trust in him as a reliable and dependable patient who sustained my esteem in myself had again been severely shaken. But even more upsetting for me was the loss of my trust in myself as a provider for his selfobject needs. Once again, I felt confused and foggy as my dissociative reaction prevented me from grasping the meaning of his behavior.

Mark opened the next session with two dreams from the previous night:

I have a wound near my eye. The skin is mutilated all around a large, deep hole filled with pus. No one seems to notice.

I am at a family gathering, maybe a picnic at a park. I am playing with a long, furry animal like a ferret. I want to show my mother what I'm doing but she is talking to some people and doesn't look at me. At one point my finger gets caught in the ferret's anus. There are little teeth in the anus and as I try to pull my finger out it bites me. I see that my finger is badly cut and show it to my mother. She says, "Oh, it's nothing to worry about. See, it's hardly bleeding." But I worry that it will get infected.

Without attempting his usual systematic exploration of his dream, Mark said that he had lost all romantic interest in Sheila after discovering that she wanted to marry him. Instead of feeling pleased and excited at coming so close to having the family he longed for, he had experienced a sense of dread. "For some reason I think I'd be trapped in marriage, that my life with Sheila would be bleak, dull, and burdensome," he said and then broke into sobs. In a voice barely audible he confessed that he had been sleeping with men. "I'm so ashamed, so ashamed," he said. He explained that for the past few weeks after dates with Sheila, he would go to a "gay bar" and "pick up" men for brief sexual encounters. Afterward, filled with self-revulsion, he would tell himself that it would never happen again. Recently, he observed, his urges for sex with men had become so compelling, he had begun to frequent gay bars even when he had not dated Sheila.

After a long silence in which Mark seemed to struggle to keep his composure, he said with anger ringing in his voice, "Why didn't you make sure I turned out straight? Isn't that why I'm here? I thought you'd made my disgusting homosexual fantasies disappear. Now I'm acting on them."

As before, Mark's addressing me directly in an emotionally charged way enabled me to regain my therapeutic composure. I acknowledged his anger and disappointment. "It must be very hard to show me these feelings," I said, "You've obviously been struggling with them for some time." Mark admitted that his anger had been growing over the last several weeks, and that the angrier he felt toward me, the more he thought of switching to a male therapist.

I suggested that it was hard for Mark to believe that a woman could be the target of his anger and still want to help him. As if he had not heard me, Mark said, "My mother must have known my uncle was abusing me. How could she let it happen? Why didn't she come to me after she found out that my brother had been abused? Even after I gained all that weight, she pretended nothing had happened. What does it take to get her to admit something is wrong?"

More thoughtfully and sadly, Mark added, "Ferrets are wild, mischievous animals that can't be tamed. I guess that's the way my mother feels about sexuality and it frightens her. I'm frightened too. My cut finger reminds me how terrified I am about getting AIDS. But maybe what I'm more afraid of is facing my mother. She can't even deal with me as a straight sexual person – maybe that's why I was supposed to become a priest. I could never tell her I have sex with men."

In response to my asking what he expected to happen if he told her, Mark said he thought she would "break down, cry," and although she would never say anything critical he would feel her disappointment and her disgust. "She doesn't want to see the pus-filled wound left by my uncle, she doesn't want me to rub her failure in her face."

Mark seemed to go over the same ground we had covered in relation to the convict dream but this time with much more feeling. Noting that he quickly cut short his anger at me, I suggested that he may also have feared that I, like his mother, would react with pain and revulsion to his revelation about having sex with men; he agreed. My noticing his weight gain had not been enough to assure him of my understanding and acceptance. He had needed me to know about his homosexual activities in order for him to experience me as different from his mother. In a voice breaking with pain and anger, Mark asked if I thought he was "sabotaging [his] chances for happiness" and "undoing all the benefits of therapy" by having sex with men.

I assured him that I did not, and noted his concern that I thought less of him for rejecting a conventional lifestyle. "You seem to feel you're letting me down by not staying with Sheila, that I have a stake in your being 'straight.' Perhaps you even feel I need you to take care of me by behaving like a model patient."

Mark accepted an interpretation linking his inability to trust me and the betrayals he had suffered at his mother's hands. He acknowledged worrying that he had let me down by having sex with men. "But I feel like I've let myself down, too," he said. Again he complained of feeling fat, ugly, and useless. "Maybe I can't feel worthwhile unless I'm taking care of somebody else. If I'm not the model son or the model patient, I don't know who I am."

During the next several months, Mark seemed to need little from me beyond my silent presence as he struggled to come to terms with his sexuality. He agonized over his wish to "come out" to his mother and siblings and his fear of their pain and revulsion. Although he was encouraged by Sheila's nonjudgmental reaction to his disclosure that he was bisexual, and her un-equivocal statement of love for him, Mark found it difficult to continue seeing her. Sheila increasingly represented for Mark the forces that opposed his wish to lead a free and unconventional life-style in which he might have sex with men and women.

He reported a number of "daydreams" involving his death and his mother's. For example, in one fantasy his mother weeps at his grave after he dies of AIDS, and in another he is overcome with grief on hearing of her death. We understood these waking fantasies as reflections of his wish for intensely positive feelings of connectedness with his mother at a time when his anger and his homosexual activities made him feel far from her. I also viewed his daydreams, although I did not interpret them as such to Mark at this point, as reflections of sadomasochistic fantasies by means of which he hoped to rescript the traumatic betrayals inflicted by his mother. In the AIDS fantasy, his death represents ultimate masochistic surrender at the same time as it represents sadistic punishment of his mother (she suffers over his loss). He sees her as grieving and thereby imagines himself extracting in death what he can not obtain from her in life: her loving acceptance. In the fantasy of her death, she is again (sadistically) punished for having betrayed him, but he suffers (masochistically) over his loss. Again, love and grief reunite them. Thus, both fantasies permit him to experience himself and his mother as intensely and lovingly connected, his selfobject fantasies are briefly restored.

He also reported the following dream:

> I have a cat in my hands and I'm eating it. The cat is alive and continues to be although it's disappearing, bones and all. My mother yells at me when she discovers what I'm doing. The cat, or rather, half the cat, skinned and bloody, starts fighting with me and I lose hold of it. I hit it with a broom and blood splatters all over.

We understood the dream as representing Mark's fear that his sexuality was destructive to himself and others. As a "masculine" man who "eats pussy," he felt destructive to women, a repugnant devourer like his uncle. As a "feminine" man, that is, one who became "feminized" through his sexual victimization, Mark felt "eaten alive" by the disgust he feared he aroused in others. "I tried to kill that part of myself," he said, meaning his bisexuality, "but it wouldn't die." Recalling his first dream in therapy of himself and Lisa in the boys' bathroom, Mark understood that she represented his disavowed experience of himself as a feminized man who desired sex with men.

As Mark continued to overeat and gain weight, we explored the many meanings of food and obesity in his life. We discovered that through eating Mark was enabled to maintain his sense of connection to his father. Aside from Mark's happy recollections of their shared pleasure in eating unusual food, the act of eating calmed and soothed him and so reminded him of the peace he once felt in his father's protective presence.[2] Mark's relationship with his mother was also involved. Because being fat enabled Mark to hide his sexuality, his obesity represented a way of taking care of her (he remained for her an asexual little boy who had never been molested by his uncle) and therefore it helped him maintain his bond with her. Mark also experienced being fat as a protective padding that made him feel more substantial, less like a helpless victim. Thus, in a curious way, being fat also served to rescript trauma scenarios in which he, as the skinny helpless boy, had been abused.

While traveling abroad after his graduation from medical school, Mark lost a great deal of weight. Free from the stresses of life as a medical student and filled with excitement at encountering new places and people, he found he had little desire to overeat. Returning to treatment looking fit and attractive, he was clearly pleased when I noticed the changes in him. He proudly displayed an earring he wore in one ear, a style he copied from gay acquaintances. He mentioned that on his travels he had frequented gay bars and dances without any shame or furtiveness. He also mentioned a brief affair with an attractive woman.

Shortly after beginning his internship, however, he complained of feeling depressed and anxious. He soon regained all of the weight lost on his trip. Finally, in response to my questions about problem areas in his life, Mark revealed his passionate attraction to Mustapha, a Turkish doctor. Mark had fallen in love with Mustapha at first sight; he seemed to him the oriental priest in his dream come to life. They quickly agreed to a monogamous sexual relationship.

Mark accepted my interpretation that his weight gain had represented an attempt to disguise his commitment to a homosexual lifestyle. Fearing that I, like his mother, would recoil from him in disgust if I discovered his relationship with Mustapha, he had beaten me to the punch by withdrawing from me.

"You don't really want to hear about Mustapha, do you?" he asked in disbelief. When I assured him that I did, Mark revealed his deep admiration for him; he seemed to possess all the qualities Mark wished for in himself. Mustapha had known he was homosexual early in life and had participated in a gay lifestyle from the time of early adolescence. Slim and muscular, he took

---

[2]Ulman & Paul (1989, 1990, 1992) include food in their description of addictive trigger mechanisms, which they define as "an animate or inanimate thing or activity that arouses 'selfobject fantasies' and moods of narcissistic bliss" (1992, p. 110).

excellent care of his body. Mark could not believe that someone as beautiful as Mustapha could find him attractive too. Yet, as Mark's relationship with Mustapha deepened, he seemed to grow more troubled. He complained of insistent suspicions about Mustapha that seemed to have no basis in reality. For example, after having found a telephone bill listing calls to various places around the world, Mark imagined that Mustapha was part of an international terrorist organization. When he was late for a date, Mark imagined that he had been arrested for some unspeakable crime.

I soon discovered that although Mustapha was hardly a terrorist or criminal, Mark's suspicious fantasies were rooted in events that disrupted Mark's trust in him as a provider of selfobject experiences for him. Extremely handsome, charming, and flirtatious, Mustapha attracted men wherever he went. His glib, lighthearted manner made it difficult for Mark to tell when he was lying about his whereabouts. Mark spoke of feeling frightened that Mustapha was sleeping with other men and furious over his obstinate refusal to have an AIDS test. Mark also feared that Mustapha was taking advantage of him financially. Since he was dependent on checks his mother sent him from abroad, he was often short of cash. He would withdraw and sulk if Mark refused to treat him to meals or buy him gifts.

I suspected that Mustapha not only embodied qualities that Mark wished to possess, but also those he disavowed in himself; that is, he served Mark as an alter ego selfobject. To the extent that Mark still disavowed his sexual attractiveness, his sense of entitled self-interest, and his hostility, and embraced an image of himself as the family "priest," he reconnected with these hidden aspects of himself by finding them in Mustapha. When he felt that his relationship with Mustapha was endangered, he developed paranoid fantasies of him as a sadistic abuser. In response to my noting that he seemed to feel abused by Mustapha, he responded with fresh memories of humiliating sexual scenes with his uncle.

Mark's mood seemed to swing between despair and elation depending on where he was in the cycle of fights and reconciliations that patterned his relationship with Mustapha. Before long I noticed that the dark, depressed periods were lasting longer. Because Mark had remained fairly reserved with me, I was prepared when he again expressed doubts about the value of continuing therapy. This time, feeling confident that the treatment was still on track, I accepted his doubts without comment.

Later in that session, Mark reported the following dream:

> My brother Steve and I are at my mother's house. We're carrying big glass objects. The one I'm carrying breaks into tiny fragments and I realize that my

arms and hands are covered with splinters of glass and that blood is dripping all over. I feel terrible at having been so careless. I also think, "All of this blood is dangerous. It's infected."

Mark's first association to the dream concerned his dread of AIDS and his concern about possibly infecting others. Then he reflected on the fact that the glass objects were transparent. He wondered how the enormous changes in him since he met Mustapha could be so completely ignored in his family. I commented on his longing to be noticed and appreciated as he really was. He spoke of hoping that his mother would ask him directly about his sexual life and thus relieve him of the need to hide what felt to him like a shameful defect. He had even brought Mustapha to a family party in the hope that his mother would ask about him, but she had ignored his presence. "I'm always protecting her, taking care of her feelings. Why doesn't she take care of me for once? The blood on my arms and hands makes me think of Christ on the cross. I always feel that I sacrifice myself to keep her from being hurt." I asked if he worried about hurting me by speaking about leaving therapy. Mark responded, "You don't seem hurt to me. Are you?" I assured him that I was not. "That's good," Mark said, but I thought I detected a hint of disappointment in his voice.

On discovering that Mustapha had been seeing someone else, Mark felt his pain was unbearable. Alarmed by his uncontrolled weeping in sessions and his reports of breaking down at work, of sleepless nights, and of drinking heavily, I suggested he consult a psychiatrist to evaluate his need for medication. Mark rejected my suggestion but mentioned feeling glad that I had "taken [his] pain seriously." Although Mustapha ended his affair after a few weeks and they quickly reunited, Mark remained mistrustful of him. "I can't tell my mother I'm gay unless I'm in a stable relationship with a man," he said. "Somehow that would make me feel less disgusting to her and to myself. But that probably won't happen with Mustapha."

Soon after, I noticed that Mark had begun to arrive late for our sessions and then for the first time, he failed to show up for an early-morning appointment. He mentioned in an offhand way that he had simply overslept and seemed annoyed by my attempts to discuss this radical change from his characteristic punctuality. After missing three consecutive sessions on account of oversleeping, I told Mark that I could not help connecting his uncharacteristic absences with the stresses he experienced in his relationship with Mustapha.

"I don't see how coming late or missing sessions has anything to do with him," Mark said testily. He then launched into an account of Mustapha's giving him the "silent treatment" after an argument. "He knows that kills me," Mark said, "I told him how I suffered when my brother didn't talk to me for a year." Mark said he worried that Mustapha's behavior probably meant that he wished to see someone else. "I don't know what I'll do if he disappears on me again," Mark moaned.

I mentioned that Mustapha's silences as well as the prospect of his disappearing must be particularly painful given that the two most important men in his childhood, his father and his uncle, had both suddenly vanished from his life. Tears sprang to Mark's eyes, and he said, "It isn't as if he doesn't know how hard that is for me. I've told him the story of my early life."

"Once again you seem to see Mustapha as an abusive person," I said. Mark then revealed that Mustapha had accused *him* of being abusive. "He says I hurt him by withdrawing emotionally from time to time," Mark said, "and I guess I do withdraw when I feel hurt by him."

I suggested to Mark that we might understand what happened between him and Mustapha in terms of his need to make sure that he would not be hurt by another man's leaving him. "Perhaps you distance yourself as a way of striking first, to guard yourself against the blow of being left by him." Mark confessed that he had taken some satisfaction in Mustapha's apparent distress at his withdrawal, and that this appalled him.

"Much as you hate to be the hurtful one," I said, "it's worse to feel abused by a man you need so much." The softening of Mark's expression informed me that he felt relieved by my interpretation. Once again I returned to his lateness and absences in therapy. Immediately Mark interrupted and in an angry voice said, "I can't believe you think I'm deliberately trying to take things out on you. I thought you'd be glad that I don't have to take care of you by being so punctual."

I acknowledged my failure to appreciate that Mark had indeed found it possible at last to take care of his own needs without needing to put mine first. Mark again interrupted. "You're right, there is a connection between what goes on between Mustapha and me and my 'disappearing' on you. I always picture you sitting here when I don't show up. You're worrying about what happened to me, thinking I might have been hurt or killed in an accident." "Like your fantasies of your mother at your graveside?" I asked. Mark answered that it was upsetting to think about himself as wanting to cause anyone pain but that those feelings did make sense to him now as an alternative to feeling that he was always the one who got hurt, left, or disregarded.

As we continued to work through Mark's efforts to rescript his trauma scenarios in treatment and in his relationship with Mustapha, he spoke of his longing to have a relationship with a man whose loyalty he could trust. When Mustapha again confessed to having "cheated on him," Mark ended the relationship. Although he missed him intensely at first, Mark did not become depressed. After some months, Mark announced that he had told his family about his homosexuality. Although his mother said she had suspected it and was not shocked, that her love for him was unaffected, Mark knew she was disappointed. He also mentioned that he felt far less distressed than he imagined and he hailed this as a result of the changes in him that he attributed to therapy.

Having worked through his fears of retraumatizing betrayals within the therapeutic relationship, that is, his fear of my recoiling from him or hurting him for exhibiting his sexuality and anger, Mark had integrated these previously dissociated and disavowed aspects of himself. This enabled him to risk confronting his family with the realities of his life. The therapeutic relationship ended when Mark began his medical practice. His occasional phone calls to me indicate that he has, for the most part, sustained his positive feelings about himself, and that he has established close, caring relationships with trustworthy men and women.

DISCUSSION

Despite their very different styles of relating within the therapeutic relationship—Ruth, recklessly self-revealing, alternatively brash and helpless; Mark, initially distant and wary, determinedly self-sufficient—many similarities are to be found in their lives and in their treatment. Both patients reacted to brutal betrayals in their early lives with massive dissociative changes in their self-experience.

Ruth's efforts to reestablish trusting ties to both of her parents after their traumatizing reactions to her crippling illness involved the development of two contrasting self-perceptions. Only in the persona of the weak, suffering victim could Ruth experience her mother as a confident, self-trusting guide; only as the bold, unconventional, sexually desirable survivor could she hope to sustain the selfobject connectedness with her father. Ruth's self-trust organization varied according to the alternations in her self-perception. In her victim persona, trust-in-self was diminished, while trust-in-others and others-as-self-trusting was intensified. In her survivor persona, trust-in-self was intensified while other self-trust dimensions were diminished.

In Mark's case, his need to form a trusting selfobject bond with his mother after his father's death and his uncle's sexual abusiveness led him to disavow his experience of his mother's betrayals and his own sexuality and passion. By experiencing himself as the trustworthy provider for his mother's selfobject need, he attained a measure of self-cohesion. His self-trust organization was marked by diminished trust-in-others and intensified self-as-trustworthy.

Treatment confronted both patients with seemingly insoluable self-trust dilemmas. On the one hand, the therapeutic relationship held the promise of providing a trustworthy milieu in which the dissociated aspects of self-experience could be integrated; on the other, it posed the terrifying prospect of retraumatization. The dread of retraumatizing betrayals within the therapeutic relationship was heightened for both patients as I failed tests of trustworthiness due to the organization of my self-trust. My intense need to experience my patients as trustworthy, and myself as a trustworthy provider of selfobject experience for them, was seriously challenged by Ruth's sudden shift from blind faith in my competence to contemptuous mistrust as well as by Mark's efforts at self-sufficiency. Both patients resorted to sadomasochistic enactments both within and outside of the therapeutic relationship in the hope of rescripting trauma scenarios and averting retraumatizing betrayals.

By the conclusion of treatment, maturing self-trust enabled each to end relationships whose chief purpose was the rescripting of trauma. Both were freed to find trustworthy relationships in which previously dissociated aspects of self-experience could find expression.

Chapter 8

THE TRUSTWORTHY PATIENT

I had lost my self-confidence where you were concerned, and in its place had developed a boundless sense of guilt. . . . The mistrust that you tried to instill into me toward most people . . . turned in me to mistrust of myself. . . . it was precisely in my childhood that I did find a certain comfort in my very mistrust of my own judgment. I would say to myself; "Oh, you're exaggerating, you tend too much to feel trivialities as great exceptions, the way young people always do." But this comfort I later lost almost entirely, when I gained a clearer perspective of the world.

Franz Kafka, Letter to His Father *(1979b)*

Few self psychologists could enter the surreal world of Kafka's fiction without being reminded of Kohut's case studies. Only a modicum of poetic license appears to distinguish the psychological torment of the fictional characters from that of the self-disordered patients. Among Kohut's many references to Kafka's art is his observation that it addresses "the lonely, estranged, disintegrating and depleted individual of modern times" (Kohut, 1985, p. 89). The same certainly could be said of his own. Surprisingly, it was the author and not the psychoanalyst who explored the aspect of self-experience that serves as the subject of this chapter: the need to be trusted, or more specifically, the patient's need to be trusted to provide selfobject experiences for the therapist.

While the self psychology literature abounds with references to the patient's need for the trustworthy provision of selfobject experiences *by* others (e.g., Lichtenberg, Lachmann, & Fosshoge, 1992), little attention has been paid to the patient's need to be trusted to provide these experiences *for* others.[1] Yet disorders of self-experience are as likely to result from disturbances in the former realm of self-experience as in the latter.

> As Gregor Samsa awoke one morning from uneasy dreams he found himself transformed in his bed into a gigantic insect. (Kafka, 1979a, p. 1)

With this famous sentence, Kafka begins *The Metamorphosis*, one of the most extraordinary works of modern literature. The reader quickly discovers that, in his pre-insect life, Gregor attempted to extract trust from a paranoid world. He was employed by a firm "where the smallest omission at once gave rise to the gravest suspicion," and everyone from the chief to the porter who spied for him maligned Gregor's trustworthiness. When the chief clerk comes to investigate Gregor's first unavoidable lateness on the morning of his transformation, he expresses doubt that Gregor had ever been a "quiet, dependable person." He even hints that Gregor is suspected of making off with cash payments entrusted to him.

Gregor's life at home offered little relief from the mistrustful scrutiny he endured at work. Despite the fact that he willingly sacrificed himself for the good of his family by conscientiously applying himself to a job he detested, he was closely watched for signs that he might slack off. Gregor's demise is brought about by his family's failure to trust his benevolence. His sister, at first highly solicitous of his needs as an insect, becomes ruthlessly indifferent to them as she gradually loses faith in Gregor's ability to send her to a music conservatory. Gregor is mortally wounded by an apple hurled at him by his father who could not trust that Gregor meant his frightened wife no harm.

That one's self-esteem, well-being, and security—indeed, one's very humanness—depends on meriting and receiving the trust of others is undeniably a powerful message contained in Kafka's masterpiece. The epithet "monster" is often applied to sociopaths who exploit the trust of others out of greed or sadistic satisfaction. Self-as-trustworthy is the dimension of self-trust that pertains to the need to be trusted to provide selfobject experiences for others. To the extent that people fail to live up to criteria for this self-trust dimension,

---

[1]Shane and Shane (1989) describe "the struggle for otherhood" in which otherhood is defined as a general term for the many adult relationships wherein mature empathy and healthy altruism are seen as prerequisite to performing functions on behalf of another person. I disagree that the capacity to provide for others is achieved only after arduous labor. Under normal circumstances providing for others psychologically is highly pleasurable and satisfying. Developing the capacities necessary for this provision involves neither struggle nor pain. Rather, it is a natural, effortless process.

they can not represent themselves in their selfobject fantasies as giving, loving, caring providers.

In Chapter 2 I pointed out that children appear to be born with the capacities necessary for meeting the psychological needs of others and that they soon expect to be trusted to do so. Empathic caretakers tend to promote the optimal development of this self-trust dimension. They do so primarily by validating the child's psychological reality and by affirming the child's affective expressiveness. Children who receive these "votes of confidence" are likely to experience themselves as capable of responding appropriately to the affects of others, a central feature of selfobject experience. Empathic caretakers also encourage children to assume some responsibility for the psychological support of family members. For example, a father who bumps his head in the presence of his two-and-a-half-year-old toddler may graciously allow her to "kiss the booboo to make it better" just as she had been kissed under similar circumstances. A mother may corroborate her four-year-old child's understanding that "Mommy is sad" when he witnesses her tears after she has received distressing news. The parents of somewhat older children may applaud their expressions of concern for troubled classmates as well as their efforts to be encouraging and appreciative of others. They may include their children in discussions of family problems and welcome their contributions. Above all, empathic caretakers avoid overburdening their children with inordinate demands.

Unfortunately, many otherwise competent caretakers fail to respond empathically to this realm of their children's self-experience. Some deliberately stifle attempts by children to prove themselves trustworthy. For example, as a means of bolstering experiences of themselves as powerful providers, certain caretakers discourage their children from carrying any of the emotional weight of the family. They may deride a child's attempts at empathic responsiveness as inadequate or insufficient. Or, in a misguided attempt to prolong their children's "carefree" years, they may reject the children's giving efforts as unnecessary or even inappropriate. Still other caretakers demand more than their children are capable of providing. Overburdened by their demands, such children may search for ways to avoid responding to the adults' psychological needs.

When failures in empathic responsiveness like these are severe enough, children come to experience themselves as potential betrayers of the trust placed in them to provide for the selfobject needs of others. Depending on their subsequent alteration of subjective reality, self-as-trustworthy may be either diminished or intensified. Consequently, they may grow up feeling relatively indifferent to the psychological needs of other people or zealously devoted to serving them. Moreover, the criteria upon which self-as-trustworthy is based are likely to remain unrealistic, concrete, simple, and undifferentiated. For example, some people experience themselves as trustworthy providers only to the extent that they possess magical or superhuman powers, are unfallibly reliable and consistent, or measure up to other highly idiosyncratic standards. Intensifications or diminutions of self-as-trustworthy may also represent efforts at "self-righting" (Lichtenberg, 1989) following disturbances into the self-trust dimensions. For example, many children raised in the chaotic, unpredictable, trauma-filled households of alcoholics greatly intensify self-as-trustworthy. These precociously responsible "little adults" appear to invite others in the family to experience them as selfobjects. Because their own capacity for trustworthy giving is the only certainty in their lives, they learn to content themselves with vicarious experiences of selfobject fulfillment. For such children, many of whom are drawn to the helping professions in adulthood, their selfobject fantasies consist mainly in images of themselves providing selfobject experiences for others. Alice Miller (1981) poignantly captures their plight in *Prisoners of Childhood*.

In contrast to these paragons of altruism, certain adults who were treated with extreme cruelty or neglect as children and consequently lack models of trustworthy selfobject provision show a wanton disregard for the selfobject needs of others or even take sadistic satisfaction in betraying their trust. A drastic diminution of self-as-trustworthy permits them to commit acts of aggression and sadism without apparent guilt or shame. The loss of an experience of oneself as trustworthy often goes hand in hand with an attempt to alter subjective reality such that one perpetually assumes the posture of the betrayer instead of the betrayed, a psychological strategem Ferenzci (1949) referred to as "identification with the aggressor." Sadistic or ruthless behavior can often be understood both as concretizations of traumatizing betrayals of self-trust and as enactments undertaken in the hope of rescripting trauma scenarios (see Chapter 4). However, it is not unusual for someone with intensified self-as-trustworthy, generally recognized as a benevolent provider, to resort to sadistic enactments when retraumatization appears imminent.

THE NEED TO BE TRUSTED AND
THE THERAPEUTIC RELATIONSHIP

For patients whose need to experience themselves as trustworthy was thwarted earlier in life, the treatment situation provides a unique opportunity for resolving the resulting disturbances in self-experience. Those who begin treatment with a poor estimation of their own trustworthiness may, after a time, risk offering themselves to their therapists as providers of selfobject experience. In increasingly noticeable ways, these patients may respond empathically to the mirroring, idealizing, twinship, alterego, and myriad other selfobject needs of their therapists. Therapists who acknowledge the meaning of these efforts are most likely to help patients restore a sense of themselves as trustworthy.

Other patients begin treatment with a strong expectation of being trusted by their therapists. Because self-as-trustworthy was intensified as part of an earlier self-restitutive effort, they are accustomed to acting as trustworthy providers in relationships. Convinced that their only hope of receiving selfobject experiences from their therapists lies in their demonstrations of trustworthiness, they may tend to their therapists' psychological needs with astonishing sensitivity. With the strengthening of the other dimensions of self-trust as disturbances are worked through in treatment, the self-experience of these patients is likely to become less exclusively organized by selfobject fantasies in which they represent themselves as providers.

In therapy, as in childhood, empathy is the key to addressing disturbances in this realm of self-trust. All too often, however, instead of responding empathically to their patients' need to be trusted in the therapeutic relationship, therapists regard this need with suspicion. They may interpret expressions of this need as "reaction formations" that cover hostile or envious feelings for the therapist, as maneuvers to "buy" love, or as efforts to prolong dependency. The fear of exploiting patients by accepting their gifts, whether material or psychological, may also interfere with empathic acceptance of the need to be trusted.

Therapists who find ulterior motives in their patients' bids to be experienced as trustworthy are just as likely to disrupt the therapeutic relationship as those who fail to recognize expressions of a patient's need to be trusted. Certain manifestations of this need are difficult to detect, especially among patients who attempt to prove themselves trustworthy by producing symptoms their therapists know how to cure or by feigning improvement in compliance with their therapists' wishes. In "The Two Analyses of Mr. Z," Kohut (1979) suggests that Mr. Z responded to him with this kind of compliance. He referred to the apparent improvement in Mr. Z's condition at the conclusion of the first analysis as a "transference success." The patient, Kohut claims, produced oedipal issues in compliance with Kohut's theoretical convictions at the time. He then suppressed his masochistic fantasies and changed his behavior in order to mimic "the appearance of normality as defined by the maturity morality" to which Kohut then subscribed. From the perspective of self-trust, we could say that Mr. Z's intensified need to be experienced as a trustworthy selfobject for Kohut led him to produce the oedipal issues Kohut required and to act as though he had been cured. He apparently hoped that by serving Kohut in these ways, Kohut would be transformed into the idealized paternal selfobject he longed for. In returning for a second analysis, Mr. Z clearly gave Kohut another chance. It is hard to know if his return represented a masochistic enactment by means of which he hoped to rescript his trauma scenarios, or if Kohut had simply proved himself trustworthy enough during the first analysis to keep alive his hope for a lasting cure (see Brothers, 1994).

Impediments to therapists' empathic responsiveness when confronted with their patients' difficulties in this realm often derive from intensifications and diminutions in the therapists' self-as-trustworthy. We have already seen how a patient's intensified need to be trusted affected the therapeutic relationship in the case of Mark (Chapter 7). In response to numerous betrayals of Mark's self-trust, his self-experience was strongly organized by his experience of himself as a trustworthy provider. Because my own self-trust is similarly organized, serious disruptions occurred at the outset of treatment. Although this self-trust configuration greatly affected the unfolding of our relationship, it became less prominent with time.

In the two clinical examples that follow, issues related to the need to be trusted strongly colored the entire treatment process. I present the cases of Beverly and James with my clinical focus narrowed to an almost exclusive concern with the therapeutic vicissisitudes of self-as-trustworthy.

Beverly

Tall and strikingly attractive, Beverly, a self-employed businesswoman, entered twice-weekly treatment with me when she was 47. She fairly exuded cheerful self-confidence. Her handshake was firm, her smile open and warm, and she appeared to invite eye contact. Although considerably overweight, she dressed in bright colors and assertive patterns that seemed to indicate her comfort with her size. The liberal sprinkling of coarse words and folksy expressions in her speech added to my impression of her as a plain-spoken, honest, and tough-minded woman.

During the initial stage of our relationship, I could not have explained exactly why Beverly had decided to enter treatment. Although she vaguely mentioned a troubled marriage and feeling "lost" since her mother's death 15 years earlier, she seemed high-spirited in my presence. If she had one mission as a patient, it appeared to be to bolster my self-esteem. She seemed bent on learning all she could about me in order to assure herself an ample supply of fresh data for her unfailingly positive comments about me. "You really chose the right colors for your office—so restful," she might say, or "How thoughtful of you to keep such a wide variety of magazines—something for everyone." Needless to say, she paid close attention to changes in my appearance. Most sessions began with a comment like "Oh, you like the longer hemlines, don't you? I think they're so much more graceful too," or "Great new shade of lipstick!" Beverly also reacted to my every intervention as if it were a brilliant revelation and even turned my mistakes into clever psychological strategies. For example, after I kept her waiting for a session, Beverly said, "You wanted to see how I dealt with frustration, didn't you?"

I was startled to discover that her strenuous efforts to take care of my psychological needs were far from characteristic of her other relationships. In fact, by her own admission she had betrayed the trust of all of the people closest to her. Curiously, Beverly offered accounts of her deceitfulness and manipulation of others without the slightest hint of shame or guilt. On the contrary, she seemed to expect my applause for what she would call "taking good care of number one," a term she applied to a wide range of behaviors that included lying to friends and relatives as a means of gaining their compliance with her wishes, blatantly resorting to guilt-inducing scenes to control her teenage children, and short-changing business associates.

Of all her relationships, it was with her husband, Harry, that Beverly seemed least like the psychological cheerleader she was with me. She criticized him continually for being selfish, inconsiderate, an inadequate lover, and a "hothead" who could not control his temper. Moreover, she revealed that she had tortured him with a string of extramarital affairs during their 20 years of marriage. She explained that although she had never been in love with him, she had believed her mother's assessment that he would make a "good match." He was handsome, an accomplished dancer, and, at the time they met, a junior executive on the brink of a lucrative career in a large corporation. In addition, he bore a striking similarity to Beverly's father in a number of respects and she felt a sense of comforting familiarity with him. Unfortunately, Beverly's hopes for marital happiness were dashed soon after their wedding. Highly critical and demanding, Harry blamed her for his many disappointments in life and regarded her as likely to bring them to ruin if he ever relaxed his vigilant scrutiny of all she did.

Shortly before Beverly's involvement with Harry she had fallen in love with a man her mother had called a scoundrel. "My mother was right, the guy was a scoundrel," she said, "but it broke my heart to leave him. Of course I Iistened to Mom, I always did." I learned that Beverly had followed her mother's advice in all matters, large and small, throughout her life. Even after her mother's death, Beverly still attempted to live by what she called "Mother's guidelines for good living." Much of Beverly's self-presentation, from her determinedly cheerful manner to her choice of attention-getting clothing, had either been copied from her mother or directly prescribed by her. Even her marriage seems to have been patterned on her mother's failed relationship with her father.

Beverly explained that she had always been close to her mother but it was not until after her parents' stormy divorce when she was 12 that they had become an inseparable duo. Forced to choose between her parents, she had chosen her mother "since Dad seemed almost as angry at me as he was at her." She had only recently reestablished contact with her father who had moved to a distant city. Beverly's mother had been depressed, preoccupied, and withdrawn during the time of her divorce. "Sometimes I worried that Mom was losing it," she remarked. "I had to keep an eye on her all the time." I learned that what Beverly meant by keeping an eye on her mother was literally watching her mother vigilantly for any sign of psychological collapse. When such collapse seemed imminent, she would do whatever it took to rescue her. This usually involved showering her with protestations of love, admiration, and loyalty.

When her mother died, Beverly worried that she would make "a hopeless mess" of her life. Yet, Beverly never cried for her mother. "I knew she would have wanted me to be strong, to hide my tears," she said. Then she added thoughtfully, "Maybe I never cried for her so that I could pretend she wasn't really gone. I have imaginary conversations with her all the time."

After several months I realized that Beverly experienced me as a therapeutic reincarnation of her mother. She treated me to the same kind of attentiveness and flattery she had previously bestowed on her mother. And she would report on everything that she had done between sessions in an obvious bid to obtain my "seal of approval" as a replacement for her mother's. She seemed convinced that I, like her mother, would praise her for putting her own needs ahead of those of others. "Look out for number one," it turned out, had been one of her mother's favorite expressions. "Smile and the world smiles with you" was another. He mother's maxims became the criteria against which she measured her trustworthiness as a selfobject. The first time she broke into tears during a session after describing some detail of her mother's death, she apologized profusely. "I don't know what's wrong with me today," she said. "Forgive the display." Told that her tears were certainly understandable and welcome, Beverly responded, "Oh, you expect me to cry when I talk abut death. That makes sense—like everything else you say."

During the first year of therapy Beverly tested the therapeutic relationship, tentatively at first and then more boldly, by expressing pain and despair about the loss of her mother, her troubled marriage, problems with her children, and concerns about her business dealings. Concomitant with her growing freedom to express negative feelings was the lessening of the idealized glow that had surrounded her reminiscences of her relationship with her mother. She came to realize that she had had little choice but to follow her mother's dictates. Rejecting them would have been tantamount to betrayal since she had felt her mother depended on her compliance to feel wise, powerful, and above all, indispensible.

In the second year of treatment I noticed that Beverly had begun to make small decisions without consulting me. Some weeks later she would reveal her accomplishment in a quiet, mumbling voice. Soon her initial reluctance to call my attention to her deeds gave way to proud trumpetings of her boldness. I surmised that Beverly now trusted that I would appreciate her efforts to act on her own initiative and that, in contrast to her mother, I did not need her to make me feel indispensible. Her criteria for self-as-trustworthy appeared to be maturing. Then, in one dramatic session during this period, Beverly tearfully confessed feeling responsible for her mother's death. Despite her mother's protestations that she was in good health, Beverly had observed signs of her deterioration. She suspected that her mother's blood pressure was dangerously high and she worried about her mother's failure to exercise and restrict her diet. "Why didn't I do something?" Beverly cried. "We were both supposed to take care of one another, but I didn't have the guts to challenge her. I really let her down." Sobbing convulsively, Beverly seemed to abandon herself to her grief.

I pointed out that Beverly had been placed in a difficult predicament. She had learned to take care of her mother's feelings by allowing her to believe her word was law. How could she contradict her mother's assurances that she was well without feeling that she betrayed her mother's trust in her as the guardian of her omniscience? After listening to me intently, Beverly sighed as if she had been relieved of a heavy burden. She acknowledged that it was at least an oversimplification to feel she had caused her mother's death. She also admitted feeling angry that her mother had "put me in that bind."

Since I expected Beverly to feel better after confronting what she had long believed to be a cruel betrayal of her mother, it took several sessions for me to fully appreciate the extent to which her mood had darkened. She seemed listless and preoccupied and she complained of feeling exhausted. Fortunately, a dream she presented during this period helped us understand the change in her:

> I am walking down the street with a very tall man. We pass a soda shop and decide to go in. The man orders an ice cream sundae for me. It's just what I want and it tastes delicious. The man says something like "you deserve it." Somehow I realize that my mother is sitting next to me and I'm overjoyed. I offer her some of my ice cream. But she's staring at me with an ugly, angry look on her face. I want to finish eating but I feel too scared. I wake up just as I'm about to run out.

Beverly decided that the tall man in the dream represented her father. The evening before the dream she had received a phone call from him. Something in his tone reminded her of the way he sometimes spoke to her as a child, "like I was his little princess." She recalled her mother's jealous rages when he bought Beverly presents or praised her. Beverly also remembered feeling she was bad and hurtful for wanting to be close to him. At the time of the divorce, her father had warned that her mother might make excessive demands on her and suggested that she live half the time with him. Although Beverly sensed he was looking out for her best interest, she feared that her mother would abandon her if she did not sever all ties to him. Besides, she could not trust him to control his temper, nor to provide for her with any more consistency than he had shown her mother.

I suggested that her current depression was the result of my inadvertently having put her in the same situation her father once had. By relieving her of responsibility for her mother's death, I made her feel less connected to her. With the loosening of her bond to her mother, she was forced to rely on someone who seemed far less likely to meet her needs. She had experienced my interpretation much as she had experienced her father's real-life gifts, or the ice cream sundae in the dream. It was an invitation to abandon her selfobject fantasies in which she served as selfobject for her mother, an invitation she feared would lead to psychological catastrophe. Beverly elaborated on my explanation. "Wonderful as you are," she said, "it's hard for me to trust that you'll always be there when I need you. You're not my mother."

In the third year of treatment, Beverly decided to separate from her husband and to initiate a divorce. Around the same time she began to attend meetings of a well-known therapeutic group organization at the urging of some business associates and became greatly attracted to the program. In response to her attempts to learn what I thought of the program, I explained that despite my reservations about its underlying philosophy, I trusted her feeling that it had much to offer her. After she decided to join, I congratulated her for doing what seemed right for her.

Despite my belief that it was a sign of therapeutic progress for Beverly to have joined the group program on her own initiative, I felt concerned about her involvement in an organization I distrusted. I also felt disappointed. Although I had not been fully aware of it until then, I had enjoyed Beverly's celebration of my competence as a therapist. Her songs of praise for the group program left me feeling that I could no longer count on her to sing mine. My trust in her as a provider of selfobject experiences for me was shaken. Moreover, the gains she had made in treatment with me seemed to compare unfavorably with the benefits she claimed to derive from the program. My trust in myself as a competent clinician was also disturbed.

For the next several months, Beverly's apparent cheerfulness in sessions contrasted with my feelings of depression and loss in her presence. Much as I tried, I could not regain my former sense of confidence in treating her. I disliked hearing about the friends she had made in the program and how much of her free time she had devoted to recruiting new members. Eventually, I realized that Beverly, too, felt differently about therapy. At times she would seem to run out of things to talk about and would ask if we could end early. She would assure me that she was feeling fine and really had nothing on her mind. My efforts to explore the wish to cut short the sessions proved futile.

I was startled by Beverly's announcement that she and her husband had reconciled. Several months after they reestablished their home together, Beverly decided to leave treatment. Although I was well aware that our therapeutic relationship had gotten off track, Beverly's decision to terminate came as an unexpected blow. I felt angry at Beverly, at the organization she had joined, and at myself. Confused and miserable, I merely indicated my respect for her decision and said I would welcome her back if she ever deemed it necessary.

In the preceding few months of therapy, Beverly had failed to pay my fee, and, by the time of her last sessions, she owed me a considerable amount of money. The diminutions in my self-trust had made it difficult for me to confront her missed payments as a treatment issue. As our final session came to a close, Beverly indicated that she would pay me in monthly installments. Every month thereafter I received a check for a portion of her debt, often accompanied by a brief note "to catch you up on my life." Then, several months after making her final payment, Beverly phoned to ask if I had time to see her. She said that she had become very depressed because Harry had not lived up to his promises. He had reverted to his critical, blaming manner, had exploded in rage at her over seemingly trivial matters and, even worse, he seemed to regard her as needing, more than ever, close surveillance lest she fail him as a wife and businesswoman.

During her first session after returning to therapy, Beverly described her disenchantment with the group program. She was annoyed by their pressured demands that she demonstrate greater allegiance to the program than she felt. Beverly confirmed my suggestion that the philosophy espoused by the program was much like her mother's. She said, "They agreed with Mom that I should be strong and put my own needs first. They said I could be anyone I wanted to be and do anything I wanted to do. But only if I did just as they advised and swore complete loyalty to them. I guess I always knew they were coercive but I saw only what I wanted to see."

Suddenly looking at me shrewdly, Beverly said, "You didn't really want me to join the program, did you? I wish you had advised me against it." These words were barely out of Beverly's mouth before she began to apologize for doubting my conduct of the treatment. "After all," she added quickly, "you wanted me to feel good about making my own decision."

Interrupting, I told her that I knew it was hard for her to criticize me. "You worry that, like your mother, I need you to take care of me by acting as if I'm above criticism." I acknowledged that my failure to advise her against joining the program had led to a serious rupture in our relationship. Nodding in agreement, she said, "I guess I was so used to having Harry act like my watchdog, it was scary to make decisions on my own."

I reminded her that she had not only left Harry, but that the treatment had resulted in her feeling less connected to her mother as well. Having been scrutinized and treated as if she were untrustworthy for so long, she was undoubtedly afraid that she could not do without my guidance. "I *was* feeling very shaky," Beverly responded, "like I couldn't be trusted to make the right moves. I needed you to tell me what to do but you didn't. Maybe I joined the program and got back with Harry to make up for what you weren't giving me."

I then interpreted Beverly's leaving treatment as a means by which she had hoped to avert retraumatization in the therapeutic relationship. I had let her down by failing to alert her to the dangers of joining the group program just as her mother had failed her by encouraging her to marry her husband. Beverly experienced the group program, like her husband, as an extension of her mother's possessiveness and control over her. "You had just begun to feel that you didn't have to take care of my feelings so vigilantly when I let you down." I said. "No wonder you decided to leave therapy." Her eyes full of tears, Beverly explained why she could not return to treatment until she paid back all she owed me. "I needed to show you that you could count on me again. That's my way isn't it? I show how strong and dependable I am and get someone to lean on me when I really need them to be strong for me."

The working through of the disturbance in Beverly's experience of herself as trustworthy continued to occupy center stage in the treatment for quite a while. For the most part, this involved Beverly's attempts to make certain calamity would not befall her if she relaxed her vigilant attempts to serve my psychological needs. A good example of this process occurred in the final stages of Beverly's treatment, soon after she separated from her husband for the second time. Her children had become angry with her and had rallied around their father. In an effort to regain her connection to her eldest son, she had written him a letter, a copy of which she read in a session. In the letter Beverly listed many of the wonderful qualities she saw in her son and told him repeatedly about the depth of her love for him. I wondered is she were not attempting to relate to her son as she had with her mother and with me earlier in treatment. By using flattery and assurances of undying devotion, she was attempting to persuade her son that she was indispensable to his psychological well-being.

Beverly seemed to respond well to my interpretation, and even acknowledged that perhaps her effusive praise was meant to make her son feel so guilty he would no longer vent his anger at her. However, in the following session Beverly seemed extremely depressed. She also expressed hopelessness about her chances for happiness without Harry and suggested that perhaps it was wrong to go through with the divorce.

I wondered if there had been a disturbance in our relationship. "You were dead wrong," she finally blurted out. "Things are great between me and my son. He loved the letter. He needed to hear all those good things in it." Beverly had been afraid to tell me that my comments on her letter to her son had felt like disparaging criticisms. Once again she feared that expressing her own views and feelings without regard for mine, in this case being critical of me, would be tantamount to losing me. She had needed my vote of confidence in her efforts to reconnect with her son. Lacking it she felt that I had doubted her trustworthiness in relation to him. Soon after I conveyed my understanding of this disturbance between us, her depression lifted.

By the conclusion of our therapeutic relationship after six years, Beverly's experience of herself as trusted and trustworthy had matured considerably. We had successfully worked through a paralyzing dilemma created by her need to comply with her mother's directive that she "look out for number one," and her fear that only flawless attention to another person's selfobject requirements would guarantee a relationship. Her self-confidence was no longer a studied posture adopted as means of serving her mother's needs – it had become an authentic expression of her now genuinely vital self.

James

After arriving 15 minutes late for his first session, James, a fairly successful actor in his late thirties, introduced himself to me as "Old Unreliable." "Why didn't you start without me?" he joked. James's youthful features, somewhat ungainly way of moving, and his "uniform" of jeans, a tee shirt, and a battered baseball cap lent a strongly adolescent cast to his appearance. Despite his elaborately casual and offhand way of addressing me, he seemed ill at ease. He folded and unfolded his arms and legs restlessly and his eyes darted quickly from place to place as if he were searching the room for some means of escape.

The steady stream of jokes and wisecracks James produced throughout the session reduced me to helpless laughter. When I observed to him that therapy and therapists were the frequent targets of his mocking wit, James admitted having serious doubts about treatment. His mother, he explained, had spent years in therapy without being helped. His only reason for consulting me was to appease Amy, his girlfriend. She had threatened to leave him unless he resolved his ambivalence about getting married. He flatly rejected my suggestion that he should have two sessions a week. "I don't need a second career," he said. "Besides, I'll never make it to the top as a patient." As he prepared to leave the office he hummed the melody of "I Won't Grow Up," from the musical *Peter Pan*. "Now, that pretty much sums up my attitude," he said. "I just want to be an irresponsible kid for the rest of my life. You can't say I'm not a challenge."

In subsequent sessions James provided only the sketchiest outline of his life, claiming that he had a "lousy memory." He mentioned growing up in a working-class suburb of a large city, and that he had been indistinguishable from the other neighborhood children in all respects expect for his burning desire to be a performer. James spoke nostalgically of having devised "shows" for which he wrote the scripts, directed the other children, played the music, sang, and danced. One of his shows was especially memorable, he noted, because his father, mother, and older sister joined the other parents to watch the performance, one of the rare times he remembered their all being together. He explained that his father traveled extensively as part of his job and that his mother periodically had to be hospitalized for severe depression. He recalled that her hospitalizations often followed suicide attempts. Asked what that was like for him, James snapped, "I told you I don't remember much of my childhood."

I soon learned that any attempt to elicit more information than James had volunteered upset him a great deal. Invariably he would express his distress in sarcastic, humorous language. For example, in response to a particularly probing question, James said in a mock-angry voice, "You're never satisfied, are you? I give you a short story, you want an epic novel." After several months had elapsed, James let me know that he was not any closer to resolving his difficulties with Amy. He explained that from the beginning of their relationship, periods of relative calm alternated with violent fights that usually ended with one of them leaving the apartment. Amy would often resort to throwing dishes, smacking him, and even banging her head against the wall in frustration. Nevertheless, James described her as "the single most stabilizing influence in my life—until she takes off on me."

James seemed to have little doubt that Amy's outbursts were caused by her dissatisfaction with him. "I'm a selfish, moody guy," he said. "Things go okay for a while and then I seem to get turned off. I just stop ₁ring about her. Amy says I'm withholding, but I always feel that she's asking for more than I want to give. For instance, she wants an engagement ring. But, that means I'd have to spend the rest of my life with her. I'm not even sure I want to spend the rest of my life with me."

I soon became aware that James's relationship with me recreated the on-again, off-again pattern of his relationship with Amy. James would keep his appointments for about a month, although rarely on time, and then fail to appear for several sessions. On returning he would make no effort to explain his sudden disappearances from treatment except to make casual references to out-of-town trips. My efforts to explore the meaning of his unannounced absences would lead to irritated outbursts. "I don't know why I didn't show up and I couldn't care less. You're wasting my time with these questions," he would say.

James's absences and latenesses, his unwillingness to discuss them, as well as his frequent expressions of doubt about the usefulness of therapy took their toll on my trust in him. He was hardly the patient I counted on to reassure me of my effectiveness as a therapist. Although I suspected that his behavior represented tests of therapeutic trustworthiness, their meaning eluded me. Fortunately, the first dream James reported shed some light on our difficulties:

> There's this kid on stage, tap dancing I think. He's dancing his heart out. It's some kind of audition. A woman is sitting in the second row with a clipboard. Could be the director. She keeps yelling in this nasty voice, "Come on. You can do better than that."

Associating to the dream, James said, "I guess you could say the woman looks like you. Not that you would even think of talking to me that way. The only woman who ever really sounded that nasty was my mother." James spoke of his mother's intense but sporadic interest in him as an entertainer. Having studied acting herself as a young woman, James said, she desperately wanted one of her children to be a performer. "Why else would she have saddled me with this name. It actually says 'Jimmy Stewart' on my birth certificate. I decided to go with James because I thought my real name would be a hindrance to my career rather than a help. I'm no Jimmy Stewart. How could I ever live up to that name?"

James recalled that his mother had arranged for voice, dance, acting, and piano lessons at various points in his childhood. She would tell him that with his promise he was destined to become a star. However, her enthusiastic support rarely lasted for more than a few months at a time. Then she would criticize him for not practicing hard enough and often followed through on her threats to discontinue his lessons. "I always had the feeling I was letting her down," James said. "Even when I began to make it as an actor, she didn't seem satisfied. She complained that I never got the lead. I think I felt worse for her than I did for me."

I suggested that my implicit requirement that he show up punctually for sessions made him worry that I needed him to do better in therapy, that he was disappointing me. He acknowledged that on finding himself late for sessions he often thought to himself, "Old Unreliable strikes again!" I connected his sense of being unreliable in therapy with the image he seemed to have of himself as a disappointment to the two most important women in his life: his mother and Amy. James's description of his experience when anticipating a woman's disappointment, of "dread verging on terror, but it's sort of outside me," suggested that he entered a dissociated state at such times.

He suddenly recalled having a similar experience the morning his mother was hospitalized for the first time following a failed suicide attempt. He remembered himself as quite young—he guessed around five or six—and believed his father had been away at the time. The noisy invasion of police and emergency medical workers had awakened him. He recalled feeling paralyzed as he watched his mother, only barely conscious, being carried away on a stretcher. He remembered crying uncontrollably that evening on finding himself alone with his teenaged sister. Adding to his distress was his conviction that he was responsible for the catastrophe. In a breaking voice, he recalled that his mother had chastized him for neglecting his piano practice the previous day. "I distinctly remember thinking that if only I'd tried harder she's still be home." In response to my suggestion that he felt his mother needed more from him than he could give, James noted, "She killed herself in the hospital a few years ago," he said. "I know it sounds crazy, but I thought that if I had made it big enough, got a starring role in a Broadway show, she'd have stayed alive."

That James's difficulties with Amy reflected his earlier difficulties with his mother became increasingly clear over the next several sessions. Amy's outbursts and tendency to break off the relationship when she was disappointed in James seemed to have replicated for him his mother's depressions and hospitalizations. Just as with his mother, James felt that if only he had given more, he would have prevented the woman's emotional breakdown. Yet he felt driven to rescript his trauma scenarios again and again; he continued to behave in ways he knew would disappoint the woman in the hope that this time there would be no catastrophic abandonment.

Despite these insights, little changed between James and Amy and his intermittent attendance pattern in therapy persisted. Then, after failing to appear for a scheduled session, he arrived 15 minutes early for his next appointment. "I hope you weren't planning to take a nap," he joked, as he entered the office. "You won't believe this, but I actually wanted to be here. It used to seem like you needed to see me more than I needed to see you and I guess I felt scared about pleasing you. Maybe that's the way I feel with Amy. Even though I'm crazy nuts about her, it's scary to please her by asking her to marry me."

Recalling his early traumas, I said, "Maybe you worried that if you came reliably, I'd expect more from you than you were prepared to give. If you give your all you face the awful possibility that your best isn't good enough, that you might not be able to prevent another catastrophe like your mother's suicide." I added that it might also feel safer for him to leave or disappoint the woman before she has the opportunity to leave or disappoint him. James then observed that his worries about being left by a disappointed woman had been the cause of several failed relationships, including a brief marriage just before he met Amy. "How can I ask another woman to marry me?" he sighed. "It's a sure way to ruin a great relationship!"

In the months that followed, James seemed to find our sessions almost unbearably stressful. "This doesn't help," he would groan. "I feel worse than I ever did. What am I doing here?" Yet he kept his scheduled sessions and arrived on time for most of them. By this time he had all but abandoned his attempts to make me laugh. Clearly depressed, he spoke about his profound loathing for himself as a selfish, disappointing, unreliable person. He now devoted less time to the ups and downs in his relationship with Amy than to the unsteadiness of his career. "Sometimes, I'm good and I know it. I just flow with the role I'm playing," he said. "Then, unpredictably, I'm off. I never know when it's going to happen. But it's usually when I need to make a really good impression, like when I know a reviewer is in the audience." Evidently, fears of catastrophe should his best prove not good enough affected his professional life as well.

In one session, James seemed even more depressed than usual. He mentioned that he would be performing in a local theater. "I don't suppose you ever go to this kind of thing," he said. I asked him if he wanted me to see him perform. He emphasized his reluctance to make excessive demands on me and assured me my attendance was "no big deal" to him. Although I realized that it was risky for me to see him perform without fully understanding what meanings this had for him, I attended his opening night performance.

James arrived early for his next session looking calm and happy. I let him know how much I had enjoyed seeing him act. He said he could tell that I was pleased and wondered why he had been unable to let me know beforehand how much my attending the performance meant to him. For the first time, James's eyes filled with tears. "I was so afraid that I wouldn't be able to do well with you there. But just before I went on, I knew I wouldn't disappoint you or myself. Something felt different." We understood that by attending his play I had enabled him to test his newfound confidence in himself as a trustworthy performer and had proved my reliability as an admiring, supportive maternal figure.

In the weeks that followed, James's mood seemed to brighten appreciably. He reported a significant change in his perception of Amy. He realized that her psychological problems were similar to his mother's. "It's not normal to bang your head against the wall when you get upset," he said. He acknowledged that part of his attraction to Amy lay in her resemblance to his mother and his hope that he could be the source of a woman's happiness rather than the cause of her leaving him. His acknowledgement of her psychological problems appeared to result in a significant improvement in their relationship. Although they still fought, they now managed to resolve their differences without smashing china and slamming doors. Eventually James asked Amy to marry him. "I know I won't let her down," he said. "She doesn't need very much. Just my being there."

Feeling concerned about James's apparent mission to rescue Amy from mental illness by marrying her and thereby rescripting the traumas of his mother's suicidal depressions, I urged him to postpone the wedding until his gains in therapy were consolidated. He refused, noting that he had kept her waiting long enough. "She really wants kids," he said. "I don't want us to look like their grandparents."

As James put it, "The honeymoon was over before the honeymoon began." Amy and James had their first big fight as a married couple on their wedding day and many more in the weeks that followed. Although James reacted to news that Amy was pregnant with excitement and pride, he feared they would fail dismally as parents. Unfortunately, the birth of James's son, Scott, coincided with a dry spell in his career. Amy blamed James for the financial difficulties they encountered. Accusing him of shirking his duties as a husband and father, she challenged him to give up his acting career for "a real job" that would provide them with more money. James chided Amy for failing to lose the weight she had gained during her pregnancy and for devoting so much of her energy to child care that she neglected him. He confessed to feeling overcome with sexual longings for other women. In addition he turned to marijuana and cocaine, as he had done in adolescence, for "escape."

Extremely depressed, James berated himself for being a "loser." "I just can't get the hang of being a grown-up," he moaned. "I wasn't cut out for anything but an extended adolescence." He also expressed increasing doubts about therapy and his attendance again became erratic. The following is a significant dream from this period:

I'm with Scott in a fun house. Suddenly he darts away from me and I scream for him to stop because there's a hole in the floor ahead of him. But he keeps running and falls through the hole. I look down and see him lying motionless. As I try to rescue him, I catch a glimpse of your reflection in a distorting mirror. Then, I look again, and to my horror, I see flesh peeling away from your bones. You turn into a grotesquely leering skeleton.

James's first association to the dream was to traveling with his father on a business trip when he was a child. His initial excitement had changed to boredom and acute homesickness when he realized that his father regarded him as a burden. One day his father grudgingly acquiesced to his pleas to stop at a carnival they passed along the road. Although his father brought him cotton candy and let him go on many rides, James noticed that he seemed preoccupied and distant. James remembered deliberately slipping away and getting lost in an effort to shock his father into paying more attention to him. But his plan backfired; his father seemed even more remote and depressed after they were reunited. Later his father confided to him, "I told your mother it was crazy to have kids. Neither one of us was cut out to be a parent."

James wept at this memory. "The old guy probably felt just as rotten about himself as I feel about myself." He accepted my suggestion that his father's failure to offer James a model of reliable paternal care had contributed to his inability to feel trustworthy in his caretaking roles. James noted that his relationship with his father had improved in later years. Unlike his mother, his father had unfailingly expressed pride in James's accomplishments as an actor. James said he had been grief-stricken when he died a short time after his mother killed herself.

Associating to the dream image in which I became a leering skeleton, James remarked that once again a woman who looks like me in a dream reminded him more of his mother. "Maybe I feel that even in her grave she's still disappointed in me, contemptuous," he mused. "I know she would agree with Amy that I'm hopelessly unreliable as a husband and father, that I should give up show business and admit I'm washed up professionally." I asked if he was worried that I shared these sentiments, that I too felt disappointed that he had not done "the right thing" by leaving show business. "Well, isn't becoming a '9-to-5 man' the mature, healthy thing to do?" James asked. I told him that he undoubtedly needed stronger assurances of my confidence in him during this stressful time than I had managed to convey, and I again suggested that he might benefit from seeing me more often. James argued that he found it hard enough to show up for his once-weekly sessions. Then he mentioned that he had refused Amy's request that he accompany her to marital therapy. "This is about as much therapy as I can stand."

After a while James seemed to regain, to some extent, his experience of himself as a reliable adult. He was buoyed by having received a leading role in a show that allowed him to display his talents as a dancer and singer as well as an actor. In addition, he found himself greatly enjoying the time he spent with Scott while Amy worked. However, when the show closed and he once again had difficulty finding acting jobs, the strains in his marriage worsened. Despite his trying circumstances, James managed to give up his dependence on drugs and to resist the temptation to have affairs with other women. He noted that he had become better able to withstand Amy's criticism without losing his confidence in himself. Moreover he felt his steady presence had enabled her to become a wonderful mother. "I'm a real family man," he said. "Imagine that!"

James was tearful in what turned out to be our final session. He acknowledged the validity of my assertion that he needed to come more frequently to finish treatment. However, he said he could not pay for additional sessions and still afford marital therapy, which he now felt was necessary for the survival of his marriage. He proposed stopping our sessions for a time before returning to finish up "the way it should be done." "You've helped me to grow up," he said. I congratulated James on making a mature but difficult decision and I assured him that I would welcome him back when he was ready to return.

Discussion

The cases of Beverly and James illustrate the working through of disturbances in self-as-trustworthy in the therapeutic relationship. For both patients, disturbances in this realm resulted from failed efforts to serve as trustworthy providers for their mothers' selfobject needs. Beverly's attempt to bolster her mother's self-esteem placed her in a difficult dilemma: In order to reinforce her mother's cherished self-image as an omniscient advisor, Beverly sought to follow her advice in all matters, even her confusing insistence that Beverly "look out for number one." She could not simultaneously put her mother's needs first and follow her advice. Unable to contradict her mother's false assurances about her health without failing to provide mirroring selfobject experiences for her, Beverly blamed herself when her mother died. At the same time, her mother's death represented a traumatizing betrayal of Beverly's self-trust.

On entering treatment, Beverly initially experienced the therapeutic relationship as recreating her relationship with her mother. She tried to provide for my selfobject needs as she once did her mother's by lavishing me with praise and assuring me of my omniscience as a therapist. Gradually she tested the therapeutic trustworthiness by making decisions on her own and by expressing an ever greater range of feelings. Unfortunately, I inadvertently threatened her with a retraumatizing betrayal by failing to share my reservations about a group program she had joined. Like her husband whom her mother had encouraged her to marry, the program represented an extension of her mother's possessiveness and control.

Beverly's decision to drop out of therapy represented her only hope of preserving her connection to me. After paying off her debt to me and thereby symbolically reestablishing herself as a trustworthy caretaker of my needs, she was enabled to resume treatment. Fortunately, Beverly was able to reveal her disappointment in me despite her fears of abandonment. Once the meaning of the disruption in our relationship was understood, we were able to resume the working-through process.

Named for a movie star whose fame he could scarcely hope to equal, James's childhood was burdened by his mother's need for vicarious success as a performer. Attributing his mother's suicidal depressions to his failure to work hard enough for her, James felt that more was required of him than he could possibly provide. James's father's inability to model pride in paternal trustworthiness further contributed to his sense of being a disappointment to others.

Fearing retraumatizing betrayals on the order of his mother's suicide attempts in childhood, James developed the persona of "Mr. Unreliable." By disappointing others before they could disappoint him, James hoped to find some measure of safety. However, the resulting diminution of self-as-trustworthy adversely affected his self-esteem, his career, and his relationships with women.

James's thwarted need to be trusted quickly claimed the foreground of therapy. He tested the therapeutic relationship by coming late, missing sessions, and cynically questioning the value of treatment. As a result of my initial failure to comprehend the meaning of these tests, my trust in myself and in him eroded. Only after his dream of the dissatisfied director did I understand his behavior as attempts to avert a retraumatizing betrayal within the therapeutic relationship. Working through disruptions in the therapeutic relationship resulted in a strengthening of James's experience of himself as trustworthy and a reduction of his fear of catastrophic desertion by a woman needed as a selfobject if his best proved to be not good enough.

Chapter 9

MOVING FORWARD

To suffer woes which Hope thinks infinite;
To forgive wrongs darker than death or night;
To defy Power which seems omnipotent;
To love, and bear; to hope till Hope creates
From its own wreck the thing it contemplates

Percy Bysshe Shelley, Prometheus Unbound, *IV:1.570*

With self-psychological theory as my Baedeker, I have explored virtually uncharted terrain in psychoanalysis. The preceding chapters record my reconnaissance of self-trust, the realm of trust that is vital to the experience of selfhood. Nearing the end of my travels, I find that I have not ended up in some distant outpost of self psychology but, rather, at its core. Moreover, from my new vantage point, the theory that guided me appears changed in a number of respects. I will now summarize these changes by answering some pertinent questions about self-trust and its clinical application. I will then examine some implications of employing a self-trust perspective, and finally, suggest a number of areas for future expeditions.

A SUMMARY OF SELF-TRUST AND ITS CLINICAL APPLICATION

What is Self-Trust?

Self-trust is defined as the hope or wishful expectation of obtaining and providing the selfobject experiences necessary for cohesive selfhood. Four dimensions of self-trust have been identified:

1. Trust-in others—the tendency to view others as trustworthy providers of selfobject experiences

2. Trust-in-self—the tendency to view oneself as capable of eliciting selfobject experiences from others

3. Self-as-trustworthy—the tendency to view oneself as a trustworthy provider of selfobject experiences for others

4. Others-as-self-trusting—the tendency to view others as trusting of their capacity to obtain and provide selfobject experiences

What Is the Role of Self-Trust in Mental Life?

Insofar as self-trust mediates between the world of subjective reality and the world of selfobject fantasy, it serves as the glue of self-experience. The unconscious selfobject fantasies that organize self-experience (Ulman & Brothers, 1988) consist of affect-laden images of others providing selfobject experiences for oneself and of oneself providing selfobject experiences for others. Only those deemed trustworthy are represented in selfobject fantasies. Trustworthiness is determined by experiences that demonstrate affectively attuned responsiveness to selfobject need.

How Does Self-Trust Develop?

Recent infancy research confirms Kohut's (1977) and Tolpin's (1980) assertions that we are born with trust. The four self-trust dimensions appear in nascent form in earliest infancy. Self-trust matures over the course of development as the criteria used to evaluate self-trust in the four dimensions become more realistic, abstract, complex, and differentiated. Everyone develops a unique self-trust organization as a consequence of inevitable developmental traumas.

What Is the Relationship Between Self-Trust and Trauma?

Betrayals of self-trust lie at the heart of trauma. When the meaning of an event is construed as a betrayal of any of the four self-trust dimensions, the glue of selfobject relatedness between self and others is loosened causing selfobject fantasies to shatter. As self-experience disorganizes, survivors suffer unbearable disintegration anxiety and excruciating feelings of shame and rage.

Striving to restore selfobject fantasies and quell these overwhelmingly negative affects, they dissociatively alter their experience of subjective reality in an attempt to reestablish trust in themselves and/or others.

Why Does Trauma Involve Dissociation?

Selfobject fantasies depend on what Noy (1980) called the self-centered organizational mode (primary process) whereas the experience of subjective reality depends on the reality-oriented organizational mode (secondary process). Ordinarily these two modes function simultaneously and harmoniously. Traumatizing betrayals of self-trust lead to profound changes in both realms of self-experience and cause arrests in their development. The resulting imbalances between the two organizational modes are responsible for dissociative phenomena such as depersonalization and derealization.

How is the Experience of Subjective Reality Altered in the Wake of Traumatizing Betrayals of Self-Trust?

The following changes in self-experience contribute to the alteration of subjective reality following self-trust betrayals:

1. Affected dimensions of self-trust are either diminished or intensified (self-trust disturbance is bidirectional).

2. Immature criteria for self-trust are retained or reinstated.

3. Aspects of self-experience antithetical to the survivor's dissociatively altered reality (e.g., memories of traumatizing betrayals, their meaning, or affects associated with them) are eliminated from consciousness (repressed) creating "black holes" in self-experience.

4. Various psychological strategems may be employed as a means of filling in these black holes (e.g., the dissociated aspects of self-experience may be expressed in alternating states of consciousness, they may be elaborated into alter personalties as in multiple personality disorders, or they may be attributed to others, contact with whom provides alter ego selfobject experiences).

5. Attempts may be made to rescript trauma scenarios, often by means of sadomasochistic enactments.

How are Disorders of Self-Experience Viewed from a Self-Trust Perspective?

Betrayals of self-trust are seen as elements of all disorders of self-experience. This view derives from Kohut's (1984) assertion that the "flaws in the self," which underlie all psychopathological conditions, result from disturbances in "self-selfobject" relationships in childhood. Viewed in terms of self-trust, disturbances severe enough to cause flaws in the self are likely to be experienced as self-trust betrayals. The dissociative alteration of subjective reality concomitant with traumatizing betrayals of self-trust are, to varying degrees, also common to all self-disorders.

What Role Does Self-Trust Play in Therapeutic Relationships?

Since subjectivity is greatly influenced by the unique way in which self-trust is organized in any given person (i.e., by the varying degrees to which each self-trust dimension is intensified or diminished and the varying levels of maturity of the self-trust criteria used), it follows that the intersubjective field (Atwood & Stolorow, 1984) of treatment is profoundly affected by the self-trust organizations of therapist and patient. These self-trust configurations affect all that transpires in the therapeutic relationship. Both participants face a self-trust dilemma: Much as they wish to establish trustworthy selfobject relations, they fear retraumatizing self-trust betrayals. Threats of retraumatizing betrayal often lead to behaviorally enacted rescriptings of trauma scenarios both within and outside of the therapeutic relationship.

How is Treatment Conceptualized from a Self-Trust Perspective?

There are three interconnected elements that recur throughout treatment: testing, reconstructing, and working-through. Testing tends to be most prominent in the initial phase of treatment; reconstructing, in the middle phase; and working-through, in the final phase. Testing refers to the fact that patients and therapists construe events that occur in the therapeutic relationship to test its trustworthiness. "Empathic failures" are construed as failed tests of therapeutic trustworthiness and signal the imminence of retraumatizing betrayals. Reconstructing involves the analysis of past betrayals of self-trust in the lives of patients and the ways in which subjective reality was dissociatively

altered. Working-through refers to those responses to failed tests of trustworthiness within the therapeutic relationship that reduce fears of retraumatizing
betrayal and promote the maturation of self-trust.

How Does a Self-Trust Perspective Change the Focus of Self-Psychological Treatment?

Although treatment is guided by intersubjectivity theory and conducted in
accordance with familiar self-psychological principles, greater emphasis is
placed on the quality of selfobject relatedness between patient and therapist.
Attention is focused on changes in the various dimensions of self-trust in both
patient and therapist as they confront their self-trust dilemmas. A major goal
of treatment is to promote the maturation of the patient's self-trust. In successful treatment, extreme diminutions and intensifications in the various dimensions of self-trust are reduced and more realistic, abstract, complex, and
differentiated criteria are used. These changes in self-trust enable patients to
establish trustworthy relationships that promote vital and cohesive experiences of self.

IMPLICATIONS OF EMPLOYING A SELF-TRUST PERSPECTIVE

The Positive Quality and Particularity of Selfobject Experience

According to Lichtenberg, Lachmann, and Fosshage (1992), the term "negative selfobject" makes sense only when selfobjects are personified. Since the
term "selfobject experience" refers to a vitalizing or cohesion-producing affective state, this experience, by definition, cannot be negative. A self-trust
perspective is consistent with this view insofar as only those experienced as
trustworthy will be represented in selfobject fantasies: There are no untrustworthy, failing, bad, or traumatizing selfobjects. However, using the term
"selfobject experience" does not necessarily imply that those represented in
selfobject fantasies are interchangeable. On the contrary, we are very choosy
about those from whom we wish to receive selfobject experiences and those
for whom we wish to provide selfobject experiences. A self-trust perspective
helps explain why this is so. Highly idiosyncratic self-trust criteria are used to
determine the trustworthiness of self and others; those who fail to live up to

our self-trust criteria will not be represented in selfobject fantasies. In other words, selfobject experience involves oneself in relation to highly specific others.

The Therapeutic Effect of Empathy

According to Kohut (1981), "empathy per se, the mere presence of empathy, has also a beneficial, in a broad sense, a therapeutic effect—both in the clinical setting and in human life in general" (p. 544). This position becomes understandable when empathy is viewed as integral to selfobject experience. For example, Lichtenberg et al. (1992) observe that "when empathic responsiveness ensures an experience of cohesion and vitality of the self, we designate it as a selfobject experience" (p. 132). When does empathic responsiveness ensure an experience of cohesion and vitality of the self? Again, a self-trust perspective clarifies the issue. Empathic responsiveness is an almost universal criterion for self-trust. Those who fail to respond empathically are unlikely to be experienced as trustworthy and represented in selfobject fantasies. Hence, when viewed from the vantage point of self-trust, empathy is therapeutic to the extent that it promotes self-trust.

The Language of Self-Trust

In this book I have avoided using the terms *transference* and *countertransference* and have instead referred to various aspects of the therapeutic relationship. Instead of transference, I speak of the patient's thoughts or feelings for the therapist. Instead of countertransference, I speak of the therapist's thoughts or feelings for the patient. My main reason for doing so is that I believe the terms transference and countertransference are imbued with meanings inimical to a self-trust perspective, meanings that primarily reflect Freud's drive theory formulations. For example, Stolorow and Lachmann (1980) and Stolorow et al. (1987) have persuasively demonstrated the theoretical drawbacks associated with conceptualizing transference as regression, repetition, displacement, projection, and distortion. They argue in favor of reformulating transference as "organizing activity":

> [T]he concept of transference may be understood to refer to all the ways in which the patient's experience of the analytic relationship is shaped by his own psychological structures—by the distinctive, archaically rooted configurations of self and object that unconsciously organize his subjective universe. . . . The

transference is actually a microcosm of the patient's total psychological life, and the analysis of the transference provides a focal point around which the patterns dominating his existence as a whole can be clarified, understood, and thereby transformed. (Stolorow et al., p. 36)

In a similar vein, they conceptualize countertransference as a manifestation of the analyst's psychological structures and organizing activity. Since, as far as I can tell, there is *no* way in which the therapeutic relationship is not shaped by the patient's and the therapist's "organizing activity," I believe the terms transference and countertransference are superfluous and should be dispensed with; they contribute little beyond possibly unintended meanings. Moreover, when the therapeutic relationship is conceptualized in terms of self-trust, a clearer understanding is gained of much that transpires between patient and therapist.

I have also avoided using the term *resistance*. Although I prefer Kohut's (1970, 1984) view that resistance is undertaken as a means of safeguarding self-experience and motivated by fears of self-disintegration or depletion, to a more traditional view of resistance as a means of preventing anxiety- and guilt-provoking aggressive and sexual drive-wishes from becoming conscious, I believe a pejorative aura still clings to the term. The complex set of behaviors, attitudes, and expectations commonly known as resistance can be understood as responses to fear of retraumatizing betrayals of self-trust within the therapeutic relationship. Responses prompted by these fears usually take the form of tests of therapeutic trustworthiness.

Therapeutic Hopefulness

Hope, a close semantic cousin of trust, is defined as "a wish or desire supported by some confidence of its fulfillment" (*The American Heritage Dictionary*, 1980). The concept of self-trust helps to create an atmosphere of hope and optimism within the therapeutic relationship. Self-trust is seen as an inherent part of human psychological existence. No matter how catastrophic the consequences of past self-trust betrayals on one's self-experience, the longing to regain trust in self and others as providers of experiences needed for selfhood is never extinguished. It is basic to what Kohut (1984) called "*the principle of the primacy of self preservation*" (p. 143). Applying a self-trust perspective to the therapeutic relationship, therefore, promotes confidence that the mutual desire of patient and therapist for a successful outcome will be fulfilled.

SUGGESTIONS FOR FUTURE EXPLORATION

Although traumatizing betrayals of self-trust play a contributing role in all disorders of self-experience, they appear to assume special importance in the development of obsessive compulsive disorders, in which diminished trust-in-self is so prominent, and in the development of phobias, in which diminished trust-in-others and others-as-self-trusting are often found. Therefore, I believe a self-trust perspective should be particularly useful in furthering understanding of these conditions and their treatment.

In recent years, traditional psychoanalytic notions with respect to gender have been challenged by exciting and innovative investigations (e.g., Crawford, 1994). The assumption that gender is established once and for all as masculine or feminine in early life no longer seems tenable in light of this work. Because self-trust and gender organize self-experience so basically and profoundly, it stands to reason that a special relationship exists between them. An examination of this relationship might help to explain my (1982) finding that both men and women experience women as more trustworthy.

In recent years, many psychoanalysts have questioned the utility of the technical principles of therapeutic neutrality and abstinence. Although guidelines meant to replace these principles have been proposed (e.g., Lichtenberg et al., 1992), many questions still remain. For example, how much should therapists reveal about their personal lives? When is it advisable for therapists to disclose the reasons for their errors in empathic responsiveness? Should they reveal aggressive or sexual feelings for patients? Should they ever hug their patients? Employing a self-trust perspective, one might attempt to address these questions by evaluating the extent to which the therapists's actions promote or detract from the trustworthiness of the therapeutic relationship. Obviously, a great deal more study is needed in this area.

Most importantly, the concept of self-trust itself requires further investigation. The ideas set forth in this book have little value unless they are tested and refined to suit the individual needs of any reader who has been persuaded of their usefulness.

REFERENCES

Abraham, K. (1908). The psychosexual differences between hysteria and dementia praecox. In D. Bryan, & A. Strachey (Trans.), *Selected papers of Karl Abraham* (pp. 64–79). New York: Brunner/Mazel, 1927.

Adler, A. (1927). *Understanding human nature*. New York: Permabooks.

Ainsworth, M. D. S., & Eichberg, C. (1991). Effects on infant-mother attachment of mother's unresolved loss of an attachment figure, or other traumatic experiences. In C. M. Parkes, J. Stevenson-Hinde, & P. Marris (Eds.), *Attachment across the life cycle* (pp. 160–183). London: Routledge.

The American heritage dictionary of the English language. (1980). New College Edition. Boston: Houghton-Mifflin.

American Psychiatric Association. (1980). *Diagnostic and statistical manual of mental disorders* (3rd ed.). Washington, DC: Author.

American Psychiatric Association. (1994). *Diagnostic and statistical manual of mental disorders* (4th ed.). Washington, DC: Author.

Angyal, A. (1941). *Foundations for a science of personality*. New York: Commonwealth Fund.

Angyal, A. (1965). *Neurosis and treatment*. New York: John Wiley & Sons.

Arlow, J. A. (1969). Unconscious fantasy and disturbances of conscious experience. *Psychoanalytic Quarterly, 38*, 1–27.

Aronson, T. A. (1989). Paranoia and narcissism in psychoanalytic theory: Contributions of self psychology to the theory and therapy of the paranoid disorders. *Psychoanalytic Review, 76*, 329–352.

Atwood, G. E., & Stolorow, R. D. (1984). *The structures of subjectivity*. Hillsdale, NJ: Analytic.

Bacal, H. A. (1985). Optimal responsiveness and the therapeutic process. In A. Goldberg (Ed.), *Progress in self psychology* (Vol. 1, pp. 202–227). New York: Guilford.

Bacal, H. A. (1990). Does an object relations theory exist in self psychology? *Psychoanalytic Inquiry, 10*, 197–220.

Bacal, H. A., & Newman, K. M. (1990). *Theories of object relations: Bridges to self psychology*. New York: Columbia University Press.

Bach, S., & Schwartz, L. (1972). A dream of the Marquis de Sade: Psychoanalytic reflections on narcissistic trauma, decompensation, and the reconstruction of a delusional self. *Journal of the American Psychoanalytic Association, 20,* 451–475.

Bak, R. (1946). Masochism in paranoia. *Psychoanalytic Quarterly, 15,* 285–301.

Balint, M. (1935). Critical notes on the pregenital organization of the libido. In *Primary love and psycho-analytic technique* (pp. 49–72). London: Hogarth Press, 1952.

Balint, M. (1952). *Primary love and psycho-analytic technique.* London: Hogarth Press.

Balint, M. (1957). *Problems of human pleasure and behavior.* New York: Liveright.

Balint, M. (1968). *The basic fault: Therapeutic aspects of regression.* New York: Brunner Mazel.

Balint, M. (1969). Trauma and object relationship. *International Journal of Psycho-Analysis, 50,* 429–435.

Basch, M. F. (1983). The perception of reality and the disavowal of meaning. *International Journal of Psycho-Analysis, 11,* 125–153.

Baumeister, R. F. (1989). *Masochism and the self.* Hillsdale, NJ: Lawrence Erlbaum.

Baumeyer, F. (1956). The Schreber case. *International Journal of Psycho-Analysis, 37,* 61–74.

Beebe, B., Jaffe, J., & Lachmann, F. (1994). A dyadic systems model of mother-infant regulation: Implications for the origins of representations and therapeutic action. *Psychologist Psychoanalyst, 14,* 27–33.

Beebe, B., & Lachmann, F. M. (1988a). Mother-infant mutual influence and precursers of psychic structure. In A. Goldberg (Ed.), *Progress in self psychology* (Vol. 3, pp. 3–25). Hillsdale, NJ: Analytic.

Beebe, B., & Lachmann, F. M. (1988b). The contribution of mother-infant mutual influence to the origins of self and object representation. *Psychoanalytic Psychology, 5,* 305–338.

Beebe, B., & Stern, D. (1977). Engagement-disengagement and early object experiences. In M. Freedman, & S. Grand (Eds.), *Communicative structures and psychic structures* (pp. 35–55). New York: Plenum.

Benedek, T. (1938). Adaptation to reality in early infancy. In *Psychoanalytic investigations: Selected papers of Therese Benedek, M.D.* (pp. 113–128). New York: Quadrangle/N.Y. Times Book Co., 1973.

Benedek, T. (1952). *Studies in psychosomatic medicine: psychosexual functions in women.* New York: Ronald.

Benedek, T. (1956). Toward the biology of the depressive constellation. In *Psychoanalytic investigations: Selected papers of Therese Benedek, M.D.* (pp. 356–376). New York: Quadrangle/N.Y. Times Book Co., 1973.

Benedek, T. (1959). Parenthood as a developmental phase: a contribution to the libido theory. *Journal of the American Psychoanalytic Association, 7,* 389–417.

Benedek, T. (1960). The organization of the reproductive drive. *International Journal of Psycho-Analysis, 41,* 1–15.

Benjamin, J. (1988). *The bonds of love.* New York: Pantheon.

Benjamin, J. (1990). An outline of intersubjectivity: The development of recognition. *Psychoanalytic Psychology, 7*(Suppl.), 33–46.

Bettelheim, B. (1976). *The uses of enchantment: The meaning and importance of fairy tales.* New York: Knopf.

Block, D. (1989). Freud's retraction of his seduction theory and the Schreber case. *Psychoanalytic Review, 76,* 185–202.

Bottome, P. (1939). *Alfred Adler: Apostle of freedom.* London: Faber & Faber.

Bowlby, J. (1973). *Attachment and loss: Vol. 2. Separation.* London: Hogarth.

Bowlby, J. (1984). Violence in the family as a function of the attachment system. *American Journal of Psychoanalysis, 44,* 9–27.

Brenner, C. (1959). The masochistic character: Genesis and treatment. *Journal of the American Psychoanalytic Association, 7,* 197–226.

Brome, V. (1982). *Ernest Jones: Freud's alter ego.* London: Norton.

Brothers, D. (1982). *Trust disturbances among rape and incest victims.* (Unpublished doctoral dissertaion Yeshiva University). *Dissertation Abstracts International,* 1247, *43,* 4B.

Brothers, D. (1989, October). *Treating trust pathology in trauma survivors: A self-psychological approach.* Paper presented at The Twelfth Annual Conference on the Psychology of the Self, San Francisco.

Brothers, D. (1990, October). *The recollection of incest as a consequence of working through trust disturbances in the transference.* Paper presented at the Sixth Annual Meeting of the Society for Traumatic Stress Studies, New Orleans.

Brothers, D. (1992). Trust disturbance and the sexual revictimization of incest survivors: A self-psychological perspective. In A. Goldberg (Ed.), *Progress in self psychology* (Vol. 8, pp. 75–91). Hillsdale, NJ: Analytic.

Brothers, D. (1993). The search for the hidden self: A fresh look at alter ego transferences. In A. Goldberg (Ed.), *Progress in self psychology* (Vol. 9, pp. 191–207). Hillsdale, NJ: Analytic.

Brothers, D. (1994). Dr. Kohut and Mr. Z. Is this a case of alter ego countertransference? In A. Goldberg (Ed.), *Progress in self psychology* (Vol. 10, pp. 99–114). Hillsdale, NJ: Analytic.

Browne, A., & Finkelhor, D. (1986). The impact of child sexual abuse: A review of the research. *Psychological Bulletin, 99,* 66–77.

Buckley, P. (Ed.). (1986). *Essential papers on object relations.* New York: New York University Press.

Bunselmeyer, H. W. (1989, October). *Freud as a trauma survivor.* Paper presented at the Fifth Annual Meeting of the Society for Traumatic Stress Studies, San Francisco.

Bunselmeyer, H. W., & Ellerby, J. (1991). *Traumatic implications of Eckstein surgery on Sigmund Freud.* Unpublished manuscript.

Caplan, P. J. (1985). *The myth of women's masochism.* New York: E. P. Dutton.

Chun, K., & Campbell, J. (1974). Dimensionality of the Rotter interpersonal trust scale. *Psychological Reports, 35,* 1059–1070.

Cicero. (1966). In Verrem. In L. H. G. Greenwood (Trans.), *The Verrine Orations I* (Vol. 1). Cambridge, MA: Harvard University Press.

Cohen, J. (1980). Structural consequences of psychic trauma: A new look at "Beyond the Pleasure Principle." *International Journal of Psycho-Analysis, 61,* 421–432.

Cohen, J. (1981). Theories of narcissism and trauma. *American Journal of Psychotherapy, 35,* 93–100.

Cohen, J., & Kinston, W. (1984). Repression theory: A new look at the cornerstone. *International Journal of Psycho-Analysis, 65,* 411–422.

Collodi, C. (1987). *Pinocchio* (M. A. Murray, Trans.). New York: Children's Classics, Division of Dilithium Press. (Original work published in 1883).

Condon, W. S., & Sander, L. (1974). Neonate movement is synchronized with adult speech. *Science, 183,* 99–101.

Corrazini, J. (1977). Trust as a complex multi-dimensional construct. *Psychological Reports, 40,* 75–80.

Crabtree, A. (1993). Multiple personality before "Eve." *Dissociation, 6,* 66–73.

Crawford, J. (1994, October). *The severed self: Gender as trauma.* Paper presented at The Seventeenth Annual Conference on the Psychology of the Self, Chicago.

Davies, J. M., & Frawley, M. G. (1994). *Treating the adult survivor of childhood sexual abuse: A psychoanalytic perspective.* New York: Basic.

DeCasper, A., & Carstens, A. (1980). Contingencies of stimulation: Effects on learning and emotion in neonates. *Infant Behavior and Development, 4,* 19–36.

de Forest, I. (1954). *The leaven of love.* New York: Harper.

deMause, L. (1991). The universality of incest. *Journal of Psychohistory, 19,* 123–164.

Detrick, D. W. (1985). Alterego phenomena and the alterego transferences. In A. Goldberg (Ed.), *Progress in self psychology* (Vol. 2, pp. 240–256). New York: Guilford.

Detrick, D. W. (1986). Alterego phenomena and the alterego transferences: Some further considerations. In A. Goldberg (Ed.), *Progress in self psychology* (Vol. 2, pp. 299–304). New York: Guilford.

Deutsch, H. (1944). *The psychology of women*. New York: Grune & Stratton.

Deutsch, M. (1973). *The resolution of conflict: Constructive and destructive issues*. New Haven: Yale University Press.

Elder, G.(1985). Problem behavior and family relationships: Life course and intergenerational themes. In A. Sorenson, F. Weinert, & L. Sherrod (Eds.), *Human development: Multidisciplinary perspectives* (pp. 293–340). Hillsdale, NJ: Lawrence Erlbaum.

Emde, R. N. (1981). Changing models of infancy and the nature of early development: Remodeling the foundation. *Journal of the American Psychoanalytic Association, 29,* 179–219.

Emde, R. N. (1988a). Development terminable and interminable. I. Innate and motivational factors. *International Journal of Psycho-Analysis, 69,* 23–42.

Emde, R. N. (1988b). Development terminable and interminable. II. Recent psychoanalytic theory and therapeutic considerations. *International Journal of Psycho-Analysis, 69,* 283–296.

Emde, R. N. (1990). Mobilizing fundamental modes of development: Empathic availability and therapeutic action. *Journal of the American Psychoanalytic Association, 38,* 881–913.

Erikson, E. H. (1950). *Childhood and society*. New York: Norton.

Erikson, E. H. (1959). Identity and the life cycle. In G. S. Klein (Ed.), *Psychological issues* (pp. 54–78). New York: International Universities Press.

Erikson, E. H. (1964). Growth and crises of the "healthy personality." In C. Kluckhorn, & H. Murray (Eds.), *Personality in nature, society, and culture*. New York: Wiley.

Erikson, E. H. (1968). *Identity, youth and crisis*. New York: Norton.

Erikson, E. H. (1982). *The life cycle completed: A review*. New York: Norton.

Fantz, R. (1963). Pattern vision in newborn infants. *Science, 140,* 296–297.

Ferenczi, S. (1919). Technical difficulties in an analysis of hysteria. In J. Rickman (Ed.), J. I. Suttie (Trans.), *Further contributions to the theory and technique of psycho-analysis* (pp. 189–197). London: Hogarth, 1960.

Ferenczi, S. (1920). The further development of active technique. In J. Rickman (Ed.), J. I. Suttie (Trans.), *Further contributions to the theory and technique of psycho-analysis* (pp. 198–217). London: Hogarth, 1960.

Ferenczi, S. (1932). Note. In M. Balint (Ed.), E. Mosbacher (Trans.), *Final contributions to the problems and methods of psycho-analysis* (p. 270). New York: Basic, 1955.

Ferenczi, S. (1933). Confusion of tongues between adults and the child. In M. Balint (Ed.), E. Mosbacher (Trans.), *Final contributions to the problems and methods of psycho-analysis* (pp. 156–167). New York: Basic, 1955.

Ferenczi, S. (1955). *Final contributions to the problems and methods of psycho-analysis*. (M. Balint, Ed.; E. Mosbacher, Trans.). New York: Basic.

Finkelhor, D., & Dziuba-Leatherman, J. (1994). Victimization of children. *American Psychologists, 49,* 173–183.

Franklin, M. (1981). Play as the creation of imaginary situations: The role of language. In S. Wapner, & B. Kaplan (Eds.), *Toward a Holistic Developmental Psychology* (pp. 197–220). Hillsdale, NJ: Lawrence Erlbaum.

Frieze, I. (1983). Investigating the causes and consequences of marital rape. *Signs, 8,* 532–553.

Freud, A. (1966). *The ego and the mechanisms of defense*. New York: International Universities Press.

Freud, S. (1895). Letter to Fliess, Draft H. In J. M. Masson (Ed.), *The complete letters of Sigmund Freud to Wilhelm Fliess 1887–1904* (pp. 107–113). Cambridge, MA: The Belknap Press of Harvard University Press.

Freud, S. (1896). Further remarks on the neuropsychoses of defense. In E. Jones (Ed.) & J. Riviere (Trans.), *Sigmund Freud: Collected papers* (Vol. 1, pp. 155–182). New York: Basic, 1959.

Freud, S. (1900). The interpretation of dreams. In J. Strachey (Ed. and Trans.), *The standard edition of the complete psychological works of Sigmund Freud* (Vols. 4, 5). New York: Norton, 1953.

Freud, S. (1905). Three essays on the theory of sexuality. In J. Strachey (Ed. and Trans.), *The standard edition of the complete psychological works of Sigmund Freud* (Vol. 7, pp. 135–243). New York: Norton, 1953.

Freud, S. (1908). Hysterical phantasies and their relation to bisexuality. In J. Strachey (Ed. and Trans.), *The standard edition of the complete psychological works of Sigmund Freud* (Vol. 9, pp. 159–166). New York: Norton, 1959.

Freud, S. (1911). Psycho-analytic notes on an autobiographical account of a case of paranoia (dementia paranoides). In J. Strachey (Ed. and Trans.), *The standard edition of the complete psychological works of Sigmund Freud* (Vol. XII, pp. 3–82). New York: Norton, 1958.

Freud, S. (1913). On beginning the treatment (Further recommendations on the technique of psycho-analysis I). In J. Strachey (Ed. and Trans.), *The standard edition of the complete works of Sigmund Freud* (Vol. 12, pp. 123–144). New York: Norton, 1959.

Freud, S. (1914a). On narcissism: An introduction. In J. Strachey (Ed. and Trans.), *The standard edition of the complete psychological works of Sigmund Freud* (Vol. 14, pp. 67–102). New York: Norton, 1957.

Freud, S. (1914b). On the history of the psycho-analytic movement. In J. Strachey (Ed. and Trans.), *The standard edition of the complete psychological works of Sigmund Freud* (Vol. 14, pp. 7–66). New York: Norton, 1957.

Freud, S. (1919a). The uncanny. In J. Strachey (Ed. and Trans.), *The standard edition of the complete psychological works of Sigmund Freud* (Vol. 17, pp. 217–252). New York: Norton, 1957.

Freud, S. (1919b). A child is being beaten. In J. Strachey (Ed. and Trans.), *The standard edition of the complete psychological works of Sigmund Freud* (Vol. 17, pp. 175–204). New York: Norton, 1957.

Freud, S. (1920). Beyond the pleasure principle. In J. Strachey (Ed. and Trans.), *The standard edition of the complete psychological works of Sigmund Freud* (Vol. 18, pp. 3–64). New York: Norton, 1955.

Freud, S. (1924). The economic problem of masochism. In J. Strachey (Ed. and Trans.), *The standard edition of the complete psychological works of Sigmund Freud* (Vol. 19, pp. 153–170). New York: Norton, 1961.

Freud, S. (1925). Some psychical consequences of the anatomical distinction between the sexes. In J. Strachey (Ed. and Trans.), *The standard edition of the complete psychological works of Sigmund Freud* (Vol. 19, pp. 243–258). New York: Norton, 1961.

Freud, S. (1933 [1932]). New introductory lectures on psycho-analysis. In J. Strachey (Ed. and Trans.), *The standard edition of the complete psychological works of Sigmund Freud* (Vol. 22, pp. 1–182). New York: Norton, 1964.

Freud, S. (1937). Analysis terminable and interminable. In J. Strachey (Ed. and Trans.), *The standard edition of the complete psychological works of Sigmund Freud* (Vol. 23, pp. 216–253). New York: Norton, 1964.

Freud, S. (1940 [1938]). An outline of psycho-analysis. In J. Strachey (Ed. and Trans.), *The standard edition of the complete psychological works of Sigmund Freud* (Vol. 23, pp. 139–207). New York: Norton, 1964.

Garfield, D. A. S., & Havens, L. (1991). The treatment of paranoid phenomena: The development of the self. *American Journal of Psychotherapy, 47*, 75–89.

Gay, P. (1988). *Freud: A life for our time*. New York: Norton.

Gilligan, C. (1982). *In a different voice*. Cambridge, MA: Harvard University Press.

Glover, E. (1945). Examination of the Klein system of child psychology. In R. Eissler et al. (Eds.), *The psychoanalytic study of the child* (Vol. 1, pp. 75–118). New York: International Universities Press.

Goldberg, A. (1988). *A fresh look at psychoanalysis: The view from self psychology*. Hillsdale, NJ: Analytic.

Goldstein, K. (1947). *Human nature in the light of psychopathology*. Cambridge, MA: Harvard University Press.

Goleman, D. (1989, March 28). Researchers trace empathy's roots to infancy. *The New York Times*, p. C1.

Goleman, D. (1994, January 14). 1 in 2 experience a mental disorder. *The New York Times*, p. A20.

Greenacre, P. (1957). The childhood of the artist. In *Emotional growth* (pp. 479–504). New York: International Universities Press, 1971.

Greif, A. C. (1989). Introduction: historical synthesis. In J. D. Montgomery, & A. C. Greif (Eds.), *Masochism: The treatment of self-inflicted suffering* (pp. 1–15). Madison, CT: International Universities Press.

Grosskurth, P. (1991). *The secret ring: Freud's inner circle and the politics of psychoanalysis*. Reading, MA: Addison Wesley.

Grossman, W. I. (1982). The self as fantasy: Fantasy as theory. *Journal of the American Psychoanalytic Association, 30*, 919–937.

Grossman, W. I. (1984). The self as fantasy: Fantasy as theory, In J. E. Gedo, & G. H. Pollack (Eds.), *Psychoanalysis* (Vol. 1, pp. 395–412). New York: International Universities Press.

Gruber, P. (1992). *Trauma and the role of disavowal*. Unpublished manuscript.

Guntrip, H. (1969). *Schizoid phenomena, object relations and the self*. New York: International Universities Press.

Hartmann, H. (1950). Comments on the psychoanalytic theory of the ego. In R. Eissler et al. (Eds.), *The psychoanalytic study of the child* (Vol. 5, pp. 74–96). New York: International Universities Press.

Herman, J. L. (1992). *Trauma and recovery*. New York: Basic.

Herman, J. L., & Hirshman, L. (1981). *Father-daughter incest*. Cambridge, MA: Harvard University Press.

Herman, J. L., Perry, J. C., & van der Kolk, B. A. (1989). Childhood trauma in borderline personality disorder. *American Journal of Psychiatry, 146*, pp. 490–495.

Herman, J. L., & van der Kolk, B. A. (1987). Traumatic antecedents of borderline personality disorder. In B. A. van der Kolk (Ed.), *Psychological trauma* (pp. 111–126). Washington, DC: American Psychiatric Press.

Hoffer, W. (1952). The mutual influences in the development of ego and id: Earliest stages. In R. Eissler et al. (Eds.), *The psychoanalytic study of the child* (Vol. 7, pp. 31–41). New York: International Universities Press.

Hoffman, R. (1981). Is altruism part of human nature? *Journal of Personality and Social Psychology, 40*, 121–137.

Homans, P. (1988). Disappointment and the ability to mourn: De-idealization as a psychological theme in Freud's life, thought, and social circumstance, 1906–1914. In P. E. Stepansky (Ed.), *Freud: Appraisals and reappraisals. contributions to Freud studies* (Vol. 2, pp. 3–101). Hillsdale, NJ: Analytic.

Horney, K. (1924). On the genesis of the castration complex in women. In H. Kelman (Ed.), *Feminine psychology* (pp. 37–53). New York: Norton, 1967.

Horney, K. (1926). The flight from womanhood: The masculinity-complex in women as viewed by men and women. In H. Kelman (Ed.), *Feminine psychology* (pp. 54–70). New York: Norton, 1967.

Horney, K. (1933). The problem of feminine masochism. In H. Kelman (Ed.), *Feminine psychology* (pp. 214–233). New York: Norton, 1967.

Isaacs, K. S., Alexander, J. M., & Haggard, E. A. (1963). Faith, trust and gullibility. *International Journal of Psycho-Analysis, 44,* 461–469.

Israëls, H. (1989). *Schreber: Father and son.* Madison, CT: International Universities Press.

Janet, P. (1887). L'anesthésie systematisée et la dissociation des phénomenes psychologiques [Systematic anesthesia and dissociation of psychological phenomena]. *Revue Philosophique, 23,* 449–472.

Jones, C. (1989). Problems of separation and clinging in masochism. In J. D. Montgomery, & A. C. Greif (Eds.), *Masochism: The treatment of self-inflicted suffering.* Madison, CT: International Universities Press.

Jones, E. (1955). *The life and work of Sigmund Freud* (Vol. 2). New York: Basic.

Jones, E. (1961). *The life and work of Sigmund Freud* (Edited and abridged in one volume by L. Trilling & S. Marcus). New York: Basic.

Josephs, L., & Josephs, L. (1986). Pursuing the kernel of truth in the psychotherapy of schizophrenia. *Psychoanalytic Psychology, 3,* 105–119.

Jung, C. (1912). Transformations and symbols of the libido. In H. Read, J. Fordham, G. Adler, & W. McGuire (Eds.), R. F. C. Hull (Trans.), *The collected works of C. G. Jung.* Princeton, NJ: Princeton University Press.

Kafka, F. (1979a). The metamorphosis. In E. Heller (Ed.), *The basic Kafka* (pp. 1–53). New York: Washington Square Press. (Original work published 1915)

Kafka, F. (1979b). Letter to his father. In E. Heller (Ed.), *The basic Kafka* (pp. 186–235). New York: Washington Square Press. (Original work published 1958)

Kahn, E. (1985). Heinz Kohut and Carl Rogers: A timely comparison. *American Psychologist, 40,* 893–904.

Kahn, E. (1989). Heinz Kohut and Carl Rogers: Toward a constructive collaboration. *Psychotherapy, 26,* 555–563.

Katan, M. (1959). Schreber's hereafter: Its building up (aufbau) and its downfall. In W. G. Niederland, *The Schreber case: Psychoanalytic profile of a paranoid personality* (pp. 127–150). Hillsdale, NJ: Analytic, 1984.

Kendall-Tackett, K. A., Williams, I. M., & Finkelhor, D. (1993). Impact of sexual abuse on children. A review and synthesis of recent empirical studies. *Psychological Bulletin, 113,* 164–180.

Kernberg, O. (1966). Structural derivatives of object relationships. *International Journal of Psycho-Analysis, 47,* 236–253.

Kernberg, O. (1987). Projection and projective identification: Developmental and clinical aspects. In J. Sandler (Ed.), *Projection, identification, projective identification* (pp. 93–115). New York: International Universities Press.

Khan, M. (1963). The concept of cumulative trauma. In R. Eissler et al. (Eds.), *The psychoanalytic study of the child.* (Vol. 18, pp. 286–306). New York: International Universities Press.

Kinston, W., & Cohen, J. (1986). Primal repression: Clinical and theoretical aspects. *International Journal of Psycho-Analysis, 67,* 337–356.

Klein, M. (1946). Notes on some schizoid mechanisms. *International Journal of Psycho-Analysis, 27,* 99–110.

Klein, M. (1968). *Contributions to psycho-analysis 1921–1945.* New York: McGraw-Hill.

Klein, M. (1973). *The psycho-analysis of children* (A. Strachey, Trans.). London: Grove Press. (Original work published 1932)

Kligerman, C. (1972). Report on panel of "creativity." *International Journal of Psycho-Analysis, 53,* 21–30.

Kohlberg, L., Yaeger, J., & Hjertholm, E. (1968). Private speech: Four studies and a review of theories. *Child Development, 39*, 691–735.

Kohut, H. (1959). Introspection, empathy, and psychoanalysis: An examination of the relationship between mode of observation and theory. In P. H. Ornstein (Ed.), *The search for the self: Selected writings of Heinz Kohut* (Vol. 1, pp. 205–232). New York: International Universities Press, 1978.

Kohut, H. (1960). Discussion of "further data and documents in the Schreber case" by William G. Niederland. In P. H. Ornstein (Ed.), *The search for the self: Selected writings of Heinz Kohut* (Vol. 1, pp. 305–308). New York: International Universities Press, 1978.

Kohut, H. (1970). Discussion of "the self: A contribution to its place in theory and technique" by D. C. Levin. In P. H. Ornstein (Ed.), *The search for the self: Selected writings of Heinz Kohut* (Vol. 2, pp. 577–588). New York: International Universities Press, 1978.

Kohut, H. (1971). *The analysis of the self.* New York: International Universities Press.

Kohut, H. (1972). Thoughts on narcissism and narcissistic rage. In P. H. Ornstein (Ed.), *The search for the self: Selected writings of Heinz Kohut* (Vol. 2, pp. 615–658). New York: International Universities Press, 1978.

Kohut, H. (1974). Remarks about the formation of the self: Letter to a student regarding some principles of psychoanalytic research. In P. H. Ornstein (Ed.), *The search for the self: Selected writings of Heinz Kohut* (Vol. 2, pp. 737–770). New York: International Universities Press, 1978.

Kohut, H. (1976). Creativeness, charisma, group psychology. In C. B. Strozier (Ed.), *Self psychology and the humanities: Reflections on a new psychoanalytic approach* (pp. 171–214). New York: Norton, 1985.

Kohut, H. (1977). *The restoration of self.* New York: International Universities Press.

Kohut, H. (1979). The two analyses of Mr. Z. In P. H. Ornstein (Ed.), *The search for the self: Selected writings of Heinz Kohut* (Vol. 4, pp. 395–446). New York: International Universities Press, 1991.

Kohut, H. (1981). Introspection, empathy, and the semicircle of mental health. In P. H. Ornstein (Ed.), *The search for the self: Selected writings of Heinz Kohut* (Vol. 4, pp. 537–568). New York: International Universities Press, 1991.

Kohut, H. (1984). *How does analysis cure?* Chicago: University of Chicago Press.

Kohut, H. (1985). *Self psychology and the humanities: Reflections on a new psychoanalytic approach.* C. B. Strozier (Ed.), New York: Norton.

Kohut, H., & Wolf, E. (1978). The disorders of the self and their treatment: An outline. In P. H. Ornstein (Ed.), *The search for the self: Selected writings of Heinz Kohut* (Vol. 3, pp. 359–386). New York: International Universities Press, 1990.

Kris, E. (1956). The personal myth. *Journal of the American Psychoanalytic Association, 4*, 653–681.

Krugman, S. (1987). Trauma in the family: Perspectives on the intergenerational transmission of violence. In *Psychological trauma* (pp. 127–151). Washington, DC: American Psychiatric Press.

Krystal, H. (1971). Psychotherapy after massive traumatization. In J. Krystal, & W. G. Niederland (Eds.), *Psychic traumatization* (pp. 223–229). Boston: Little, Brown.

Kuhn, T. (1962). *The structure of scientific revolutions.* Chicago: University of Chicago Press.

Laub, D., & Auerhahn, N. C. (1993). Knowing and not knowing massive psychic trauma: Forms of traumatic memory. *International Journal of Psycho-Analysis, 74*, 287–302.

Levinson, E. (1983). *The ambiguity of change.* New York: Basic.

Lichtenberg, J. D. (1983). *Psychoanalysis and infant research.* Hillsdale, NJ: Analytic.

Lichtenberg, J. D. (1987). Infant studies and clinical work with adults. *Psychoanalytic Inquiry, 7*, 311–330.

Lichtenberg, J. D. (1988). Infant research and self psychology. In A. Goldberg (Ed.), *Progress in self psychology* (Vol. 3, pp. 59–64). Hillsdale, NJ: Analytic.

Lichtenberg, J. D. (1989). *Psychoanalysis and motivation*. Hillsdale, NJ: Analytic.

Lichtenberg, J. D., Lachmann, F. M., & Fosshage, J. L. (1992). *Self and motivational systems*. Hillsdale, NJ: Analytic.

Liotti, G. (1992). Disorganized/disoriented attachment in the etiology of the dissociative disorders. *Dissociation, 5*, 196–204.

Lothane, Z. (1992). *In defense of Schreber: Soul murder and psychiatry*. Hillsdale, NJ: Analytic.

Lunt, D. (1993, October). *A case of multiple personality disorder from a self psychological perspective*. Paper presented at the Sixteenth Annual Conference on the Psychology of the Self, Toronto.

Macalpine, I., & Hunter, R. A. (1953). The Schreber case: A contribution to schizophrenia, hypochondria, and psychosomatic symptom-formation. *Psychoanalytic Quarterly, 22*, 328–371.

Mahler, M. S. (1967). On human symbiosis and the vicissitudes of individuation. In P. Buckley (Ed.), *Essential papers in object relations* (pp. 200–221). New York: New York University Press, 1986.

Mahler, M. S. (1972). On the first three subphases of the separation-individuation process. In P. Buckley (Ed.), *Essential papers in object relations* (pp. 200–221). New York: New York University Press, 1986.

Mahler, M. S. (1979). *The selected papers of Margaret Mahler: Vol. 2. Separation-individuation*. New York: Jason Aronson.

Mahler, M. S., Pine, F., & Bergman, A. (1975). *The psychological birth of the human infant*. New York: Basic.

Main, M. (1981). Avoidance in the service of attachment. In K. Immelmann, G. Barlow, L. Petrinovitch, & M. Main (Eds.), *Behavioral development: The Bielefeld interdisciplinary project* (pp. 651–693). Cambridge: Cambridge University Press.

Main, M., & Hesse, E. (1990). Parents' unresolved traumatic experiences are related to infant disorganized attachment status: Is frightened and/or frightening behavior the linking mechanisms? In M. T. Greenberg, D. Cicchetti, & E. M. Cummings (Eds.), *Attachment in the preschool years* (pp. 161–182). Chicago: University of Chicago Press.

Main, M., & Hesse, E. (1992). Attaccamento disorganizzato/disorientato Nell infanza e stati mentali dissociata nel genitorl [Disorganized/disoriented infant behavior in the strange situation, lapses in the monitoring of reasoning and discourse during the parents' adult attachment interview, and dissociated states]. In M. Ammaniti, & D. Stern (Eds.), *Attacamento e psicoanalisi* [Attachment and psychoanalysis] (pp. 86–140). Bari: Laterza.

March, J. S., & Amaya-Jackson, L. (1993). Post-traumatic stress disorder in children and adolescents. *PTSD Research Quarterly, 4*(4)4, 1–3.

Maslow, A. H. (1954). *Motivation and personality*. New York: Harper.

Masson, J. M. (1984). *The assault on truth*. New York: Farrar, Straus and Giroux.

Masson, J. M. (Ed.). (1985). *The complete letters of Sigmund Freud to Wilhelm Fliess 1887–1904*. Cambridge, MA: The Belknap Press of Harvard University Press.

McGuire, W. (Ed.). (1974). *The Freud/Jung letters: The correspondence between Sigmund Freud and C. G. Jung* (Bollingen Series 94). Princeton, NJ: Princeton University Press.

Meares, R. (1988). The secret, lies, and the paranoid process. *Contemporary Psychoanalysis, 24*(4), 650–666.

Meissner, W. W. (1978). *The paranoid process*. New York: Jason Aronson.

Meissner, W. W. (1986). *Psychopathology of the paranoid process and treatment*. New York: Jason Aronson.

Meltzoff, A., & Moore, M. (1977). Imitation of facial and manual gestures by human neonates. *Science, 198*, 75–78.

Menaker, E. (1953). Masochism: A defense reaction of the ego. *Psychoanalytic Quarterly, 22*, 205–220.

Miller, A. (1981). *Prisoners of childhood* (R. Ward, Trans.). New York: Basic. (Original work published 1979)

Miller, A. (1986). *Thou shalt not be aware* (H. Hannum, & H. Hannum, Trans.). New York: Meridian. (Original work published 1984)

Mitchell, S. A. (1988). *Relational concepts in psychoanalysis: An integration.* Cambridge, MA: Harvard University Press.

Natterson, J. (1991). *Beyond countertransference.* Northvale, NJ: Jason Aronson.

Niederland, W. G. (1951). Three notes on the Schreber case. In *The Schreber case: Psychoanalytic profile of a paranoid personality* (pp. 39–48). Hillsdale, NJ: Analytic, 1984.

Niederland, W. G. (1959a). Schreber: Father and son. In *The Schreber case: Psychoanalytic profile of a paranoid personality* (pp. 49–62). Hillsdale, NJ: Analytic, 1984.

Niederland, W. G. (1959b). The "miracled-up" world of Schreber's childhood. In *The Schreber case: Psychoanalytic profile of a paranoid personality* (pp. 69–84). Hillsdale, NJ: Analytic, 1984.

Niederland, W. G. (1960). Schreber's father. In *The Schreber case: Psychoanalytic profile of a paranoid personality* (pp. 63–67). Hillsdale, NJ: Analytic, 1984.

Niederland, W. G. (1963). Further data on the "historical truth" in Schreber's delusions. In *The Schreber case: Psychoanalytic profile of a paranoid personality* (pp. 93–100). Hillsdale, NJ: Analytic, 1984.

Niederland, W. G. (1968). Schreber and Flechsig: A further contribution to the "kernel of truth" in Schreber's delusional system. In *The Schreber case: Psychoanalytic profile of a paranoid personality* (pp. 93–100). Hillsdale, NJ: Analytic, 1984.

Niederland, W. G. (1984). *The Schreber case: Psychoanalytic profile of a paranoid personality.* Hillsdale, NJ: Analytic.

Noy, P. (1980). The psychoanalytic theory of cognitive development. In R. Eissler et al. (Eds.), *Psychoanalytic study of the child* (Vol. 35, pp. 169–216). New York: International Universities Press.

Nurnberg, G. H., & Shapiro, L. M. (1983). The central organizing fantasy. *Psychoanalytic Review, 70,* 493–503.

Nydes, J. (1963). The paranoid-masochistic character. *Psychoanalytic Review, 50,* 215–251.

Orange, D. M. (1993). The restoration of Schreber's stolen self. In B. Magid (Ed.), *Freud's case studies: Self-psychological perspectives* (pp. 135–156). Hillsdale, NJ: Analytic.

Ornstein, A. (1974). The dread to repeat and the new beginning. In G. Pollack et al. (Eds.), *The annual of psychoanalysis* (Vol. 2, pp. 231–248). Madison, CT: International Universities Press.

Orenstein, A. (1991). The dread to repeat: Comments on the working-through process in psychoanalysis. *Journal of the American Psychoanalytic Association, 39*(2), 377–398.

Prelinger, E., & Zimet, C. (1964). *An ego-psychological approach to character assessment.* Glencoe, IL: Free Press.

Putnam, F. W. (1989). *Diagnosis and treatment of multiple personality disorder.* New York: Guilford.

Puysegur, A. Marquis de. (1784). *Memoirs pur servir a l'histoire et a l'establissement dur magnetisme animal* [Memories that serve history and the establishment of animal magnetism]. Paris: Dentu.

Rapaport, D. (1960). The Structure of psychoanalytic theory: A systematizing attempt. *Psychological Issues, 2*(2) (Monograph 6).

Rempel, J. K., & Holmes, J. G. (1986). How do I trust thee? *Anthropology and Education Quarterly, 20,* 28–34.

Rich, A. (1979). *On lies, secrets, and silence: Selected prose 1966-1978.* New York: Norton.

Ritter, A. (1936). *Schreber: Das bildungssystem eines arztes erlangen* [Developing a system for the training of a doctor]. Inaugural Dissertation.

Roazen, P. (1976). *Erik H. Erikson: The power and limits of a vision.* New York: Free Press.

Rogers, C. R. (1970). *Carl Rogers on encounter groups.* New York: Harper & Row.

Rogers, C. R. (1980). *A way of being*. Boston: Houghton Mifflin.

Rogers, C. R., & Sanford, R. C. (1984). Client-centered psychotherapy. In H. I. Kaplan, & B. J. Sadock (Eds.), *Comprehensive textbook of psychiatry* (Vol. 4, pp. 1374–1388). Baltimore: Williams & Wilkins.

Ross, J. (1975). The development of paternal identity: A critical review of the literature on nurturance and generativity in boys and men. *Journal of the American Psychoanalytic Association, 23*.

Rotter, J. B. (1967). A new scale for the measurement of interpersonal trust. *Journal of Personality, 35*, 651–665.

Rotter, J. B. (1980). Interpersonal trust, trustworthiness, and gullibility. *American Psychologist, 35*(1), 1–17.

Russell, D. E. H. (1986). *The secret trauma*. New York: Basic.

Ryan, W. (1971). *Blaming the victim*. New York: Random House.

Sagi, A., & Hoffman, M. L. (1976). Empathic distress in newborns. *Developmental Psychology, 12*, 175–176.

Sander, L. W. (1977). The regulation of exchange in the infant-caretaker system and some aspects of the context-content relationship. In M. Lewis, & L. Rosenblum (Eds.), *Interaction, conversation, and the development of language*. New York: Wiley.

Sander, L. W. (1983). To begin with: Reflections on ontogeny. In J. Lichtenberg, & S. Kaplan (Eds.), *Reflections on self psychology*. Hillsdale, NJ: Analytic.

Sandler, J. (1967). Trauma, strain and development. In S. Furst (Ed.), *Psychic trauma*. New York: Basic.

Sandler, J. (1976). Countertransference and role responsiveness. *International Review of Psycho-Analysis, 3*, 43–47.

Schad-Somers, S. P. (1982). *Sadomasochism: Etiology and treatment*. New York: Human Sciences.

Schilling, K. (1960). *Letters to Dr. Niederland of March 6, May 4, September 27, October 30, 1960*. Washington, DC: Library of Congress (Niederland Collection, Manuscript Division).

Schmideberg, M. (1931). A contribution to the psychology of persecuting ideas and delusions. *International Journal of Psycho-Analysis, 12*, 331–367.

Schreber, D. P. (1903). *Memoirs of my nervous illness* (I. Macalpine, & R. A. Hunter, Eds. and Trans.) London: Dawson, 1955.

Schreber, D. G. M. (1842). *Die kaltwasser-heilmethode in thren grenzen und ihrem wahren werthe* [The cold water therapeutic method: Its limits and true value]. Leipzig: Bernh. Hermann.

Schreber, D. G. M. (1852). *Die Eigenthümlichkeiten des kindlichen organismus in gesunden und kranken zustande: Eine propädeutik der speciellen kinderheilkunde* [A particular type of organism found in children, healthy or ill. It is a distinctly pediatric condition]. Leipzig: Friedrich Fleischer.

Schreber, D. G. M. (1858). *Kallipadie oder erziehung zur schönheit durch naturgetreue und gleichmässige förderung normaler körperbildung, lebenstüchtiger gesundheit und geistiger veredlung und insbesondere durch möglichste benutzung speciellier Erzlehungsmittel: Fur aeltern, erzieher und lehrer* [Upbringing to beauty, true to nature, and an equal measure of body building, health and mind improvement, particularly through the possible use, especially European, for parents as raisers and teachers]. Leipzig: Fleischer.

Schwaber, E. (1981). Empathy, a mode of analytic listening. *Psychoanalytic Inquiry, 1*, 357–392.

Schur, M. (1972). *Freud: Living and dying*. London: Hogarth.

Searles, H. F. (1965). *Collected papers on schizophrenia and related subjects*. New York: International Universities Press.

Selman, R. L., Jaquette, D., & Lavin, D. R. (1977). Interpersonal awareness in children:

Toward an integration of developmental and clinical child psychology. *American Journal of Orthopsychiatry, 44*(1), 264–274.

Shainess, N. (1984). *Sweet suffering*. Indianapolis, IN: Bobbs-Merrill.

Shakespeare, W. (1981). King Lear. In G. K. Hunter (Ed.), *William Shakespeare. King Lear*. New York: Penguin. (Original work registered 1607c)

Shane M., & Shane, E. (1989). The struggle for otherhood: Implications for development in adulthood. *Psychoanalytic Inquiry, 9*, 463–482.

Shapiro, D. (1965). *Neurotic styles*. New York: Basic.

Shelley, P. B. (1820). Prometheus unbound. In L. J. Zillman (Ed.), *Prometheus unbound*. St. Louis: University of Washington Press, 1959.

Socarides, D. D., & Stolorow, R. (1985). Affects and selfobjects. In C. Kilgerman (Ed.), *The annual of psychoanalysis* (Vols. 12/13, pp. 105–119). Madison, CT: International Universities Press.

Spruiell, V. (1975). Three strands of narcissism. *Psychoanalytic Quarterly, 44*, 577–593.

Steele, B. F. (1970). Parental abuse of infants and small children. In E. J. Brown, & T. Benedek (Eds.), *Parenthood: Its psychology and psychopathology*. Boston: Little, Brown.

Stekel, W. (1953). *Sadism and masochism: The psychology of hatred and cruelty* (Vol. 1.) (E. Guthell, trans.). New York: Liveright. (Original work published 1929)

Stepansky, P. (1983). *In Freud's shadow: Adler in context*. Hillsdale, NJ: Analytic.

Stern, D. N. (1977). *The first relationship: Infant and mother*. Cambridge, MA: Harvard University Press.

Stern, D.N. (1985). *The interpersonal world of the infant: A view from psychoanalysis and developmental psychology*. New York: Basic.

Stoller, R.J. (1975). *Perversion*. New York: Pantheon.

Stoller, R. J. (1979). *Sexual excitement*. New York: Pantheon.

Stolorow, R. D. (1975). The narcissistic function of masochism (and sadism). *International Journal of Psycho-Analysis, 56*, 441–448.

Stolorow, R. D. (1994). The intersubjective context of intrapsychic experience. In R. D. Stolorow, G. E. Atwood, & B. Brandchaft (Eds.), *The intersubjective perspective* (pp. 3–14). Northvale, NJ: Jason Aronson.

Stolorow, R. D., & Atwood, G. E. (1979). *Faces in a cloud: Subjectivity in personality theory*. New York: Jason Aronson.

Stolorow, R. D., & Atwood, G. E. (1992). *Contexts of being: The intersubjective foundations of psychological life*. Hillsdale, NJ: Analytic.

Stolorow, R. D., Atwood, G. E., & Brandchaft, B. (Eds.). (1994). *The intersubjective perspective*. Northvale, NJ: Jason Aronson.

Stolorow, R. D., Brandchaft, B., & Atwood, G. E. (1987). *Psychoanalytic treatment: An intersubjective approach*. Hillsdale, NJ: Analytic.

Stolorow, R. D., & Lachmann, F. M. (1980). *Psychoanalysis of developmental arrests: Theory and treatment*. New York: International Universities Press.

Strozler, C. B. (1983). Fantasy, self psychology and the inner logic of cults. In A. Goldberg (Ed.), *The future of psychoanalysis* (pp. 477–493). New York: International Universities Press.

Suttie, I. D. (1988). *The origins of love and hate* (rev. ed.). London: Free Association Books. (Original work published 1935)

Sutton-Smith, B. (1971). Piaget on play: A critique. In R. E. Herron, & B. Sutton-Smith (Eds.), *Child's play* (pp. 326–336). New York: Wiley.

Szent-Gyoergyl, A. (1974, Spring). Drive in living matter to perfect itself. *Synthesis*, 12–24.

Terr, L. C. (1991). Childhood traumas: An outline and overview. *American Journal of Psychiatry, 148*, 10–20.

Thompson, C. M. (1955). Introduction. In M. Balint (Ed.), *Sandor Ferenczi: Final contributions to the problems and methods of psycho-analysis* (pp. 3–4). New York: Basic.

Thomson, P. (1994). Countertransference. In R. D. Stolorow, G. E. Atwood, & B. Brand-chaft (Eds.), *The intersubjective perspective* (pp. 127–144). Northvale, NJ: Jason Aronson.

Tolpin, M. (1980). Discussion of "Psychoanalytic developmental theories of the self: An integration" by M. Shane and E. Shane. In A. Goldberg (Ed.), *Advances in self psychology* (pp. 47–68). New York: International Universities Press.

Tolpin, M. (1986). The self and its selfobjects: A different baby. In A. Goldberg (Ed.), *Progress in self psychology* (Vol. 2, pp. 115–128). New York: Guilford.

Tolpin, M., & Kohut, H. (1980). The disorders of the self: The psychopathology of the first years of life. In S. I. Greenspan, & G. H. Pollock (Eds.), *The course of life: Psychoanalytic contributions toward understanding personality development* (Vol. 1, pp. 425–442). Washington, DC: U. S. Printing Office.

Tolpin, P. (1985). The primacy of the preservation of self. In A. Goldberg (Ed.), *Progress in self psychology* (Vol. 1, pp. 83–87). New York: Guilford.

Tompkins, S. (1963). *Affect, imagery, consciousness.* New York: Springer. (Original work published 1962)

Tronick, E., Als, H., Adamson, L., Wise, S., & Brazelton, T. B. (1978). The infant's response to intrapment between contradictory messages in face-to-face interaction. *Journal of Child Psychiatry, 17,* 1–13.

Ulman, R. B., & Brothers, D. (1988). *The shattered self: A psychoanalytic study of trauma.* Hillsdale, NJ: Analytic.

Ulman, R. B., & Paul, H. (1989). A self-psychological theory and approach to treating substance abuse disorders: The intersubjective absorption hypothesis. In A. Goldberg (Ed.), *Progress in self psychology* (Vol. 5, pp. 122–142). Hillsdale, NJ: Analytic.

Ulman, R. B., & Paul, H. (1990). The addictive personality disorder and addictive trigger mechanisms (ATMs): The self psychology of addiction and its treatment. In A. Goldberg (Ed.), *Progress in self psychology* (Vol. 6, pp. 129–156). Hillsdale, NJ: Analytic.

Ulman, R. B., & Paul, H. (1992). The transitional selfobject transference and dissociative anaesthesia in the intersubjective treatment of the addictive personality. In A. Goldberg (Ed.), *Progress in self psychology* (Vol. 8, pp. 109–140). Hillsdale, NJ: Analytic.

van der Hart, O., & Horst, R. (1989). The dissociation theory of Pierre Janet. *Journal of Traumatic Stress, 2*(4), 397–412.

van der Kolk, B. (1987). The psychological consequences of overwhelming life experiences. in *Psychological trauma.* Washington, DC: American Psychiatric Press.

van der Kolk, B., Brown, P., & van der Hart, O. (1989). Pierre Janet on post-traumatic stress. Journal of Traumatic Stress, 2, 365–378.

Watkins, M. (1986). *Invisible guests: The development of imaginal dialogues.* Hillsdale, NJ: Analytic.

Watson, G. (1972). Nonverbal activities: Why? When? How? In W. G. Dyer (Ed.), *Modern theory and method in group training* (pp. 154–163). New York; Van Nostrand Reinhold.

Watson, J. (1985). Contingency perception in early social development. In T. Field & N. Fox (Eds.), *Social perception in infants.* Norwood, NJ: Ablex.

Weinberg, T., & Levi Kamel, G. W. (1986). S & M: An introduction to the study of sadomasochism. In T. Weinberg, & G. W. Levi Kamel (Eds.), *S and m: Studies in sadomas-ochism* (pp. 17–24). Buffalo, NY: Prometheus.

Weininger, O. (1975). *Geschlecht und charakter [Sex and character].* London: Heineman. (Original work published 1906)

Weiss, J. (1986). The patient's unconscious work. In J. Weiss, H. Sampson, & The Mount Zion Psychotherapy Group (Eds.), *The psychoanalytic process: Theory, clinical observation, and empirical research* (pp. 101–116). New York: Guilford.

Werner, H. (1948). *Comparative psychology of mental development.* New York: International Universities Press.

White, R. B. (1961). The mother-conflict in Schreber's psychosis. In *The Schreber case: Psychoanalytic profile of a paranoid personality* (pp. 155–158). Hillsdale, NJ: The Analytic Press, 1984.

Williams, T. (1971). Camino Real. *The theater of Tennessee Williams* (Vol. 11). New York: New Directions (Original work published 1953)

Winnicott, D. W. (1951). Transitional objects and transitional phenomena. In *Through paediatrics to psycho-analysis* (pp. 229–241). New York: Basic, 1975.

Winnicott, D. W. (1954). The depressive position in normal emotional development. In *D. W. Winnicott, Collected papers: Through paediatrics to psycho–analysis* (pp. 202–77). London: Tavistock, 1958.

Winnicott, D. W. (1960). The theory of the parent-infant relationship. In M. Khan (Ed.), *The maturational processes and the facilitating environment* (pp. 37–55). New York: International Universities Press.

Winnicott, D. W. (1967). The location of cultural experience. In *Playing and reality* (pp. 95–103). London, New York: Tavistock/Routledge, 1992.

Wispe, L. (1978). *Altruism, sympathy and helping: Psychological and sociological principles*. New York: Academic.

Wolf, E. S. (1980). On the developmental line of selfobject relations. In A. Goldberg (Ed.), *Advances in self psychology* (pp. 117–132). New York: International Universities Press.

Wolf, E. S. (1988). *Treating the self*. New York: Guilford.

Yates, J. L., & Nasby, W. (1990). Dissociation, affect, and network models of memory: An integrative proposal. *Journal of Traumatic Stress, 6*(3), 305–326.

Zahn-Wexler, C., Radke-Yarrow, M., Wagner, E., & Pyle, C. (1988). *The early development of prosocial behavior*. Paper presented at the International Conference on Infant Studies, Washington, DC.

INDEX